MiCK
RONSON

MICK RONSON

THE SPIDER WITH THE PLATINUM HAIR

WEIRD & GILLY

MUSIC
PRESS

Published by Music Press Books,
an imprint of John Blake Publishing
The Plaza,
535 Kings Road,
Chelsea Harbour,
London, SW10 0SZ

www.johnblakebooks.com

www.facebook.com/johnblakebooks **f**
twitter.com/jblakebooks **t**

First published in 2003 by Independent Music Press
First published in paperback in 2009
This edition published in 2017

ISBN: 978-1-78606-268-0

British Library Cataloguing-in-Publication Data:
A catalogue record for this book is available from the British Library.

Design by www.envydesign.co.uk

Printed and bound in Great Britain by Clays Ltd, Elcograf S.p.A.

5 7 9 10 8 6 4

John Blake Publishing is an imprint of Bonnier Books UK
www.bonnierbooks.co.uk

TABLE OF CONTENTS

ACKNOWLEDGEMENTS

We are extremely grateful to all of the family, artists, friends and fans who graciously donated their time to be interviewed for this biography. A special nod to Gus Dudgeon, Cyrinda Foxe, Frankie LaRocka and Mick 'Johnny Average' Hodgkinson who passed away before the completion of this project.

A Very Very Special Thanks to: Sven Gusevik.

Wham Bam Cheers to:
John 'JohnO' Oreskovich, Sean & Deb Doherty, Steve Williams, Madeline Bocaro, Naomi Fujiyama, Justin Purington and Jim Noury.

Weird Thanks:
Craig, Gracie, Jean, Jasper, Moose, JoJo, Danny Boy, Jareth, Teddy & Boomer, Bill & Lois Demattio, Mary Demattio & Ray BonGini, Melody & Tim Smith, Erica & Matt Campbell,

WEIRD & GILLY

Katie Campbell, Ashley & Adam Leirer, Will Hamma, Tana Silla, Jake Hamma, Madison Smith, Grandma D, Grandma Betty, Grandma Smith, Andrea (Henry) & Antonia Demattio and all their descendants, Jim & Deb Tucker, Kit & Blue, Fred Klara, Gloria, Janet, Gary & Barb, Paul Von Kaenel and his yellow van, and God.

Gilly Thanks:
Jesus Christ, Brian 'Wonderboy' Laney, Sandy McFeeders, Gary McFeeders, Mary McFeeders, Ralph Swonger, Abbie Joy, Fern Heater, Stacey Grove, Thomas & Sami, Jenny & JR Geers, Jim Dixon, Bill & Mary McGovern, The Fisk Family, George & Karen Soldo, Zoltan The Wizard, Shelby & Chuck, Flyin' Fred & Bobbie, and Anthony & Monica Kaiser-Leung.

"W&G Thank The Band":
Rod Sherrell, David Butler, Char Bandi, Martin & Kaye Roach and Dave Hanley at Independent Music Press, Kevin Cann, Violet, Tricia Devine, Neil Prime-Coote, Daria, Charles at My Mind's Eye, Dave Swanson, Frank & Holly Vazzano, Jim Donadio, Tim Dralle, Dave Saunders, Bill Peters, John Koury, Tony Crimaldi, Craig Conti, James Short, Party Marty, Mike Hodgkiss, George Bertovich at Checkered Records, Tom Weigand, Steve & Tracey Smith, Tim Buckley, Leslie Burton, Lou Williams, Paul Simone, Dan Kane, Don, Paul Kirby, Jon Haverman, Jackyl Jim, Mary Jane, Kristen Konicki, Jessica Roach, Jessica Broz, Mark Tidrick, Terry Keating, Faith Nezovich, Jim Raishart, Rick Garratt, Robin Kochur, Matt Verba, Eric Anders, Shawn Michalak, Monica Pocci, Ronda & John Williamson, Pete & Cindy Olson, Karl Kalk, Mark Schiefer, Mark Kratzer, Kathy Toomey, Dana Manist, Susie Kizler, Chris Beadle, Jim Thompson, Doug Martin, Allen Johnson, Michael & Julie Devine, Rob & Tara Branz, Heather

Wilson, Bob Best, Cyndi & Melissa and all of our past and present friends at the Quonset Hut, Lee Ruhrkraut, The Post Office, Dr. Robert, John Slaven, Mike Harvey, Campbell Devine, Martyn Hammond, Roeland Suurmond, Anastasia Pantsios, Neil Harris, John Kirk, Larry Smiley, Julie Stoller, Joy Gorino, Eric Olsen, Laurie Woolsoncroft, Trevor and the entire road crew on the YUI Orta tour, Cheryl Wright, Jim Veltri, David & Lenny at the James Dean Gallery, Dorothy Sherman, George Gibson, Robert Santelli, Hanna de Heus, Ralph Heibuizki, Peter Purnell at Angel Air, Dagmar, Rupert Pumpkin, Robin Davies, Jane Scott, Carlton Sandercock At NMC, MainMan, TripleX, Tenth Planet, The Voyeur, Q-Prime, BowinMan, Bowienet, Isolar, Sister Ray Management, Mick Rock, Repertoir, John Easdale, Clem Burke, Pat Pierson, Greg Dwinnel, *Goldmine* Magazine, *MOJO*, *Classic Rock*, David Spero, MrTwain, Vern Morrison, Jimmy McInerney, Randy Wheeler, JoAnneO, Gregg Yoder, all of our S.O.T.S.A pals, Luchitas, Arnold Printing, Canton Graphic Arts, Dave Thompson, Zeee, Jayne County, Tony Martell, Ed Di Gangi, Judy Mantyla, Randy & Brenda Romig, Mike Kerry, Susan Ashworth and Marc Coker at Spontanuity, John Melville, John Petkovic, Dennis Yurich, Chris Viola, Erhardt Bell, Sherry Rose, Mike Wilkinson, Karen Kilroy, Frank Famiglietti, Colin Blades, Mark Atkinson, Versa Manos, Ashley Studer, Edward Marks, Hilly Michaels, John, Paul, George & Ringo, and by all means YOU!

~ Mick Ronson ~ This is for you ~

**This book is dedicated in loving memory to
friend, manager and Big Brother**

JohnO
John P. Oreskovich

1955–2000

CAST OF CHARACTERS INTERVIEWED BY WEIRD AND GILLY FOR THIS BIOGRAPHY:

(all recorded via the telephone or in person, unless otherwise noted)

01. -Geoff & Moi Appleby – translated by Moi – via written correspondence – April 1998
02. Karen Barakan – June 1999
03. Rodney Bingenheimer – autumn 1994
04. Eric Bloom – Internet – August 1995
05. Trevor Bolder – October 1997
06. Chris Carter – autumn 1994
07. -Michael and Andru Chapman via audio recorded correspondence – July 1996
08. Leee Black Childers – June 1999
09. Phil Collen – November 1997
10. Billy Corgan – via faxed transmission – July 1999
11. Lisa Dalbello – January 1998
12. Gus Dudgeon – July 1999
13. Dennis Dunaway – Internet correspondence – October 2007
14. Joe Elliott – March 1995 and via Internet correspondence in March 2009
15. Morgan Fisher – Internet correspondence from Japan – March 1998
16. Ellen Foley – March 1995
17. Mike Garson – July 1998
18. -Sandra Goodare – November 1997 and February 2002 – written contributions July 1999
19. Dale 'Buffin' Griffin – July 1999
20. Steve Harley – via faxed transmission – October 1997
21. Bob Harris – May 1999

22. Laurie Heath – Internet correspondence – c/o Madeline – May 2009
23. -Youichi Hirose – translated by Robin Davis – via faxed transmissions – summer 1999
24. Mick Hodgkinson – June 1999
25. John Holbrook – July 1999
26. Ian Hunter – April 1995
27. Chrissie Hynde – August 1998
28. Mick Jones – August 1995
29. Rick Kemp – via written correspondence – summer 1998
30. Pat Kilbride – April 1995
31. Frankie LaRocka – autumn 1994
32. Sam Ledderman – March 1995
33. Russell Mael – Internet correspondence – c/o Madeline – spring 1999
34. Edward Marks – Internet correspondence – March 2009
35. Benny Marshall – February 1998
36. Glen Matlock – August 1997
37. Roger McGuinn – Internet correspondence – February & March 1996
38. Cody Melville – Internet correspondence – February 2009
39. Steve New – August 1997
40. Graham Parker – April 1995
41. Annette Peacock – July 1998
42. Steve Popovich – February 1995
43. -Lou Reed – Internet correspondence – c/o Sister Ray Management – March 1999
44. David Ronson – November 1997
45. Joakim Ronson – Internet correspondence – March 2009
46. Lisa Ronson – Internet correspondence – March 2009
47. Maggi Ronson – February & November 1997
48. Minnie Ronson – October 1997 & November 2001

WEIRD & GILLY
Michael Picasso

Once upon a time, not so long ago,
People used to stand and stare, at the spider with the platinum hair,
They thought you were immortal,

We had our ups and downs,
Like brothers often do,
But I was there for him,
He was always there for me,
And we were there for you,

How can I put into words, what my heart feels?
It's the deepest thing, when somebody you love dies,
I just wanted to give something back to you, gift to gift,
Michael, Michael Picasso, Goodnight,

You used to love our house,
You said it was relaxin',
Now I walk in the places you walk,
I talk in all the spaces you talked,
It still hasn't sunk in,

Are the words real that come into my head on a mornin' walk?
Do the shadows play tricks with my mind?
For it feels like nothing has changed but I know it has,
Michael, Michael Picasso, Goodnight,

Heal me, won't you heal me,
Nothin' lasts forever, set me free,
Heal me, won't you heal me,
I'm the one who's left here,
Heal me, heal me, heal me,

THE SPIDER WITH THE PLATINUM HAIR

You turned into a ghost, surrounded by your pain,
And the thing that I liked the least, was sitting 'round Hasker Street,
Lyin' about the future,
And we all sing, in a room full of tears, on a windy day,
And I look down, but none of these words seem right,

I just wanted to give something back to you, gift to gift,
Michael, Michael Picasso, Goodnight.

by Ian Hunter, taken from the album, The Artful Dodger

INTRODUCTION

Word of the 1988 Hunter/Ronson reunion couldn't have come at a better time. We had just released our first David Bowie fanzine (*Sons Of The Silent Age - Kit #1*) and quickly sold out the measly fifty copies we'd assembled by hand. Its focus was primarily on Bowie, but we couldn't resist sticking in news and reviews about our other favourite stars of the Glam Rock era as well. Since both Ian and Mick had been involved with Bowie at certain points in their careers, it seemed appropriate to report on their tour. On a purely selfish level, we were both more than a little anxious to experience Mick Ronson's guitar genius in person, having spent years listening to his work with Bowie, Lou Reed, Ian Hunter and all the other artists he collaborated with.

A little detective work turned up the name and phone number of Ian and Mick's management company. When the call was made, we were surprised to find that Vault Management were keen to have a little grass roots support from fans. They quickly supplied the concert dates and the photos we requested. Armed with our new mailing list, we announced the news in a Halloween card to our readers. Vault later called to let us know that Ian and Mick both sent their thanks for our efforts, and asked whether we needed any tickets for the shows.

It was clear from the first note we heard Mick play at Graffiti's (a small club in Pittsburgh) that we would not be disappointed. His solo spots during 'Sweet Dreamer' and 'Slaughter on 10th Avenue' sent chills down the spine with their subtle beauty, yet he also delivered the hard rock goods with an authority we'd never seen displayed before. When the incredible concert came to an end, we were ushered backstage to meet the band, thanks to a prior arrangement set up by Vault. To say we were nervous would be something of an understatement.

Fans surrounded Mick while he carefully signed autographs and posed for photos with everyone. When we introduced ourselves, he immediately thanked us for the plug in our card and seemed impressed that we had plans to attend four more concerts. It wasn't long before we hatched the plan to do an entire book dedicated to the 1988 shows and the recording of their upcoming album. Ian and Mick were both supportive of the idea, so we used the time on the road to photograph the concerts and meet with other fans that could provide photos and reviews of the shows in other cities we couldn't attend. In June of 1989, while in New York to see Tin Machine's debut concert, we were invited by Mick to come to the recording studio where they were working on their new album. As he had done on the tour, Mick made sure everyone felt comfortable and at home. The *Scrapbook Of A rock 'n' roll Fan* was released to coincide with the *YUI Orta* album and the incredible tour that followed. Once again we attended a string of shows and were given the royal treatment from Mick.

It's impossible to express the so-simple yet so-divine impact

Mick Ronson had on our lives and the lives of the fans that he touched through his generosity and down-to-earth nature. On one hand, you had Mick the larger-than-life rock star with the records, the videos and his presence on the stage. On the other hand Mick was the caring friend with his laughter and jokes, his distinctive accent, the offer of an extra bed or a meal for safe touring, his smile, the invites, the 'be good' bye bye's, and all the rest. Truly, he never made us feel like the fans that we were - he treated us (and every other star-struck fan) like long-lost friends.

Annette Peacock compares Mick to one of her favourite Dylan Thomas quotes, noting that he sang and changed like the sea. "I always felt like he was confined. He had this heart and soul and spirit that was larger than himself. Like the sea in its boundaries, right? They're always trying to move past the borders. It's larger and more vast than its containment." This touching statement couldn't be more true and best expresses the way we remember him. It's one of the many reasons we committed ourselves to tell Mick's story.

Upon returning from the Mick Ronson Memorial Concert, we decided to begin our own tribute to the man who touched so many lives. It's been an absolute joy and honour for us to weave the expressions of those who loved Mick together into this biography. Mick left a long and lasting impression on those whose paths he crossed. In fact, everyone we approached leapt at the opportunity to share memories of Mick, which made this project all the more rewarding. It's a testimony, really. A testimony to the music he made and the life that he lived.

Musically speaking, if there is a common thread throughout these pages, it's that he was a passionate player, the master of melody and a huge Jeff Beck fan. During the making of this book, we talked to Jeff Beck after his Akron, Ohio performance at the E.J. Thomas Hall on March 31, 1999. He thought that this book was "a great thing" and added that, "Mick was a real innovator". Though a proper interview never materialized, it's certainly worth noting that Mick's guitar hero recognised the talents of one of his most earnest fans.

In closing, we hope that you will find this book useful in your exploration of Mick Ronson, the music and the man. We encourage you to seek out his music for yourself, that is... if you haven't already. We hope that you enjoy the story of The Spider With The Platinum Hair. Mick had some of the most devoted fans on Earth and he knew it. We're proud to have been a part of that... then and now.

Mick, this is for you. Thanks for the music and the memories.

Sincerely,
Weird and Gilly
January, 2003

FOREWORD

I am thrilled to be writing an introduction for a book that shows the fascinating life of an unusual musician: Mick Ronson.

In June 2007 Spontanuity, a small film company from Blackheath, south-east London, approached me, wanting to make a documentary about my late husband, Mick Ronson.

Mick has been but a memory for fifteen years now. I thought I was the only one who still thought about him. Wrong!

November 2007, Mick was given, by *Classic Rock*, The Tommy Vance Inspirational Award; this made me certain that I had to make the documentary. Spontanuity interviewed musicians at the *Classic Rock* Awards and everyone had wonderful things to say about him. Lisa and I were happy to accept the award from Ian Hunter and Joe Elliott.

I went and talked about Mick with old friends, fans and contemporaries. The artists who interviewed with me had such great stories to tell and such funny moments it was a real pleasure to revisit those heady days.

I asked help from fans via www.mickronson.co.uk, so brilliantly run by Justin, and the response was great, really opened up my heart and mind to making this documentary the best that I can. I am so grateful for the wonderful stories, from fans that met him and their thoughts about him.

I enjoyed this book; it gives a factual accounting of Mick Ronson's life and times.

P.S. I use it in the documentary as my time line, thanks Weird and Gilly!

Love and music, Long Live Mick!

Suzi Ronson – March 2009

CHAPTER 1

GROWING UP
AND I'M FINE

Nestling on the north-east coast of Britain, Hull is a tough old town. Built on woollen exports, whaling, ship-building and a historic fishing fleet, Hull is the first major port on the coast of England if you're travelling north from London. Bombed mercilessly through two World Wars, and perennially learning to live with many of its industries in decline, it is not an obvious stop on rock's superhighway.

Hull has little of the romance associated with Liverpool, the great port of the western coastline. Likewise, its famous sons and daughters are fewer and more modest in their achievements than the Lennons, McCartneys and other notable Scousers born on the shimmering post-war Mersey. Actress Maureen Lipman, actors John Alderton and Ian Carmichael hail from Hull, as did anti-slavery campaigner William Wilberforce. Poet Philip Larkin was a university librarian there for many years, while the Beautiful South and Housemartins frontman Paul Heaton is another famous resident. HMS *Bounty* was built here and

Robinson Crusoe set sail from Hull on his famously ill-fated fictional voyage. Another famous traveller, the aviatrix Amy Johnson, started her life here, but one of the most exciting and public journeys of all from this hard-working town was made by a gentle and shy Hull lad, born to shine brighter than all these stars... Michael 'Mick' Ronson, the platinum-haired Spider from Mars.

George Ronson was not so different from most young men in Hull in the mid-1940s. The son of a North Sea fisherman, nineteen-year-old George was working as a labourer for a chemical lab when he was called up for active service in the war against Germany. Leaving his hometown for the army meant leaving the new love of his life, Minnie Morgan, the fifteen-year-old girl that George had just met and with whom he would stay in constant touch throughout the war years. The pair lived near each other on the Hessle Road in Hull, where most of the fishermen lived, including George's father. "When I say fishermen," Minnie recalls, "you might think of somebody with a rod, but I mean they went out to sea for three weeks at a time. They came home for twenty-four hours and then they went back again. It was a hard life."

George's attentions were initially too much for the girl, as Minnie fondly remembers now: "I was only fifteen, and he was nineteen, and I thought, 'I don't like you.' Yet when the war came it broke my heart when he went because he was called up straight into the army. No 'next week' - it was 'right now'... immediately. When he went to war, that's when I realised how much he meant to me."

George and Minnie were married on January 26, 1944. Making their home on the Greatfield Estate in Hull, the couple's first child Michael Ronson was born on May 26, 1946, in a nursing home on Beverley Road. Born a Gemini, with fair skin and the lightest hair, baby Michael came into a disciplined home. Minnie remembers that George was a very strict man. Unimpressed by materialism, he cared deeply for family life and for the rules by which it should be lived. Michael's father had himself suffered a difficult childhood. By the time George was eleven, his parents had separated and his mother had died, so growing up as an only child in the home of a guardian relative gave him a sense of both discipline and of the value of having a family around him - lessons that all his children would learn.

Minnie: "George had nobody of his own, so he felt, as he grew older, that if you've got a bed to get into and plenty of food... then you had a lot to be thankful for. It didn't matter about posh homes, we had the necessities. He was a very strict man, but was quite content with his lot. He didn't care about new carpet, we had our priorities right!"

Within the new Ronson household, mother and the young Michael were both nervous of George. Michael in particular "never answered back and was very obedient," Minnie recalls. "His father was terribly strict with him. Too strict. All the time. When his father said 'bed' he meant 'now.' It didn't mean, 'Oh, can I stay up?' Michael had to rise from the chair and go straight to bed, no questions asked."

Despite George's ruling with an iron fist, it was a happy home and Minnie was delighted with her new son. Aged twenty two when Michael was born, she went on to have more children who she loved equally, but she remembers Michael's coming into the world with a clear fondness: "We just have to be grateful. I was chosen to be Michael's mother. The Lord didn't give him to anybody else. He sent him to me!"

From an early age, Michael showed an interest in music and musical instruments. Minnie remembers his animation as a baby when music was played in the house. "He would jump up and down to music. We didn't have a television, just a wireless, but he seemed to respond to the music on there. He'd jump up and down on his little rocking horse." A second-hand accordion lying around the house proved to be Mick's first instrument. Although money was tight, when they did have a little spare cash the family would go to the cinema, and often Michael would come home and figure out the theme tune on the old accordion.

Minnie recalls how she recognised her son's abilities and tried her best to develop them from an early age: "When he was five I was working then, so I got a piano. It was quite a lot of money and I paid so much a week (for it). It was £73, which doesn't sound like much but in them days a working mum's wage was £4 (a week)." Minnie tried to arrange piano lessons for her talented young son, but was initially turned away. "He's too young," she was told, and was encouraged to keep him back for another year. The reasoning behind this decision turned out to be that, despite his youth, Michael was memorizing perfectly any tune that the teacher gave him, instead of slowly working through a course book at the expected rate. "In other words," remembers Minnie, "he wasn't really doing it by the book."

Her son seemed so talented that Minnie resolved not to give up and found him a new teacher. Of all the people available in Hull, she chose the grandmother of future Spiders From Mars bass player Trevor Bolder, another Hull boy. This older lady loved Michael and the pair hit it off, especially as she recognised that he needed a more open-minded approach to learning. She welcomed his ambition and allowed him the space to learn for himself as well as to learn what she could teach him. Mick lived just around the corner from her, so this was a great opportunity for him to nurture his musical abilities. It is easy at this point to recognise a nervous child ("he was very shy," remembers Minnie), loved but held under an authoritarian thumb by his father, burning at an early age with a creative spark that had no easy outlet. In music Mick had found a way out of himself and he was quickly liberated by his hobby. Michael's teachers, remembers Minnie, would be paid for a half hour lesson and end up gladly keeping him on for longer and longer as his talent developed.

"When he played the piano it was out of this world," says Minnie. "There was a tune that (Trevor Bolder's grandmother) gave him called 'Black Hawk Waltz' that was so pretty. Anybody that would ever hear it... it did to them what his guitar does to people now." Surprisingly, Trevor Bolder was totally unaware of Mick's friendship with his grandmother until the recording of (1972's) *The Rise and Fall of Ziggy Stardust and the Spiders from Mars* album. Trevor recalls, "Mick just happened to mention it to me. He wasn't sure that she was my grandmother but he asked and I told him, "Oh yeah, she used to give piano lessons."

Michael's primary education was at Maybury Junior School. Here another instrument caught his attention. "He was a very nervous child," says Minnie. "Yet when he went (to school) he played the violin. Being shy, if anybody took the mickey he'd be a bit embarrassed about it, as if there was something wrong with him for playing the violin." The school recognised his talent for the instrument though, and it was evident to anyone that this boy had a remarkable 'ear' for music. At the same time Mick was developing an eye for his own status too.

"Violin was quite fun," he told *Guitar Player* in 1976, "but after about three years I got fed up with it because people used to make fun of you if you carried a violin case. All the big lads were getting motorbikes and I wanted to go out into the streets and into the bowling alleys and things. I used to pay people to carry my violin because I was afraid to myself... there were some tough lads there!" (was he already employing roadies in his tender early teens?). Competent with strings, accomplished on keyboards, and with the guitar still to come, Mick was already finding a way to tough it out in the outside world as a musician. There was really only one future for him already.

His early training on the piano and violin would play an important role in his future musical endeavours, as so many of his tracks featuring strings and piano arrangements will testify. At this stage, however, a pre-adolescent Michael had an unusually deep desire to learn and a passion for playing that set him apart from other students. Despite his own desire to blend in with the motorbike crowd, he was, in fact, well on his way to what might have become a classical career, shaping and sharpening his musical skills.

When Michael was eleven years old, Minnie gave birth to her second child, Margaret, on January 7, 1957. Margaret was a blessing to her older brother. Lonely, and an only child in a tempered household, the joy of a baby girl in father George's life meant that childhood lightened up for Mick too. Minnie remembers that, "George was over the moon because it was a little girl. I think it helped relieve the atmosphere with Michael, (having) another baby in the house. Margaret was the apple of George's eye. Anything she did was right - she could do no wrong. George never showed Michael affection or understanding like fathers should do."

While many children might have grown resentful in these circumstances, Mick's reaction was quite the opposite. He adored baby Maggi, and delighted in entertaining her. Maggi herself has great memories of her childhood as the kid sister: "He was always up on his hands, walking around. He used to walk downstairs on his hands and do lots of gymnastic type things." Mick was an ace roller skater, and a keen magician. "He could have been a really good magician," remembers Maggi, "...he always had a few tricks up his sleeve!"

At fourteen, like many young men of his generation, Mick

left school and went out to look for work. He got a job working on the mobile grocery van that toured the neighbourhood council estates, selling goods to residents from door to door. He gave money to Minnie for his board and lodgings and always paid his way in the Ronson household from his small wages. "And then he would give me pocket money," remembers his mother. "He was a lovely boy!"

On November 25, 1962, Mick's brother David was born into the family. Sixteen years older than his new sibling, Mick nevertheless took his big brother role seriously, and all the family remember his tenderness and caring attitude to David and Margaret alongside his helpfulness towards Minnie. "David cried all the time," Minnie remembers. "So when Michael came home (from work) on his lunch hour, he would mind to the baby while I got him something to eat... As they got older, he was like a father to them both."

Mick himself once recalled how his love affair with the guitar started: "I played classical piano, violin and recorder. Then I stopped playing the violin because I wanted to be a cello player but I soon fell in love with the guitar at age seventeen, after getting hooked on Duane Eddy, The Yardbirds and the Stones." His first six string was a Rosetti acoustic guitar costing £14 and soon after he began involving himself in the local band scene. It appears that Mick was largely self-taught.

Mick steadily developed as a guitar player such that by 1963 he was ready to join his first band, The Mariners. Various sources give different line-ups for The Mariners, so it is likely that during their short time together, the members of the band came and went pretty regularly. According to bassist Rick Kemp, The Mariners was started by John Griffiths: "(They) were a pretty neat R&B band doing covers of blues and rock. Chuck Berry, the Rolling Stones, Gene Vincent, Eddie Cochran - the usual material for provincial English bands of the time." Rick can tie up his first memory of Mick Ronson appearing with the band easily. He was on his way to Beverley, a town to the north-west of Hull, where the band had a pub gig: "I had stopped for petrol in my Morris 1000, and the pump attendant told me of the shooting (of JFK). It really cast a cloud over the night."

During Mick's debut with The Mariners, Rick Kemp remembers a man in the front row of the audience shouting out during the sound check that Mick "was the best player around," and that they were lucky to have him in the band. Sure enough, Mick had quietly become an excellent guitarist. He had found a means of expressing himself on the guitar, something that he found difficult in his everyday life. Shy, humble yet wide-eyed, friends noted how he sensed that there was a space for him somewhere in a rock band that he couldn't find elsewhere. The rehearsals and gigs that The Mariners diligently played fuelled Mick's confidence in his own abilities.

Meanwhile, out in the big, wide world, it was clear that the old world order was breaking down. As The Beatles' third successive #1, 'I Want To Hold Your Hand' stormed across Britain, Mick Ronson's future as a lead guitar player was quietly being etched out for him.

Bridlington Spa, a fabulous dance hall near enough to Hull to be included in the local circuit, held legendary all-night shows. Fans of good bands and bad could dance through the night, do breakfast at 5am and make their way home as the sun came up over the North Sea. Early in 1964 the new kids on the block from London, the Rolling Stones, topped the bill. Getting a reputation but by no means famous yet, the Stones had just released their first single, 'Come On,' and were an exciting draw at this big all-nighter. Down at the bottom of the bill were The Mariners, the first group on stage.

THE SPIDER WITH THE PLATINUM HAIR

Sandra Goodare remembers the night well, for a variety of reasons. As a teenager, she spent the night joking around with her girlfriend and spotting male talent both on and off the stage. The one guy who struck her the most was the young guitar player with The Mariners. A couple of weeks later, the two girls were at another disco where Sandra's friend chatted up the drummer from a band called John Tomlinson and The Buccaneers. Hoping to get a lift home with the group in their van, she tried to get Sandra interested in the singer. Sandra wasn't particularly enamoured, but she went along with it to keep all parties happy. This went on for about three weeks and then one day The Buccaneers told her, "We're going to interview a new guitarist tomorrow night, do you want to come?" She went out of curiosity and was pleasantly surprised to see that the guitarist in question was the same young man from The Mariners who had caught her eye that night at Bridlington Spa. "So," she says, "I thought 'Hmmm, I might stick around!'"

Sandra and Mick liked each other instantly, yet Sandra remembers Mick being very shy. Of course, there were the personal politics, as Sandra was supposed to be going out with The Buccaneers' singer even though she recalls it was against her better judgement. Meanwhile, Mick was eager for any musical opportunity, as his own band The Mariners were not getting the work or experience he craved. It's not clear whether Mick officially left The Mariners before gigging with John Tomlinson and The Buccaneers or not. The Buccaneers were a short-lived project and apparently Mick had associations with John Tomlinson prior to this noted meeting. It's been said that Mick played with John and Bob Welton in a three piece called The Insects before he joined The Mariners, although this hasn't been confirmed.

Every Sunday afternoon, the group used to go to Scarborough, a seaside resort further north, and just mess about

9

on the beach. On one such occasion, they all decided to go out to sea on a fishing boat but as neither Sandra nor Mick wanted to go, they were left behind on their own for a couple of hours. Sandra remembers how, "it was a magical afternoon. We were both dumbstruck with shyness and embarrassment, being young and everything. We just did funny things like played crazy golf and we went on dodgem cars and then we kissed. I thought I would collapse!"

When the group returned from their fishing trip, Mick and Sandra acted as if nothing had happened. They knew they were in a dilemma. That night, Sandra told the singer she didn't want to go out with him anymore and he quickly replied, "Well, you needn't think Mick fancies you, because he doesn't." Sandra flattered him with an "OK, alright," but they didn't make any future arrangements.

Things came to a head at the interval of the next gig, when the band went to a nearby pub for a swift drink. "Michael never drank alcohol when I knew him, so he didn't go," Sandra remembers. She didn't drink either, so they both stayed behind and sat with their arms around each other, chatting. When one of the lads returned and saw them, he ran back to the pub, broadcasting, "Mick and Sandra are together!"

The singer reacted to this news by declaring, "Well, I'm not going to sing anymore tonight then." Mick went back to the pub and told him, "Don't be stupid, get yourself on, we've got a contract to meet. Sing!" He agreed to sing on condition that Sandra wouldn't come home in the van afterwards, at which point Michael threatened to not play guitar. After this impasse, a resolution was eventually found, the gig was on and Sandra was allowed in the van. Sandra recalls, "This is how it all started, really. Over the next two years, Michael and I saw each other every night and rang each other two or three times a day."

THE SPIDER WITH THE PLATINUM HAIR

Mariners bassist Rick Kemp remembers Mick and Sandra babysitting his kids at his house in Hessle (a district of Hull) shortly after they first started dating. "Oh yeah, we used to do different things," Sandra recalls. "We would often go ten-pin bowling. Most of the time they were playing gigs, but I had a flat and he used to come around to paint my window frames and decorate for me. We used to go around to his flat too. We had so much fun and I recall he even used to laugh a lot on stage. His jokes were groaning jokes but he had quite a wicked sense of humour, really. He'd recount a joke and then crack up giggling when he'd told you. We were so young. I shared a flat with a 21-year-old girl and we both thought that was really, really old."

Aside from DIY, Mick was quite talented at art. "He could draw. I've got a few of his little drawings and he's quite the artist," Sandra says. Mick definitely had the arts in him. "His piano playing was amazing. Sometimes, he'd play and my flat mate and me would just sit around and sing. Nice times. He'd play whatever was around at the time. Another friend of mine had an acoustic guitar that he'd pick up and we would sing along to that as well."

Mick was also very generous. Sandra's first flat was so damp and dank that the wallpaper was actually falling off. She always had aches and pains in her joints as a result of sleeping in the freezing flat. "He bought me an electric blanket which I thought was really kind, not least because he didn't have very much money. He bought me something that I actually needed and it would never have occurred to me to buy one."

Sandra wasn't the only one reaping the generous rewards of Mick's innate kindness. "He always gave money to the buskers and beggars and people that were homeless," Sandra recalls. "He never walked past any of them without dropping some money for them. At Christmas he used to buy a little present for the lads in the group just because he wanted to. The lads were kind of embarrassed, not really knowing how to say 'thank you.' Mick had a huge heart."

Mick and Sandra had great weekends together. "We used to spend some Saturday afternoons in the musical instrument shop. All the lads that were in local groups used to hang out there, lovingly touching these expensive guitars," Sandra says. On Sundays they would go to church together. Mick was brought up Mormon and told Sandra about the church. She became interested and started attending herself shortly thereafter – she's been going ever since.

At this time, Mick began numerous associations with other local groups, including The King Bees and The Crestas, during a period where his musical allegiances seem rather complex. Suffice to say, a 1964 *Hull Times* clipping actually lists him as a member of The King Bees, although it seems most likely that Mick joined this act on stage only for an occasion or two later in that year, after having first joined The Crestas.

Justin Purington, author of the Mott the Hoople Fanzine *Just A Buzz,* has written at length about The Crestas, with excellent interviews and research that are referenced here. Crestas joint vocalist Johnny Hawk told *Just A Buzz* that it was Mariner John Griffiths who suggested he check out their guitarist Ronson in mid-1964. This naturally implies that, in spite of his flirtation with other groups, Mick was still a Mariner up until that point. Griffiths told Hawk that he "thought this young man deserved better" and invited Hawk to a show. Hawk was introduced to Mick after the gig and, seeing the enthusiasm he had, asked him to join himself and co-vocalist Eric Lee in the revamped Crestas. "You would have thought I had offered him a million pounds!" says Hawk about Mick's reaction to the offer. Straight away, Mick joined Johnny, Eric, Henry Temple, Tim Myers and Mike Kitching to round out the six-piece band.

Just A Buzz fanzine also reveals that the group had plenty of local work and, due to some of Johnny Hawk's previous contacts, were even promised work around Leeds, Bradford and Sheffield. Within six months The Crestas were a top attraction, getting solid bookings from promoter Derek Arnold. Covers by the Stones, The Hollies, Chuck Berry and John Lee Hooker proved to be their ace formula in winning over the audiences. In early 1965, however, The Crestas played a Sunday night gig at The Duke of Cumberland at Ferriby that nearly ended Mick's career.

Benny Marshall, lead vocalist of Hull's legendary band The Rats and himself a big Crestas fan, was at the show and has vivid recollections of what happened that night, when Mick was singing harmony to the Beatles song 'Baby It's You'. "This particular gig had a DC electric main, and when Mick put his hand on his guitar strings and simultaneously grabbed hold of the microphone stand, it gave him a nasty shock and threw him clean off the stage. He somersaulted and landed across a table before Eric Lee managed to kick the guitar away from his body. It had stuck to Mick though and burned him quite badly."

Johnny Hawk reveals the draining emotions of the incident: "I was given a severe fright. I unplugged his guitar and amplifier and shouted for someone to ring for an ambulance. I then got him into the recovery position and prayed for his well-being. Mick was taken to the hospital, while the rest of us carried on, albeit subdued, and finished the show. There were a lot of tears and emotion as people left to go home that night. I called at the hospital on my way home and was told he was comfortable and that he was a very lucky young man.

Monday was spent checking all the equipment for safety and I rang the lads and told them we would still do the gig at the Halfway House that night. I arrived at around 7.30pm with the gear and who was already waiting there but Mick Ronson! He came over, put his arms around me and said, 'Thanks, you saved my life!' I told him, 'Don't be so daft' and asked him what was he doing there when he should be at home resting? It was good to see him though, a big relief. Later that night, we were playing a song called 'Walking the Dog' when I suddenly noticed that Mick was singing too. So, I stepped back from the microphone and let Mick complete the song himself. During the interval I told him what I had done and said that in the future he could do a few numbers himself. He did so and discovered that he could in fact sing!"

In spite of the group's success Johnny Hawk announced that he was leaving the band in June of 1965 and it was around this time that Henry Temple departed as well. The Crestas continued as a four-piece with Eric Lee taking over all of the vocals.

Mick and Sandra had continued to stay close even after she went on holiday in Italy in July–August of 1965. "Mike wrote me lots of letters. He was writing from 74 Delapole Avenue, Hull. I can't actually remember him living there. He was with The Crestas by this time. Regular gigs were at the local pubs The Duke Of Cumberland and The Halfway House. Dewsbury Town Hall was another regular show. Girlfriends weren't allowed to go to that one."

Eric Lee had a girlfriend called Pat who was a long-standing friend of Sandra. They didn't like this "no girlfriends on out of town gigs" rule, so one night when The Crestas were on at Dewsbury Town Hall, they got on the train and turned up regardless. "It didn't go down well. Mike and Eric didn't seem to mind, but the rest of the lads would not even let us go home in the van. We had to go back on the train but by the end of the dance the last train back to Hull had already left, so

Pat and I slept on the table in the waiting room of the station. It was very cold, but we still thought we'd been very clever turning up."

Mick was fed up with his daytime job, working on a Co-Op van. A few months later, in December 1965, Michael found himself unemployed, living back at home and increasingly annoyed that the other lads in the group didn't want to practice as much as him. The line-up had completely changed (again) and it was obvious that The Crestas were running out of steam. Although they would remain a group until their official demise in 1966, Mick sensed that it was time to re-direct his ambitions and move forward.

After the New Year, Mick decided that if he really wanted to pursue a musical career, he should re-locate. His mother Minnie says, "He went to London on his own to try his luck there and see if he could make something. He went from working in Hull in the local band, to living down near London, his first real attempt at seeking fame and fortune. He wanted to see what work he could get and what might happen to him." Mick lived with a friend of the family called Dorothy, whose husband ran a Chinese restaurant. They lived at 32, Hookfield, Harlow, Essex. "He often raved about the wonderful food they fed him. It was probably the only good thing happening to him at first," Sandra recalls.

In one of his letters home in May 1966, Mick apologizes for not sending Sandra a birthday present: "Things aren't going so well," he tells her. Mick also frequently wrote to Sandra after he moved to the capital and she has treasured nearly fifty personal letters that he sent. "They're just like all of the letters that you send to each other when you're young and in love," she says. Sandra isn't comfortable sharing the private correspondence in full, but kindly extracted the sections that defined Mick's experiences during this trying trip to London.

Here, for the first time, these extracts are published using Mick's very own words:

16th May 1966: The people I have seen up to now are the queerest bunch I have ever seen, wise guys about forty with sunglasses and chewing gum, puffs and all the lot.

18th May 1966: Yesterday, I gave a pro group a ring and I'm sitting here waiting for a reply. The time is twelve noon and I'm by myself. I'm having my hair cut in the latest style; it will be the same as now but a lot shorter.

20th May 1966: Things are not going as well as I expected at the moment, but I think something will turn up soon. I even rang a group who are just starting, they have no gigs, no van and they said they would consider me and would write if they wanted me. I thought "of all the cheek", anyway, I shall stay here until something does turn up. By the way, I'm having some fabulous meals - in the morning, sausages, beans, eggs, bacon. Lunch - fried rice, prawns, mushrooms, veg, and all that.

24th May 1966: Do you know it costs me a pound per day travelling backwards and forwards to London? Don't you think it's expensive?

25th May 1966: Do you want to hear some good news? The group I'm with live in a great big building at West End (the group was called The Voice). There are about six floors, great big doors. The main door opens by remote control, big posh carpets, great big settees, plants, mushroom-shaped tables and funny chairs. There are about twenty five people living there and everyone is real posh. The group manager is Micky Most. He manages the Animals, Herman's Hermits, The Who, etc. The group is great. I hope everything works out OK. I don't need my amp because they provide me with equipment such as great big Marshall amps twice as big and twice as powerful as mine. So, I should be earning some real good cash shortly (I hope).

30th May 1966: Dave is coming down on Monday so I'm on the lookout for a flat.

(Authors' Note: The Dave that Mick refers to in these letters is actually Dave Bradfield, fellow band mate (drummer) in the later line-ups of both The Mariners and The Crestas. In *Just A Buzz*, Dave explained more about this band The Voice: "There was a singer, a keyboard player, a bass player, Mick and myself. The other members were all members of a religious cult. They had a big mansion in the middle of London (Park Lane) and the couple that led it were called Bob and Mary Ann." *Just A Buzz* revealed more about this rather odd set-up: "The Voice was backed by a religious organization called The Process, which was founded by a pair of disenchanted Scientologists named Robert De Grimston Moore and Mary Ann McClean. In 1964, the pair had started a therapy group called Compulsions Analysis, which soon blossomed into a religious cult called The Process Church of the Final Judgement, or The Process for short. Mick had replaced Miller Anderson as The Voice's lead guitarist. The Voice released one single in 1965 while Miller Anderson was still in the band. 'Train To Disaster' b/w 'Truth' (1965 Mercury MF905) is an expensive slice of psychedelia, fetching prices in excess of £100 in collectors' circles. Miller Anderson, coincidentally, had also been playing in bands with Ian Hunter around this time.")

1st June 1966: Somebody has just come to take me to see a flat. This flat has one bathroom and toilet, kitchen with cooker and pans and a living room with a bed in it. One wardrobe and chair. It costs £3.10.0d per week, so that would be £1.15.0d apiece. It's not bad is it?

2nd June 1966: New address - 110 Gloucester Ave., Chalk Farm, London NW1. I'm now living at the flat. It's not too bad really; in fact it is very good considering it's only £4 per week. I know I said less but the rest includes TV, refrigerator and an extra bed. I hope Dave doesn't moan and groan when he sees the place because it isn't exactly a palace.

3rd June 1966: The boys in the group want to leave for the Bahamas very shortly but I am not going. If the group go to the Bahamas, I should think that Dave and I will form a group of our own, but if we can't we might come home.

4th June 1966: At the moment I am on the train going to Harlow to collect all my things from Dorothy's. Tonight we're playing at Nottingham; we are playing in London Sunday night.

5th June 1966: We are playin' Tottenham tonight at a place called The Swan.

6th June 1966: Dave has arrived and he likes the flat.

7th June 1966: Today we received a letter from Ready Steady Go (television programme) saying that we will be on the programme soon. The group have a lot of people writing into the programme saying we're fabulous, so with that, they sent us a letter. On Monday we're going to the BBC TV Studios for an audition. Also, we're going to see Micky Most tomorrow about being signed on as one of his groups.

8th June 1966: This morning we were practicing hard again, trying to get Dave fitted in. He's fitting in very well. I heard Jeff Beck playing tonight. He's great. I hope I will come up to his standard one day.

THE SPIDER WITH THE PLATINUM HAIR

14th June 1966: *Dave and I went down to practice at Balfour Place (where the group lived) but they said they were too busy because they were getting a few things sorted out for the Bahamas.*

15th June 1966: *This morning I went down to Balfour Place to collect my wages. Tonight as there is nothing on TV I think I will paint a picture.*

18th June 1966: *We have not practiced again today.*

23rd June 1966: *Today I arrived back at the flat in quite a good mood and then much to my surprise I found my guitar and Dave found his drums up in the bedroom. With that, I thought I had better ring the group up for an explanation of why our gear was left. One of the lads at the other end said that the group had packed up, sold their gear and gone off to the Bahamas. I was fuming so I put the phone down and then decided to go down to Balfour Place and find out exactly what it was all about. When we arrived, there were only three people left in the place. They said that the group knew that they were going at the weekend and never even told me on Monday when I rang up. So now I'm deep in debt and I have no money to live on. The group owe us our wages but we haven't got a penny so I don't know what I will do. Anyway, I'm not going to give up as easy as that. I shall find a group, maybe get a job and try again.*

25th June 1966: *Today I saw Dave off to the station because he is going home.*

28th June 1966: *Martin, the boy who used to live in the flat, said that the police are (asking about) The Process and the Sunday paper* The People *have already got one story from some other people.*

29th June 1966: I collected £30.0.0d. from The Process. £15.0.0d. for me and £15.0.0d. for Dave. Well, that's a relief. Yesterday, I went for a job and the manager wasn't interested in me and I wasn't interested in him either. He was only going to pay £9.0.0d. per week. I shall try this week to get in some sort of group, if I can, I shall stay, but if I can't, I'm coming home for a while, get a job, play with a group and save up some good hard cash and then I will try again. Melody Maker comes out tomorrow so I shall see if there is anything in there, also I shall go back down to Selmer Company, because they have a book with lots and lots of advertisements in it. Also two music companies have my name and address.

30th June 1966: Today I got Dave fixed up with an audition with Lulu and the Luvvers but I still haven't found anything for myself yet. He will be all right if he gets that job.

5th July 1966: Last night I went for a job with a group (The Wanted) and I decided to take it. They are only semi-pro at the moment but they are turning pro. They are a good group and they are great showmen. They play a lot of the raving numbers like The Who. The drummer is extremely good and the bass player is good too. I have been for a job at a garage doing general work and the manager is going to let me know tomorrow. If I get this job I will be getting £13.0.0d. a week, not bad is it?

6th July 1966: On Friday night I'm going with The Wanted on a booking somewhere in the London area. They play at places like the RamJam Club, Tiles and The Marquee Club.

12th July 1966: Today I got myself a job in a garage and I will earn about £12.0.0d. I work from 8.00am to 3.30pm Monday to Friday. Tonight I have been to The Marquee Club to see The Action. They were very good.

THE SPIDER WITH THE PLATINUM HAIR

14th July 1966: I have been practicing with the group every night.

15th July 1966: Phew, work is pretty hard and I'm kept on my feet non-stop. I have ever such a lot of cars to clean, polish, etc, because they haven't had an assistant for quite a while.

17th July 1966: I'm fed up to the teeth of everything. I hate my job and the group are beginning to get me down. They are getting about one booking a week and last night we got two punctures, miles from anywhere and we didn't have a spare. What a night that was. The singer is moody and he said that he didn't fit in with the group and that he was leaving and then the next minute he wasn't leaving. The flat is getting on my wick. Paddy, Jenny and Joseph go in a room together and discuss things then come and tell me things like they hope this practicing doesn't go on too long because Paddy and Jenny can't use their room when I'm playing. Then, they said that the alarm clocks in my room wake them up in the morning. They said, "Go to work and tell them you can't go in at 8.00am in the morning but you can go in at 9.00am", so that I don't wake them until they have to get up.

19th July 1966: I feel a bit happier today because I have decided what to do. I'm going to give this group another month to sort themselves out and if they don't get on any further by then I'm going to get a pro group. It may take a few weeks to find a decent group, but I will find one, somewhere I hope. I have just finished my tea and the lads are coming down to have a little practice.

21st July 1966: Work isn't too bad now and it's getting a bit more interesting, such as I'm learning a little bit about engines.

24th July 1966: Things are going a lot smoother now and the others in the flat haven't said any more to me yet and they are quite pleasant to me. They are very friendly at work and I have made myself a couple *of decent mates. On Saturday we're getting a contract, so I shall see if it's worth taking and if it isn't, I shall have a look round for a good pro group. I think things are taking a turn for the better now and I feel a lot happier.* (with the exception of these extracts, little is known about The Wanted.)

22nd August 1966: Things are bad. I'm most probably coming home in two weeks time to settle myself down to an ordinary simple way of life for a while. I think that is the best thing to do, don't you?

12th September 1966: I'm coming home next week.

Sandra recalls Michael's first trip to London by saying "some amazing things happened to him there." Minnie Ronson, on the other hand, remembers the sort of stuff mothers tend to remember. "We didn't have a phone while Michael was away, so we didn't phone each other during this time." She was very worried, wondering how he was. "(At first) he was so delighted and so thrilled," she says, but she was well aware that the sour end in London was a great blow to her son. Minnie remembers how he struggled to earn a living and, "used to buy loaves of bread and count the slices so that he knew how many slices he could eat." He came home really skinny and absolutely penniless.

In spite of this failed attempt to get into a professional group in London, Mick remained determined and confident that he would go onto something. Meanwhile, he got a job with the parks department. "He would give me pocket money every week, which went into the house keeping," Minnie says. In turn, it "made the wheels go around." He enjoyed his time at home with his family and his brother David remembers him as a hard worker. "I was only about five years old and I can remember him pottering off to work when he used to be a gardener. He always seemed to be working too hard for a living just to make ends meet. Yet, he was always an extremely affectionate and loving kind of guy. He always had time for me, so all of my memories of those early days are very fond ones."

Mick chose to absorb himself in music and his park job. "Mick was into the simple things in life, like pottering around the garden, cutting the grass. Like, washing the car, wasn't his cup of tea, you know? He would be much happier putting on a pair of shorts and working around the garden with the lawn mower," says his brother. One-on-one either with nature or the guitar seemed to be his preference. Minnie says, "He never had the guitar out of his hand. He'd sit at the table and have the guitar lean up against him. He'd eat and then the guitar would be back on his knee. He didn't make a noise like they do these days with a big amplifier. He was just forever strumming."

David remembers how "Mick was listening to all sorts of music, including local guys like Michael Chapman and he had lots and lots of music albums around. Jeff Beck was another great favourite, obviously, and Jimi Hendrix was an influence. The mid-to-late 1960s was a very progressive time. Things were changing in the music scene and he was very keen on the new guys coming through." Unfortunately, Michael and Sandra had fallen out by this time. "It wasn't a big row or anything, just a falling out," recalls Minnie.

The times really were a-changing, so with an enthusiasm and drive that struck everyone around him, a 20-year-old Mick Ronson was ready for his first fully professional band, The Rats.

CHAPTER 2

MICK'S BOOGIE

While Mick had been in London, Hull legends The Rats were on the verge of breaking up. The band had recorded two singles for EMI's Columbia label that did very well locally, but failed to catch fire anywhere else. Two members of the group had turned in their resignations and their record label was no longer interested in them. Lesser individuals would have given up, but aforementioned lead singer and harmonica player Benny Marshall along with drummer Jim Simpson decided to form a new line-up of Rats, utilising other Hull musicians. Mick Ronson was their first choice as guitarist. "The first time I ever was conscious of him being around was in The Crestas," recalls Benny. Mick had been approached back then to join Benny's band. "He was sort of interested, but then he left The Crestas and went to London and that was the last I saw of him for quite a while. Later, when The Rats split and we were in the process of reforming the band, Mick came back from London, we just sort of got together and that was it." That only left finding a bass player to complete the new line-up. They asked part-time local agent Joe Wilkinson if he knew of any bass players. He only knew of one: Geoff Appleby.

Geoff's first meeting was a positive one. "Mick and Benny called round to my house on Hull's Dayton Road to ask if I would like to join The Rats (he said yes). Mick and I got on extremely well straight away and ended up lifelong friends." Even with new members in the fold, The Rats remained a democracy. "The Rats were more of a group thing," remembers Benny. "It wasn't like, 'Oh yeah, we've got Mick in the band now and we're going to have this super sound.' He wasn't playing feedback guitar then. He was just playing normal sort of rock guitar, that Chuck Berry-type lead guitar. He was only just experimenting with the new Eric Clapton-style of guitar playing, as it was then. You've got to remember that when we first started with Mick, we weren't playing blues stuff; we were playing Tamla/Motown songs and things like that. We had a set list and that was more or less what he stuck to. Yet, all the time we were learning new stuff and trying it out." The Rats' new bass player has different memories. Geoff was stunned when Mick first plugged in and played. "When I first heard him, I knew his guitar playing was magic and outshone any other guitarist in the area. What impressed me most was the way he handled the wah-wah pedal. According to my memory, no one else had quite got around to that in Yorkshire!"

The new Rats line-up gelled immediately and everyone got along well. They made all the group decisions together and hung out with each other when they weren't practicing or playing gigs. Going to the movies was one of the things they enjoyed and Benny remembers some surprising choices from Mick. "The films that Mick wanted to go to see were unbelievable. *Mary Poppins* and things like that. He used to really get on your nerves by singing all of the songs. It was really annoying to hear 'Supercalifragilisticexpialidocious' all of the time!"

1966 was a year of great change in rock 'n' roll music. Although the *Sound of Music* soundtrack was the biggest album of the year, The Beach Boys' *Pet Sounds* wasn't far behind. Meanwhile, England's two biggest bands were beginning to experiment. The Beatles delivered the brilliant *Revolver,* and the Rolling Stones came up with *Aftermath*, their first album entirely filled with Jagger & Richards compositions. The heavy rhythm and blues style started to give way to the more psychedelic sounds of a new breed of guitar heroes. Three guitarists in particular would have a huge influence on Mick's guitar style and provide new material for The Rats to add to their live set. The first was Jeff Beck, in particular his work with The Yardbirds; secondly, Eric Clapton on Cream's debut album *Fresh Cream*; and finally Jimi Hendrix's debut single 'Hey Joe.' The Rats wasted no time in learning 'The Nazz Are Blue' by The Yardbirds, while Cream's 'I'm So Glad' and 'I Feel Free' were also live favourites. Sister Maggi remembers, "Mick used to like Johnny Kidd & The Pirates' 'Shakin' All Over' and obviously Jimi Hendrix and Eric Clapton, but he had a wide variety of music. I remember he had 'Hall of the Mountain King' and an album of The Brandenburg Concerto. Lots of singles by The Yardbirds and The Who as well."

Mick's easy-going and generous nature during the beginnings of Flower Power almost had disastrous results when, according to Maggi, a stranger arrived at the Ronson home. "My dad was a quite strict and a very straight man. I remember somebody turning up at the doorstep once from Sheffield and he had his suitcase with him. He said to my mum, 'My name is so-and-so and I'm a friend of Mick's. He said that I could stay here.' My mum said, 'Well, I'm not sure about that, but you better come in until Michael gets home from work and we'll sort this one out.' Then he asked if we minded if he went upstairs to freshen up. When he came back down, he had all this hippie gear on and a big bell around his neck. He sat cross-legged on the floor and me mum said to me in the kitchen, 'Your dad will go mad when he comes in.' It was totally not our house at all to sit around on the floor with a bell around your neck! Thankfully, Michael got in before me dad and we sort of put it to this guy that he really couldn't stay at our house. I'll never forget the panic though, for a minute, it was like 'Bloody 'ell, Michael's inviting these people around to our house, these hippie people with bells.' It was really quite funny."

Mick's brother David similarly recalls his father not being at all enthused with his eldest son's involvement in music. "He was more inclined for us to actually go out and work for a living as such, get rid of the daydreams and get out there and earn a proper living." Mick's conflict with his father was soon to reach boiling point.

After a string of successful local shows, The Rats were approached in April of 1967 by Joe Wilkinson. He was aware of some auditions in London for a band to play four weeks of shows in Paris. The Rats passed the audition, but were informed by drummer Jim Simpson that he couldn't make the trip, so he was replaced by Clive "Spud" Taylor. Mick was approaching his 21st birthday. Minnie recalls "I didn't know how I was going to get the money (for the trip) to give him for his birthday. I thought I'd have to work something out with his father. It was £50, which doesn't sound like a lot money, but it was back then." She managed to get the money and so Mick and The Rats headed off to France in a van.

The van only got as far as Grantham in Nottinghamshire before it broke down, causing The Rats to arrive two days late on 1 May, 1967. Most of the month-long engagement was spent at The Golf-Drouot venue, playing to a rather unique crowd – the local Mafia. Benny claims, "One guy we were playing to actually had a wardrobe full of rifles, other firearms and God knows what else. He would have meetings in the café down on the corner, just opposite the club. It was just like something out of a film, really."

When they weren't playing live, Mick spent time practising and playing records. Benny recalls Mick's favourite was the Django Reinhardt/Stephane Grappelli live album. The violinist Grappelli was a firm favourite of Mick's. "When we went to France, he took that record with him as well as a small record player. He played it all the time. It got played so many times it was nearly worn into a single groove."

After completing the French gigs, the band returned home broke. Maggi remembers her brother's return home was not a pleasant one. "My dad was really, really unhappy with him because he'd basically spent the money keeping everybody in fags and making sure the band stayed on the road, repairs or petrol or whatever it was. Me dad went mad, absolutely mad and he got chucked out."

Mrs Ronson was not about to give up on her son. "When his father threw him out it, nearly finished me off. Michael would knock on the door and say, 'Mother, can I have a bath?' He would go upstairs and I would be outside the bathroom door asking, 'Would you like something to eat?' and he would say 'No, thank you Mother' and then he would go. By this time I was really beginning to hate George, to do this to my son. When he threw him out, he said 'He'll finish up selling matches in the street.' Well, he didn't end up selling matches in the street, did he?"

This was a difficult time for Mick's personal life, but professionally The Rats were picking up steam. The trip to

France had tightened them up as a band and local gigs were going down a storm. Maggi recalls they were, "the top dogs, the best band in Hull." Benny puts it into perspective. "We had a good reaction, but we were like big fish in a small pond, if you like. We were very big around Hull, but if you went away from there you would probably be pushed to find people who even knew who we were. We were never short of gigs but it was always local." Geoff adds: "Our favourite gig was the Beverley Regal. We used to strip off our friends' clothes and leave them to get home bollock-naked by jumping on the back of the van. Boys will be boys!"

Looking to find regular live work, the band travelled to London where they stayed for one incredibly difficult week, all living in the van. On the way back to Hull, they made a stop in Grantham to see if there were any gigs available at the Cat Ballou, the hottest spot in town. They passed the audition and landed some gigs there, but once again found themselves without a drummer. In came John Cambridge to replace Clive Taylor. John had been in a number of Hull bands and had always admired The Rats, so he was perfect for the newly-vacant drummer's stool.

In the winter of 1967 the boys decided to take advantage of a new recording facility in Hull called Fairview Studios, which was actually the front room of local music fan Keith Herd. The song they chose to record, 'The Rise and Fall of Bernie Gripplestone', was a group composition, but the title came from John Cambridge. John told David Wells (who wrote the liner notes for *The Rise and Fall of Bernie Gripplestone and the Rats from Hull*, a later collection of recordings by The Rats) in a December 1994 interview, "I'd just been to see the film *How I Won the War* with John Lennon. I based the name of Bernie Gripplestone on Musketeer Bernard Gripweed, the character played by Lennon. I was the Beatles fan in the group and I thought that in the wake of albums like *Revolver* and *Sgt. Pepper*, we should be trying our hand at writing our own material."

"We had a lot of trouble recording Mick because of his volume," recalls Benny. "He used quite a loud volume in those days to get the sustain. What you've got to realise is that the place we were recording at was a very basic studio indeed. In fact, it was more of a home-made studio really. It was a guy who did it more or less for fun. He had a lot of trouble getting Mick recorded without distortion. We had to cover up his amp with blankets and turn it to the wall. Keith Herd did it in the end, a reasonable job anyway. We were pleased with the final sound." Unfortunately no record companies were pleased and the track remained un-issued.

Through their success at the Cat Ballou, The Rats managed to land the opening slot when Jeff Beck (now a solo artist) played there on March 17, 1968. Benny recalls, "We stood right in front of him and nearly got our ears blown off." He also brought his tape recorder and taped the show, which featured most of the as-yet-unreleased *Truth* album. Of course, The Rats used this tape to learn the numbers for their own show. Mick's favourite songs to play were the Beck numbers: "He was into it because Beck was his idol, he was the one, as he was for us all really. We all thought he was so good."

Maggi recalls her brother's determination to get the Beck sound: "If it was 'Jeff's Boogie' that he wanted to play, which was a single he really liked, he wanted to play it brilliantly. And he did. It was note for note, just excellent. I think he always wanted to be a perfectionist at whatever he chose to do."

Around this time Mick acquired his Gibson Les Paul Custom. Maggi recalls his joy: "He was thrilled to bits, absolutely over the moon. I remember him saying to me about the action being nice and slack, it wasn't too tight and he could really get a good old bend of the strings." Mick also started to dress the part of a rocker as well: "Flares came in and I remember him getting jeans, cutting bits away and adding more bits of jeans to it." David Ronson points out, "I always said, even back then, that he was going to be a big rock star and everybody laughed it off since I was a young lad of only six or seven. I can recall taking promotional photographs to school – the kids didn't take the slightest bit of interest, but I was extremely proud of the man. He was doing what he wanted to do in life and that's the way ahead, I guess."

For a short while, The Rats changed their name to Treacle. Benny explains, "It was all down to a guy in London who had come back to Hull after their band had split. He said they had a lot of contact with the impresario Robert Stigwood and that he could get us a recording contract and all sorts of things. He said he had to change our name because it didn't fit with the image that he wanted us to put out. So we agreed." The extent of this fresh campaign was some promotional photos and a psychedelic poster for the band that featured shortened nicknames: Mike, John, Apple and Sleepy! One of Treacle's press releases states:

"Mike Ronson, aged 19, born in Hull, plays lead guitar with Treacle... is blonde and sexy in his ways, he entered show business at the tender age of 16... he raves over Beck and Hendrix, also film star Jane Fonda. Thinks politics are a real bore and Malcolm Muggeridge a drag... loves to go to raving parties and lay in the sun all day near the sea... hates English winters and dull parties. Has a constant supply of combs in his inside pocket ranging from steel to plastic... longs to own a luxury mews house in Chelsea fitted with expensive hi-fi equipment to listen to Beck and Hendrix. He is always on the lookout for sun-tanned girls in bikinis, but raves over all the English girls. He says he's backing Britain... drinksa pinta milka day."

The band weren't fooled. "It didn't take us very long to sort of suss the London guy out," recalls Benny, "so we got rid of him and decided to change the name back." Before they could revert to The Rats, there was yet another change in band personnel. This time, Geoff Appleby decided to leave the group, having recently married in November of 1968. He was replaced by Ched Cheesman before the band (still called Treacle for a little while longer) headed back to Fairview in early 1969 to try recording again.

Three tracks were recorded: 'Stop and Get a Hold of Myself', a Gladys Knight and the Pips song plus two tracks from Jeff Beck's live show, 'Jeff's Boogie' and 'Morning Dew'. There was another song from this period, 'Curry Bun', that didn't make it to the studio. Benny describes this number as "an original off-the-cuff instrumental we sometimes played live." It was named after Mick's love for Indian food. This time the tracks recorded made it as far as the acetate stage but, once again, no record companies were interested.

Shortly after these recordings were made the revolving door policy for drummers continued with the departure of John Cambridge. Guitarist Mick Wayne had asked John to join the group Junior's Eyes, who were produced by Tony Visconti.

Mick knew just who he wanted to fill the drumming vacancy, another lad from Hull, namely Mick 'Woody' Woodmansey: "I was in a band called The Roadrunners, which was a rhythm and blues band, while Mick had The Rats. I think we both played on the same bill somewhere in Yorkshire. Little did I know he was watching me that night, because I was watching him. The band I was with broke up, but it was a couple of months later when he came to the factory where I was working at the time. He just walked in one Sunday with the whole band. He says 'Hi Mick, my name is Mick Ronson and we're The Rats.' He introduced the band and said, 'We want you as our drummer.' Then he said, 'I want you to come down on Wednesday and audition. You've got the gig, we've already promised a few other drummers that they can audition, but you've got it.' We did a gig the following weekend."

Woodmansey quickly clicked with Mick and the rest of The Rats and had no trouble at all with his new position. "I knew most of the numbers they were doing, Led Zeppelin, Jeff Beck, Hendrix, that type of stuff. We also did a blues cover of something, 'Dust My Broom', I think it was." Also featured in a typical Rats set list at the time were 'Jeff's Boogie', 'Morning Dew', 'Paperback Writer', 'Red House' and 'Born To Be Wild'. Woody remembers their travels well: "The live gigs with The Rats were brilliant. Mick was very into Jeff Beck still and a lot of the Beck and Zeppelin fans would come to our gigs and say, 'Wow, you play better than them!' That was a real compliment. We did a lot of the university gigs up and down the country. We had a big old van that we called the Chocolate Wagon simply because it was a former chocolate delivery vehicle. That was our group's van and it became quite infamous wherever we played."

Mick was still a municipal gardener for Hull Council when not out with The Rats. Maggi would come by and meet her brother for lunch. "We would talk with the gardeners and have some fish and chips. When people found out that my brother was Mick Ronson, the hunky blonde gardener that worked around the corner, I was treated really well at school then. All the big girls left me alone and I was well in with them. I used it all to my advantage, so I had lots of big girlfriends!"

In the middle of Hull was Hammonds department store, whose music department was managed by local musician and former Mariners bassist Rick Kemp. "Mick was often in for strings and plectrums on Saturdays when he was in The Rats," remembers

Rick. "He was always the quiet, polite one and took his playing far more seriously than most of the other local musicians." Folk singer-songwriter Michael Chapman was another one of the store's customers and recalls the laid-back atmosphere in Hammonds. "If you were a professional musician, you used to go there on weekday afternoons because nobody had any money and there was nothing to do, so we'd go and play the guitars that we couldn't afford. Rick used to let us sometimes get a bass down off the wall, much to the annoyance of the management and we virtually had a little band although we never got a drummer in the afternoons. We just used to sit and play songs."

These informal jam sessions led to Rick being the bass player on Michael Chapman's first album *Rainmaker*. With another album in the works, Chapman now wanted something different from the first record: a red-hot, electric guitarist. He asked Rick if he knew of anyone and Mick immediately came to mind. "On my way home," recounts Rick, "I saw Mick mowing the grass on the centre verge of the main dual carriageway from Hull to Hessle. I stopped and asked him if he was interested. He asked me, 'What, a real record – one that's in the shops?'"

Chapman's first meeting with Mick was at a Rats party. "I was with another Hull guitar player who was very young at the time, a guy called Professor Sutton, or Paul Sutton as he prefers now. He took me around to a house that The Rats rented. They were having a 'young-lads-living-alone-and-are-in-a-rock-and-roll-band' party with people falling downstairs and puking in the gardens. It was typical stuff, drinking lots of beer and smoking dope. It was then that he was pointed out to me as a great guitar player." Chapman also attended one of The Rats' local shows. "I went to see them play and Mick was playing a lot of Hendrix stuff which, to be honest, I didn't really like. As usual with local bands, they were playing too loud for their equipment and so this blur came across. Every now and again Mick would solo and the whole thing would step into another gear. What he was doing was melodic and flowing and playing properly."

The two musicians hit it off and Chapman invited Mick over to his place to rehearse the material for the forthcoming album sessions. "I remember Mick coming around a couple of times, before we went down to start the album, when I was showing him bits of songs. I use a lot of different guitar tunings and my chords aren't like other people's. I tend to assemble songs differently and this was even more the case in those days. We'd just sit and play." Mick even brought his little sister Maggi along on one of these visits. "I must have gone straight from school because I had me school macintosh on and we all sat cross-legged around this real down-to-the-ground table."

At one visit, Mick's black Les Paul got a facelift courtesy of one of Michael's roadies. "My roadie was a guy called Pete Hunsley. My band was always a little too quiet for Pete's taste; he liked big, noisy rock 'n' roll bands. Ronson was Pete's hero and he wanted to be Mick's roadie, but it didn't work out like that because they already had their own people. Pete told Mick about me taking the front off my Gibson J-200. I looked around and Pete was taking his Les Paul home and taking the front off for him. Whether Mick actually wanted him to or not is open to debate! Mick finished up with the only natural Les Paul around."

Chapman's decision to use Mick on guitar was initially met with resistance from his producer Gus Dudgeon, who had just done 'Space Oddity' with David Bowie. "He wanted me to use, as he said, "London faces", they had reputations and who was I? I insisted on using the bass player from my first album and Gus agreed he was good. Then I told him about this guitar player from Hull who was really good, "You'll love him." Gus wanted to use Mick Wayne, who played that funny slide bottleneck stuff on 'Space Oddity.' However, I said, 'No, I don't want to. I'll use Barry Morgan because he's a great drummer, but I'm bringing this guitar player with me.' So, I had to kind of fight to get Mick on there because nobody had ever heard of him." Gus eventually agreed that instead of "some top notch muso", it might be better for Chapman to work with familiar faces. "Well, let's bring him down and we'll see how it works out," he conceded.

Michael's wife Andru recalls getting a phone call from Minnie Ronson right before the trip to record what would become the *Fully Qualified Survivor* album. "His mother rung us up just before we went to London and said that she was really concerned about her boy going down to the big city. 'You will make sure he wears his overcoat, won't you? He's not very strong, you know health-wise, so we want to make sure he's going to be looked after.' So we dutifully made sure that Mick wore his overcoat! Certainly, on that trip, no ill befell him." Rick Kemp remembers the ride: "We drove down to London for the sessions and, around Welwyn Garden City, Mick said he had to make a call home. The night was freezing and even though he had a big black overcoat on, I remember him shivering in the phone box by the side of the A1."

The recording sessions were to be held over four days at Regent Studios, which was basically a cellar with a modest little four-track studio. Both Chapman and Mick were a little nervous about the sessions. This was Chapman's all-important second album and for Mick it was his first recording session destined for vinyl. "That was a crucial time, me making my reputation and him making his in the same studio on the same day." They needn't have worried. Rick Kemp says that "Mick played a storm". Gus Dudgeon was won over immediately, as he recalls, "To me he seemed like a guitarist who was just so into the instrument that conversation and most of the rest of life wasn't of any great importance. Yet, as soon as he played his guitar he just totally sprang to life, he was superb."

Mick was so enthusiastic about the session that he asked Gus to keep him in mind if any further studio work was available. Michael Chapman was impressed too: "He was a professional, he learned so quick. He did all the electric stuff and I did all the acoustic stuff. It was divided because we recorded live and we just did it a few times until we got it right. On my first album, the session guitarist Clem Clemson played a bit of lead, but this was the first real time that anybody had played lead into my songs. Mick just didn't play guitar solos; he actually played for the song, which is a great art I think. He was very sympathetic, he seemed to play on what the song meant. He could hit notes that kind of expressed the emotions which the words were trying to say."

There were many highlights on *Fully Qualified Survivor* (released by the progressive Harvest label in 1970) but Chapman singles out 'Soulful Lady' and 'Kodak Ghosts' in particular. "I love Mick's playing on 'Kodak Ghosts' because I'd never seen anyone do it before, he played slide in normal tuning and was all over the chords. I just think it's a really interesting guitar part, because it's not like your normal slide playing by any means. 'Soulful Lady' is one of my favourites because as they say around here, 'it goes like shit off a shovel!'"

Once back in Hull, Mick's attention returned to The Rats. This time it was Ched Cheesman's turn to exit. Geoff Appleby returned on bass just in time for the band's last recording session at Fairview. Two songs were recorded, both featuring raw and exciting lead work by Mick. The first, 'Telephone Blues' was a gritty cover of a John Mayall tune. The second was 'Early In Spring', a group original. Geoff is the only member who can recall the recording session and remembers 'Early In Spring' as only one of a few songs he and Mick had a hand in writing together. Unfortunately, once again no record companies were sufficiently interested to release The Rats' recordings and they were to remain in the vaults for the next twenty five years.

However, the disappointment of yet another setback would shortly be erased, as Mick's circle of former band members and his growing network of contacts was about to coalesce and point him straight towards the big time.

CHAPTER 3

FACE TO FACE
WITH THE MAN WHO
SOLD THE WORLD

Between 1964 and 1967, David Bowie released nine singles (three with himself as a member of a band, the rest as a solo artist) – all of which failed to register on the charts. His first album *David Bowie* (released on Deram records in 1967) suffered a similar fate. However, mime training with Lindsay Kemp led to a sharpening of Bowie's stagecraft, and he was soon performing a solo mime spot opening for Tyrannosaurus Rex. After seeing Stanley Kubrick's *2001: A Space Odyssey*, Bowie composed the song that would reverse his fortunes, at least temporarily. The brilliant 'Space Oddity' single was released in July 1969 and took several months before it finally achieved a peak position of #5 in the British charts. When it came time to record an album, Bowie turned to producer Tony Visconti to help round up the musicians.

Brooklyn born Tony Visconti was the house record producer for The Richmond Organization in New York City. One day, he met visiting British record producer Denny Cordell.

The meeting soon led to Tony's relocation to England, where he served as Denny's assistant producer on records by Procol Harum, Denny Laine, The Move, Manfred Mann, and Joe Cocker, before branching out with his own productions. He met David Bowie in the autumn of 1967.

It was decided to use the aforementioned Junior's Eyes, a group Tony was producing that featured guitarist Mick Wayne and ex-Rat John Cambridge. Recording sessions were held at Trident studios starting July 16 and continued until mid-October. At John Cambridge's invitation, Benny Marshall of The Rats visited the recording studio and wound up playing harmonica on 'Unwashed and Somewhat Slightly Dazed'. He is mysteriously credited as 'Benny Marshall and Friends' on the sleeve of the *David Bowie* album, which was eventually released in November 1969. Could one of the 'Friends' be Mick Ronson? According to Visconti, "we were finishing off David's album and Mick Ronson was in the studio and did a little bit of guitar and some hand claps for 'The Wild-Eyed Boy from Freecloud'. He was just around. He's playing a very simple guitar line, but that was the very first time he actually recorded with us."

When it came time to promote the *David Bowie* album (re-titled *Space Oddity* on its re-issue in 1972), it was decided that David would need his own band. While discussing it with his manager Ken Pitt, they came up with the moniker The Hype, named after the type of promotion they intended to use. John Cambridge would be the drummer and Tony Visconti would play bass. The only missing ingredient was a talented lead guitarist. Cambridge (who had been singing Mick's praises to Bowie and Visconti for some time) was sent to Hull to convince Mick to join the group. He found Mick marking out the lines of a rugby pitch.

In spite of this, it took some persuading of Mick Ronson to

work with David Bowie, as his sister Maggi remembers: "He was doing quite well locally and seemed happy with his job as a gardener... but he (eventually) went for it and didn't look back." Mick's mother explains how he was "thrilled to bits" to be returning to London to play with Bowie. He asked her, as he had many other times, "Mother, do you really think that I will ever become a good musician, or that I will ever make it?" She assured her son that he would but admits to "not knowing myself how it would come about." His overwhelming need to "make it" in the music business overtook Mick's desire for the quiet life as Hull's most desirable gardener and local guitar hero. He headed back to London with John Cambridge and his guitar.

In a Hull newspaper article titled 'Ex-Rat Gets His Chance In Big Time', it's noted that "it will be quite a weekend for Michael, who today says goodbye to his work with Hull Parks Department and tomorrow announces his engagement to sixteen-year-old Denise Irvin who, like Michael, lives on Greatfield Estate at 32 Bexhill Close."

On February 3, 1970, Mick attended a gig by Bowie at The Marquee club where the latter was backed on stage by Tony Visconti, John Cambridge and Junior's Eyes' guitarist Tim Renwick. Afterwards, Visconti recalls "We had a little bit of a jam session immediately. Mick was a very, very shy person and David and I were looking at each other, not knowing what to do or say to get him out of his shell, except pick up guitars and start playing. Mick picked up the stuff immediately." Bowie was so impressed he invited Mick to join him for an upcoming radio appearance on John Peel's *Sunday Show*. It was recorded on February 5 at BBC's Paris Studio (located on Lower Regent Street in London) and broadcast three days later.

There was a lot to accomplish before the radio session. First of all, Mick needed a place to stay. There was an easy solution to this as in October 1969, David and his girlfriend Angela Barnett had taken up residence at Haddon Hall, a beautiful old house in Beckenham. Also living there were John Cambridge along with Tony Visconti and his then-girlfriend Liz Hartley. "We had nowhere to put Mick except on the floor," remembers Tony. "All the bedrooms were taken. In fact, John Cambridge was already sleeping on the floor upstairs in the gallery. It was really quite laid back." There was also the small matter of learning the songs for the radio show. Two new numbers were going to be played on the programme. The first, 'The Prettiest Star', had been recorded in January, the second tune was brand new. Visconti remembers, "We quickly got together 'Width of a Circle' which we hadn't recorded yet. Mick was quite nervous, but he fitted in fine, as you can hear."

The hour-long programme turned out to be the most interesting BBC session Bowie would ever record, presenting a fine mix of older songs, tracks from the current album and unique cover versions. The first portion of the show would feature just Bowie and his acoustic guitar performing Jacques Brel's 'Amsterdam', 'God Knows I'm Good', Biff Rose's 'Buzz the Fuzz' and 'Karma Man'. Tony Visconti and John Cambridge then joined Bowie for 'London Bye Ta Ta' and 'An Occasional Dream', before John Peel introduced the band. "We have Mick Ronson who'll be playing lead guitar, who's recorded on Michael Chapman LPs. For those of you who've heard Michael Chapman, he's one of my favourite singers." 'The Width of a Circle' (still in embryonic form) featured Mick making a powerful first impression with his muscular power chords. When the song was over, Peel asked Bowie if he and the band were going to do some gigs together, to which David replied, "Yes, we're going to do some gigs – aren't we Michael? Michael doesn't really know, he's just come down from Hull and I met him for the first time about two days

ago through John the drummer who's worked with me once."
The programme continued on with 'Janine', 'Unwashed and
Somewhat Slightly Dazed', Biff Rose's 'Fill Your Heart', Lou
Reed's 'I'm Waiting for the Man', 'The Prettiest Star', 'Cygnet
Committee' and winding up with 'Memory of a Free Festival'.
Mick told his friend Kevin Cann in *David Bowie: The Starzone
Interviews,* how "I didn't know anything, none of the material.
I just sat and watched David's fingers. I really didn't know what
I was doing, but I suppose it came across okay." Back home
in Hull, the family enjoyed the broadcast. Maggi recalls: "I
remember listening to it in the kitchen. Michael on the radio,
it was like big time, you know?"

Now the band just needed a little cash to help move things
along. Angela Barnett had managed to work out a deal with
Ralph Mace (head of A&R for Bowie's UK record label
Phillips) to sign The Hype as a separate band, in exchange for
money to buy new equipment. Tony says, "We signed a record
deal with Phillips as The Hype. The purpose of that was to get
£4000 so that we could be David's backing group. We bought
a bass amp for me, drums for John and a PA system. Our roadie
Roger (Fry) got a new set of tyres for the van, but I don't think
Mick got anything out of it."

It was decided that The Hype would make their debut
performance on February 22, 1970 at The Roundhouse in
London, opening for Fat Mattress. Musically, the two bands
were not exactly complementary. However, even more than
the music, it was the look of Bowie's band that was bound
to send the hippies running. Each member chose an alter-ego
and would dress up accordingly. Tony says, "The idea for the
costumes was definitely cooked up by David and Angela. I have
to give Angela a lot of credit because she was so instrumental in
those early days. In the late 1960s, everybody was still dressing
in flannel lumberjack shirts and wearing jeans, long hair and

were laid back with the whole flower-child hippie thing. Angela came in with a burst of energy and aggression, which was unheard of in those days. Having been raised in Cyprus, she missed the whole Flower Power thing completely."

On a tight budget, they had to make the costumes with what they had. Angela and Liz were both very good seamstresses and sewed up all the costumes between them. David was 'Rainbowman' in a tight glittery number; John Cambridge was 'Cowboyman' in his cowboy hat and jeans; Tony Visconti was clearly 'Hypeman' in white tights with a big H on his chest; Mick chose to be 'Gangsterman' and for the occasion got a double-breasted gold velour suit.

In the short time slot they were given as an opening act, they played most of the same numbers as the BBC programme like 'The Width of a Circle' and 'Memory of a Free Festival' with Tony recalling "we did all the heavy rock stuff". There was also a silent film shot of their performance. They didn't exactly convert the crowd, but one person in the audience was totally into it - Marc Bolan. It wouldn't be long before Bolan would beat Bowie to the punch and become the first British rock star of the new decade (Authors' Note: by the time Bowie released *Ziggy Stardust* in June 1972, Bolan (starting in October 1970) already had four #1 singles ('Hot Love', 'Get It On', 'Telegram Sam', and 'Metal Guru'), two #2 singles ('Ride A White Swan' and 'Jeepster') and a #1 album in the classic *Electric Warrior*. A double album repackaging of the first two Tyrannosaurus Rex albums went to #1, in March of 1972. In addition, a compilation album titled *Bolan Boogie* released in May of 1972 went to #1 as well. In comparison, Bowie had only hit the Top Ten singles chart twice, with 'Space Oddity' a #5 in 1969 while 'Starman' issued in April 1972 made it to #10. His first album *David Bowie* failed to chart at all. His second album (again titled *David Bowie*) was another commercial flop, as was

The Man Who Sold the World. To give even more perspective, in March of 1972, T. Rex filled Wembley with hysterical fans, an event documented in Ringo Starr's film of the event *Born To Boogie*. Bowie on the other hand was starting off the Ziggy Stardust tour by playing the pub and college circuit).

Unfortunately, back in the dressing room after the gig, the band discovered that their clothes had been stolen. Tony recalls a sight that must have been quite an eyeful for any passing motorists: "It was a very cold day. We had to get back into a car that had a broken window and no heater. We're talking about the whole band and the girlfriends, six or seven people in this small English car. We had to drive the fifteen miles back to Beckenham. We were very dedicated." Humble beginnings indeed for the birth of Glam Rock.

While on the road, Mick would share stories of his time in The Rats, or tell a few jokes. "One thing he shared in common with all musicians was a good mind for a dirty joke," laughs Tony. "He could get in there and really tell them. Every Northerner has that. John Cambridge was a real teller of dirty stories too, but Mick was right there behind him. He would come up with one when John would be taking a break. Mick would come in with a good filthy joke and he would have David and I rolling on the floor laughing!"

More gigs followed, with a hometown welcome for Mick and John Cambridge when the band played at the University of Hull on 6 March. Making a special appearance at the gig was former Rat Benny Marshall, who recalls, "If I ever went to any of their gigs, Bowie would always get me up during 'Unwashed and Somewhat Slightly Dazed' to do the harmonica bit." The day of the University of Hull gig also marked the release of Bowie's new single, 'The Prettiest Star', which had been recorded earlier with Marc Bolan on lead guitar. It was a beautiful record, but sadly flopped in the charts.

Around this time Mick was to witness Marc Bolan at work on one of the great 'lost' singles of the 1970s. Tony Visconti was working for David Platz, a music publisher at Essex Music. "He also had something to do with a television company who'd block-booked a recording studio. He usually recorded what was called library music, where you record things that might be used later for jingles or spots. I wrote something for that, recorded it and we still had some spare time. I said, 'I can't think of anything else, could I just go in and record some of my music?'" Platz agreed. The results of these sessions were the highly collectable Dib Cochran And The Earwigs' single 'Oh Baby/Universal Love', issued on Bell Records in 1970.

The single made no mention of the musicians involved (Marc Bolan on guitar and backing vocals, John Cambridge on drums, Tony Visconti providing the string arrangement, bass and lead vocals and Rick Wakeman on piano – Wakeman was a member of the Strawbs and had been introduced to David Bowie by Visconti. Tony and Rick first met through David Platz) and quickly disappeared from circulation. Many rumours over the years suggest that both Bowie and Ronson were involved but Tony sets the record straight: "Mick actually accompanied me to the studio for that day. He watched Marc Bolan play, it was a shame that Mick was not allowed to pick up a guitar otherwise you would have had both Marc Bolan and Mick Ronson on the same track. Mick was cool, he just wanted to learn, he just wanted to sit there and watch. He was so non-egotistical, in those days it was almost as if he was wallpaper. He would just be content to sit there and watch and listen. He would be the last person to say 'do you mind if I play guitar?' You would have to drag him across the room and put a guitar in his arms to get him to play. Contrary to what fans would like to believe, David never set foot in the studio that day. I've heard people say that he played sax on the record but there's no sax on the record!"

Another track recorded at this time under similar circumstances was a Tony Visconti composition called 'Skinny Rose'. "That was done under the same auspices of just having free time at this studio. 'Skinny Rose' is just Ronson, me and John Cambridge who, I think, was just playing brushes on the back of a guitar case or something like that." The recording would remain in the vault until 1998 when Tony re-issued his 1977 solo album *Visconti's Inventory* on CD. 'Skinny Rose' is included as a bonus track. The 1969 date attached to it in the liner notes is a typo, as Tony later confirmed it was definitely recorded in 1970.

March 23, 1970 brought another visit to the BBC, this time to the programme *Sounds of the Seventies*. Mick played with far more confidence than he had during the February BBC show, as the positively scintillating version of 'I'm Waiting for the Man' proves. Also laid down that day were 'The Wild-Eyed Boy from Freecloud' and two songs that would appear on Bowie's next album, 'The Width of a Circle' and 'The Supermen'. The broadcast was on April 6, 1970, but 'The Supermen' was deleted from the show.

Throughout this period Mick remained focussed on one thing – the music. Tony explains: "As a friend, Mick was very distant. I have one picture where we had a party at Mary Finnigan's house and John Cambridge was getting his haircut. You could see in the photos that Mick was just sitting there biding his time. You know, just a little smile on his face. I think Mick was very complicated. When he would go to a party, it seemed all he would sit and think about was 'What am I going to play in the studio tomorrow?' The most important thing in Mick's life was music." As for socializing with Bowie, Tony adds, "I don't think they were hanging out and I could see why in a way. David was already in this strange, bizarre world of his bisexual persona and Mick was a simple lad from the north of

England. That must have been hard for Mick to handle. It was hard for me to handle and I'm a native New Yorker!" To add to the ambiguity of this alternative lifestyle, Bowie and Angela were married on March 20, 1970.

Mick's first official recording with David Bowie was to be a re-worked version of the closing song from the *David Bowie* album, 'Memory of a Free Festival', captured over three days at Advision studios in early April, 1970. Visconti recalls that, "when we came to do 'Memory of a Free Festival' we were very organized. We knew who would do what and Mick was already slowly but surely becoming more powerful and more influential on David. I welcomed it because we really needed him. It hadn't shown just yet, but Mick could also play piano and arrange. I arranged the track and we used our friend, Ralph Mace, who was really the only classical keyboard player we knew. He worked at Phonogram Records. We were all in our mid-twenties and Ralph was fifty years old or so and he loved us. He played all the synthesizer parts, but we pushed Mick to the forefront and that's him playing solid electric guitar and lead guitar. It was obvious that Mick was not a run-of-the-mill guitarist. There were more dimensions to him than just being a rock or blues guitarist and that's what I think ultimately set him apart from anybody else at the time. On the B-side during that session, we finally found out through John Cambridge (who was a very funny kind of guy in pushing people forward) that Mick does some great soul singing. So, we pushed Mick in front of the microphone and he sang all that soul stuff at the end. All that 'yeah, yeah, yeah, yeah, yeah', that's Mick. He was wailing away, he was great. So our eyes kept widening and widening." The single, issued in June, was not a commercial success.

After the sessions for this single were completed, John Cambridge decided to leave the band and head back to Hull.

For the second time in his career Mick 'Woody' Woodmansey would replace him. Woody not only took over the drum stool in The Hype, but also Cambridge's place at Haddon Hall. Woody says, "You know bands like the Red Hot Chili Peppers, that now move into a house and live and record together? Haddon Hall was like that. As you went in the front door, there was a staircase like something you would see in *Gone with the Wind*. When you got to the top, there was a big stained-glass window and then the balcony went both ways around, but all the doors on the balcony were closed off, because there were flats on the other side of the walls. Mick and I had sleeping bags on the landing. We would look through the banisters at everybody that was coming into the house."

The domestic situation at Haddon Hall worked out sometimes. Visconti: "We were really hungry and we didn't have a lot of money between us, so we all sat down and budgeted how much we were going to spend on food each week. If my girlfriend and I went out and bought the food, we would have enough to last until the end of the week. If we gave the money to David and Angela, they would buy all these luxury items that you could only sit down and eat at one meal! It wasn't like bread and potatoes and carrots and all that, which you can keep making fresh for the rest of the week. They were living on a different economy than we were. David had already had a hit with 'Space Oddity' and he was spending his money on antiques and they were going out to restaurants. So the rest of us should have been on our own budget. But no, it was a commune and David insisted that we all chip in and pull together. I remember once we all had a fight with David and Angela, including Mick. It was a mutiny, we nearly tore them apart. We're talking about five hungry people all yelling! They brought home one little bag of groceries for the whole week. Angela said in a very high-class voice, 'You know, it's terrible how little £8 goes these days', and that was all we needed to hear. To us £8 was a lot of money; to her it was like a piss in the ocean. There were lovely times too, like when it was good weather, all of us would be out in the garden sunbathing."

Everything was falling into place for Bowie, he had a hot band and the undying support of his new bride. There was just one more area that needed tending to: management. In David and Angela's eyes, current manager Ken Pitt was not, in their opinion, ideal for Bowie's career. Angela sums up the dilemma in her book with Patrick Carr, *Backstage Passes*: "The words writ large on David's wall were 'Rock and Radical', not 'Cabaret and Conformity.'" They initially met up with Ralph Mace from Phillips, but it was his boss, Olav Wyper who recommended lawyer Tony Defries. Defries had already savoured a taste of the music business in 1964 when he represented Mickie Most in a case involving The Animals. Ever since then, he had been eager to move into show business. David and Angela paid him a visit and he agreed to help terminate the contract with Ken Pitt. It wasn't long before he would become David's new manager.

In the midst of all this, it was time to record a new album, the first to feature Mick Ronson as Bowie's lead guitarist. Studio time had been booked for April and May, 1970, at Trident and Advision Studios in London. Tony Visconti would be producing the project. Before beginning the album, David and Tony agreed that this was going to be as great as *Sgt. Pepper*, a true masterpiece. But once the sessions started, Tony found it difficult to get David interested in the recordings. At the time, David and Angela were still in newly-wedded bliss. Tony remembers it as "a mad love relationship, they were really crazy about each other."

At the start of the sessions, Bowie would arrive and present Tony and Mick with a couple of chord sequences, nothing more. "Then Mick and I would go in and do something with them. We wouldn't even have a style of doing it. By this time Woody Woodmansey had come into the picture, so the three of us would just thrash it out. David would come in at the end and put a lyric on and a melody. I know that makes up a lot of a song, but there wouldn't be any songs if we didn't pre-record those tracks based on David's chord changes. It was so frustrating, because the guy was mentally absent for most of it. It did lead to David and I breaking up. In the end, I said, 'Look man, I just can't make an album under these conditions.' I have to really go down on record in saying that if it wasn't for Mick and his desire to show the world that he was a great guitarist, who knows what would have happened."

Woody says, "We put all the tracks down with just guitar, bass and drums. We had no idea what song was going on top or what other instruments or weird sounds might end up on it. We treated it as 'this is it and that's all there's going to be' and it was only as we progressed through the recording that all these other sounds and harmonies and things started getting added to it. We'd really just come out of this hard rock area, that's what we were influenced by. That's what both Mick and I were into, whereas Bowie had never touched that area and I don't think Tony had either." When asked about songwriting credits during his Kevin Cann *Starzone* interview, Mick responded, "I don't know really, I can't remember. I thought I was treated fairly in a lot of ways."

The album, entitled *The Man Who Sold the World*, kicks off with 'The Width of a Circle', which had finally evolved into an eight-minute tour-de-force featuring a brutal performance from Mick. Tony remembers this track being recorded in two sections and spliced together with a unique overdub. "That was the first time backwards reverb was ever used on record. The Beatles had already used backwards sounds like a high hat on 'Strawberry Fields Forever', but this was the first time the reverb went backwards. Lots of special effects are done for reasons as simple as that, just to cover up a splice or edit."

In addition to Mick's obvious mastery of the guitar, Tony was becoming aware of his talent in other areas as well. "He had that little trick up his sleeve that he was a classically trained pianist and violinist. He played recorder, which we played together on 'All the Madmen.' I knew he could write for violins because he wanted to write a few little things on *The Man Who Sold the World* to be played on the Moog synthesizer, but he scored them as violin parts, under my tutelage, I might add. He had no idea how you actually had to lay it all out and where you begin and where you ended. He wrote out the parts on 'All the Madmen' where it goes "I'd rather stay here/with all the madmen" and in the chorus there was a violin kind of sound. It was definitely a synthesizer violin sound, but that was Mick's writing. I knew I could communicate with him in these wacky ways, and so did David by the way."

The idea to use the Moog synthesizer came from hearing Walter Carlos' groundbreaking *Switched On Bach* album, which was a staple at Haddon Hall. Once again Ralph Mace was called in to help. Ralph had the only Moog synthesizer in England at the time. It was a massive piece of equipment that, Tony remembers, "looked like three or four black refrigerators side by side with loads and loads of wires called patch cords. In spite of all of that enormous size, it was still monophonic. So all the strings that you hear on 'All the Madmen', for instance, had to be played one part at a time. You couldn't just put all of your fingers down like it was a piano and play all the notes together. You had to play one note at a time. Ralph read the pieces of music and played them very well. We wanted to be one of the first to get into the synthesizer technology."

If Tony was put off by Bowie's relative lack of participation, Mick rose to the occasion and turned in an astonishing performance that impressed the producer. "Working with him was incredible. He was one of the greatest musicians I have ever worked with. Even though he had recorded one album before us with Michael Chapman, it still didn't add up to a lot of studio experience. He acknowledged that I taught him a lot of things about how to record and score. He was asking me questions incessantly, 'how do you do this?' and 'how do you do that?' and he was such a good student on that level. On the other hand, he was teaching me about rock bass playing and guitar playing. I wasn't that great a musician then and Mick certainly was. As a consequence of playing every weekend with The Rats before he came down to play with Bowie, he had a lot more rock stage experience than me. So Mick was teaching me how to be bold and bodacious on bass and I was teaching him all of the finesse in the studio, how you get all the special effects tricks and all that."

Mick insisted that Tony needed another bass. "He didn't like my bass playing at first or my sound. He made me sit down and listen to Jack Bruce of Cream, saying, 'You've got to sound like this.' I had a Fender bass and he made me buy the same bass that Jack Bruce had, which was a Gibson EBO. It's a cherry red bass with a small neck. The charming thing about it is that you can bend the strings as if it were a lead guitar. That's the sound I'm playing on 'She Shook Me Cold', so the bass sounds like lead guitar. I'm bending those strings like mad and it was Mick getting me to do it. I know people say the bass is louder than the guitar on that track, yet it was Mick on the mix. He wasn't terribly proud of his guitar playing and he said 'push the bass up, more bass', again trying to imitate a Cream record. There is an edit right where Mick's guitar solo comes in, that was actually a take two or three. The song up to that point was one take and then the guitar solo was done separately. From the guitar solo to the end of the song was another take. It's amazing how it turned out so heavy. That was definitely Mick's dark nature. He figured if he was going to go down on record as being the guitarist in this band, it was going to be on his own terms."

When Bowie finally did put lyrics to the backing tracks, he ended up with his most dark and disturbing collection of songs yet. It was filled with unsettling images like a returning Vietnam veteran who turns his wrath on civilians ('Running Gun Blues'), his half-brother Terry ('All the Madmen') and the tale of a super-race derived from the writings of Friedrich Nietzsche ('The Supermen'). It all added up to a brilliant, but decidedly un-commercial album.

In the US, Mercury released the album first in November 1970, followed by a single release of 'All the Madmen' in December, which was quickly withdrawn. In the UK, it was decided that a track not featured on the album ('Holy Holy') was the best choice for a single in January 1971. The album followed in that country in April, but both single and album were flops. Tony Visconti believes that "the album was so innovative, but it was just a little too early. Nobody liked the album when it came out. It was just too freaky, it freaked everybody out." Certainly the sleeve (featuring David lounging on the Haddon Hall sofa in a dress) caused a bit of a stir.

While recording *The Man Who Sold the World*, Mick received an offer from Gus Dudgeon to play on a session (also at Trident Studios) for up-and-coming superstar Elton John. Gus and Elton had been struggling with the arrangement of a new song called 'Madman Across the Water' and were undecided about how to record it. When Elton played Gus the riff, Elton said he wanted to hear it on guitar instead of piano. "I knew Elton was a fan of Michael Chapman and that's the kind of thing he can do falling off a log. It's quite complicated because the riff actually winds up with a harmonic at the final note. I needed to use somebody who could execute it cleanly and wouldn't be fazed by the idea of playing what was actually, at that point, quite a complicated lick. Elton said 'Oh yeah, it would be fantastic to get Chapman in.' At that point, Elton didn't have a guitarist. I asked him, 'Are you thinking of using anything else?' and he said, 'I think I'd like this thing to be fairly psychedelic. Why don't we get another guitarist?' I said 'Well, as you like Chapman so much, why don't we get in Ronson to do it?' and he simply said 'What a great idea!' Basically, I did it because I wanted them (Chapman and Ronson) to hold each other's hands, I thought they might both be a bit freaked out by working with Elton in the first place. At least with the two of them in the room together, they're not going to feel quite so exposed, and that's essentially what happened. We wound up with this incredible psychedelic version which, ironically at the end of the day, we decided probably wasn't the best way of doing it." This amazing track (very much in the style of *The Man Who Sold the World*) would stay in the vaults until 1992, when it wound up on a collection of Elton B-sides and rarities called *Rare Masters*.

The disappointing reaction to *The Man Who Sold the World* was only one factor in Mick's decision to split from Bowie and head back to Hull. He had kept in contact with Rats frontman Benny Marshall via the post. "He'd been with Bowie for a while and got a bit disillusioned with it all," says Benny, who received several letters from Mick voicing his dissatisfaction.

Mick and Woody made their joint decision to part company with Bowie on the way to perform a David Bowie and The Hype gig. Woody: "We got talking about 'Is this what we want to do?' We had a gig in Leeds and I think Bowie was travelling in his own car, which was a Riley in those days. He seemed to crash that Riley every other day. He wasn't a very good driver. Anyway, we got in a taxi and soon after came to a crossroads which said 'Hull' one direction and 'Leeds' the other. Mick and I just kind of looked at each other and went 'Yeah, alright', and so we left Bowie and went back to Hull. He must have done that gig on his own."

Back in Hull, Mick wasted no time paying Benny Marshall a visit. "He turned up one night on the doorstep with Woody." After telling him they'd left Bowie and had no plans to return, they offered Benny the lead vocalist position in a new band. "I asked who was in it and Mick said, 'It's me, Tony Visconti and Woody'. So I said 'That sounds good, yeah, I'll do it,' and off we went."

The new line-up of The Hype was once again returning to Advision Studios to record songs for a proposed album but there was one major problem – a lack of material. Woody recalls, "None of us had ever really written. We'd had a go at writing, but we hadn't really got that side of it together at all." Tony Visconti made the first move with a song he came up with called 'Clorissa'. Tony says that this track was the very first of the few Hype sessions that ever took place. "I just wrote that song to go in and start the whole session, (since) we had no material at all." The track was sung by Tony and featured Mick on guitar, piano and backing vocals. It would remain unreleased until its use as a bonus track on the 1998 re-issue of *Visconti's Inventory*, Tony's solo album.

Another track brought to the table by Tony was '4th Hour of My Sleep', written by Tucker Zimmerman, an artist that Tony was producing for Denny Cordell's company, Straight Ahead Productions. Tony describes Tucker as "a real rebel. He had very long hair and a little beard. One day his manager said, 'I love your image, the beard looks great, don't ever shave off your beard.' Tucker immediately shaved off the beard! That's how angry he was. David Bowie was very impressed with him, he saw Tucker as the real deal. I remember he sang at the Three Tuns Pub in Beckenham, the Arts Lab that David ran. During his set, David decided to put on a light show with all these lights filled up with oil and water. Tucker screamed at him, 'Turn off those lights!' and David was staring at me horrified. I said, 'Turn them off, he doesn't like any psychedelia.' It was hilarious, but David still admired him for the outspoken/outrageous person that he was. It's a shame Tucker never really got any fame because he was amazing. So when we were looking for material, I took one of Tucker's songs and introduced it to the band." The highlight of the song is the way Mick's lead guitar licks 'answer' back the lyrics to the song, delivered by Benny in his trademark bluesy voice. A promotional film was shot for the song at The Marquee Club, but this appears to have been lost.

Mick and Benny teamed up to write another song for the album entitled, 'Powers of Darkness'. With a killer riff from Ronson that would do Black Sabbath proud and lyrics cautioning the 'Powers of Darkness' to 'stay away from my door', this stomping track sounds right in step with today's Stoner Rock movement (a newer movement of Heavy Metal that has its feet firmly planted in the style of early Black Sabbath. Fu Manchu, Queens Of The Stone Age and Electric Frankenstein are just a few of the bands that are considered to be part of this scene. The Ronno song sounds uncannily like some of the records released by this genre).

According to Benny, a few other tracks were attempted. "There was another one called 'Invisible Long Hair' and I know we did backing tracks for one or two other songs, but we didn't have names for them. They were just riffs and chords and there weren't any melodies to them."

There were troubles with the record company too. Benny had refused to sign the contract that Phillips offered. They were prepared to add him in as a member of the group, but refused to hand over any more money. They argued that the advance they paid when they signed the contract was for the entire group. Tony ironed out the situation by paying Benny as a session musician, but he felt they would get little support from Phillips. "No one was interested in us at the record company and we rapidly spent that money on musical instruments. We had no money to actually go into the studio and record, so we only did those few titles."

By this time it was decided to rename the group Ronno, (after the nickname Mick had picked up from his fellow musicians) and scout around for live work. According to Benny, "Tony couldn't commit himself to doing gigs because of his studio work. We had to get another bass player in." Enter Trevor Bolder, another Hull musician Mick knew of via the local circuit (the same Bolder whose aforementioned grandmother taught a young Mick Ronson). Trevor himself remembers seeing The Rats play at the Beverley Regal just outside of Hull. Later, he attended another gig where The Rats' bass player kept getting electrocuted on stage, so he was asked to fill in. He was, however, never a member of The Rats as popular rumour claims. "It was just a one-off, get up there and play," remembers Trevor. "Mick had been sort of an admirer of mine for quite a long time. He'd seen me play in lots of different bands."

Trevor quickly agreed to join the new band Ronno so a series of rehearsals began: "We used to rehearse in this village hall in a place called, funnily enough, Woodmansey. We'd rehearse in the daytime as we were all out of work. They had these few songs, so we'd rehearse and put together other songs for the album. I actually didn't play on the recordings, Tony Visconti did. We did that for about four months and then we went out and did some gigs. We played all over the country." Benny remembers, "We were going through the Bronze agency at the time and we played all the main places. There was a lot of hassle with the contracts because we were still under contract to Phillips and Bronze, who had their own label, didn't really want to get involved while we were tied up with Phillips so they didn't push us all that much." One memorable gig was at the legendary Cavern Club in Liverpool. Trevor proudly recalls, "The Beatles, everybody started at the Cavern. It was just an amazing place to play. It was a really tiny place, the sweat used to run down the walls. They pulled it down not long after we played, so I was really glad that we actually performed there." Benny agrees: "The Cavern Club is a good memory. There was writing on the walls and things from the different bands that had played there."

The one and only Ronno single ('4th Hour Of My Sleep/ Powers of Darkness') was released on Vertigo Records in January, 1971 and although a fine record, failed to stir up much excitement. Tony had been the one negotiating with the label and with his departure to concentrate his efforts on the rising fortunes of Marc Bolan, any future recording sessions were up in the air.

While screaming lead guitar was Mick's speciality in Ronno, there were other areas of music that he was interested in as well. Maggi Ronson recalls some of his time during this period was spent with an old piano teacher. "When he was at home during that time he'd go to Mrs White's and do a lot of theory with her, because she was amazing at that aspect. That's where he studied a lot about arrangements." These lessons would soon prove useful to Mick.

Soon after the Ronno single was issued, Mick got the call from Bowie asking if he would return and help him on his upcoming new album. With Ronno at a dead end, Mick not only agreed to return, he promised to bring along a drummer and bass player as well. Mick first called up his mates from the Michael Chapman days, Rick Kemp and Richie Dharma. Rick says that "Richie and myself met Mick soon afterwards in a village hall near Hull to make a band for David Bowie." Unfortunately, it didn't work out so the duo carried on working with Michael Chapman. Instead, the Ronno rhythm section of Trevor and Woody were recruited for the trip back to London.

Mick, Trevor and Woody found themselves back at Haddon Hall, living with David and Angela and once again there was rarely a dull moment. Bowie, fuelled by his first visit to the US, had written a batch of amazing new songs. Since manager Tony Defries was in the middle of negotiating a new recording contract for him, David looked at alternative ways of getting his songs out to the public. Two of the demos he had worked up were good so he wanted to issue them. He struck on the idea of forming a band around Freddi Burretti, a clothing designer he met at a gay club named The Sombrero. Freddi would be the singer and the band would be known as Arnold Corns. He even managed to convince B&C Records to issue a single from the group ('Moonage Daydream/Hang On to Yourself') in April, 1971.

It's been believed that these early demo recordings featured Ronson, Bolder and Woodmansey, but the recently released 30th Anniversary edition of *The Rise and Fall of Ziggy Stardust and the Spiders from Mars* credits Bowie, Freddie Burretti, Mark Carr-Pritchard, Tim Broadbent, and Pete De Somogy as the musicians.

No one knew it at the time, but from the humble seeds of Arnold Corns, great Spiders from Mars would emerge to take over the world.

CHAPTER 4

THEN WE WERE ZIGGY'S BAND

In the next year or so, "don't want to stay alive/when you're twenty-five" would ring from every household radio. Yet for Mick Ronson, this future 'All the Young Dudes' lyric couldn't ring farther from the truth at this earlier time. Having just turned twenty five, he was finally beginning to see the rewards of his determination.

Woody remembers David Bowie getting better and better as a songwriter. John Lennon and Neil Young & Crazy Horse albums were being played and they began to recognise that a lot of the instrumentation on those albums was very minimal: "We got into that way of thinking and that way of playing. When you played a note it meant something, it wasn't like fifty notes. It was the same on drums. It was very straight-ahead and when you hit a cymbal, that cymbal actually fitted and meant something, rather than hitting a cymbal all the way through. So, that's the way we got into recording the album *Hunky Dory*, it was more controlled."

Californian Rodney Bingenheimer and his then-girlfriend Melanie McDonald were at the *Hunky Dory* sessions every night at Trident Studios in London. Bingenheimer was at the time an employee of Mercury Records. Later, he opened a glam club and became a well-known DJ. He is referred to as the Mayor of the Sunset Strip. "I saw the whole thing come down," says Rodney. "David was the controller, he was always in this little booth talking on a speaker thing. Mick was incredible. I kept telling him he should come to America, that he would be a star! He laughed and said, 'Oh yeah, sure.' The studio was really weird, it was in a hole down below where they actually recorded."

This subterranean recording environment may be one of the reasons why *Hunky Dory* retains that dirty-earthy-classic quality. Imagine long-haired and bell-bottomed songwriter David against a backdrop of extraordinary Rick Wakeman moments. According to Dave Thompson, author of *David Bowie Moonage Daydream,* "*Melody Maker* was crediting Wakeman with having changed the style of the Strawbs from a fairly straight folk group to an incredibly tight and harmonic rock band." He goes on to say that, "his work on *Hunky Dory* still ranks among his best ever, seldom has he ever played as sensitively as on 'Life on Mars?'" Kevin Cann notes in *Chronology* that "David offered Rick a permanent place in his backing group but was turned down because of Wakeman's session commitments." Season that with some 'controlled' Hull rhythm and blues rock, add Ronson's brilliant arrangements and melodic guitar solos and you have a clear vision of the *Hunky Dory* sessions.

Woody: "Mick was a very direct player. When he hit a chord, he got it and when he played a solo, you got the solo. That was one of the abilities that he had. It was so natural to him that he didn't even look on it as anything special. He was a pianist and he played recorder, he was very musical, so he thought that way all the time. He was good at finding a solo that integrated with the track. It always felt like it should be there rather than, 'This is a solo and now the song continues after it.'"

Trevor adds: "I was really nervous. I'd never been in the recording studio before. It was all new to me. The other people had experienced it and seemingly done it all. Most of the time, I was just trying to think of things to play on the tracks. When we were working together, Mick was an excellent, brilliant friend. He helped me a lot and looked after me, showed me what I should and shouldn't do. I was inexperienced in those days about what went on in studios. Yet I think we learned a lot together."

There were a great number of songs recorded during this period, eleven of them etched permanently into the grooves of *Hunky Dory*. Others ended up in the Arnold Corns master-box and some remained unreleased, sure to be used as the musical blueprint for David's plan to bring his gestating new Ziggy Stardust character to life. The eleven songs that were chosen were selected with great care and, as a consequence, the album exudes a consistent flow of imagery and sound. The songs are linked together with clever arrangements that have qualified them as timeless. Mick's direct contributions include guitar, vocals and mellotron. He did the arrangements for 'Life on Mars?', 'Kooks', 'Quicksand' and the Biff Rose-composed 'Fill Your Heart', which David and Mick agreed "owes one hell of a lot to Arthur G. Wright and his prototype". Wright arranged half of the 1968 Rose record *The Thorn in Mrs. Rose's Side* which David and Mick were very fond of. Thus the fitting anecdote on the back cover sleeve. The cover photo taken by Brian Ward was brilliantly transformed into a pastel painted portrait by George Underwood and Terry Pastor of Main Artery (London). The starlet type pose and the carefully chosen colours, magnified David's androgyny, resulting in a shocking-you-softly piece of artwork. Add the polish of Ken Scott's production and it was a classic package.

Maggi remembers Mick writing at home. "I'd seen Michael working really hard on the *Hunky Dory* arrangements for 'Life on Mars?'. I even remember him sitting in the loo where he could get some peace and quiet." This focussed determination to get his contribution just right has earned Mick Ronson many plaudits from all corners of the music business. Steve New, long-time fan (later to work under Mick's wing as the guitarist for the Rich Kids) loves *Hunky Dory*: "In my opinion, Mick made David Bowie sound good. He took Bowie's songs from being sort of second-rate Donovan songs to really beautifully crafted numbers." Def Leppard's Joe Elliott raves about the guitar work: "The solo in 'Life on Mars?' is a stand-out piece, not just on that album, it's one of the all-time solos, really." Chrissie Hynde from the Pretenders says this: "The contribution that Mick made to Bowie's music was immeasurable." While sharing her own special memory about *Hunky Dory*, she validates its pivotal influence: "I was actually at a stage where I thought that maybe I should give this rock 'n' roll lark a rest, maybe it was time to move on to other things. Periodically throughout my youth, that was what I felt. When I was sixteen, I dumped all of my Beatles paraphernalia, something I still live to regret. I must have been about twenty when *Hunky Dory* came out. When I heard that, it just put me right back to where I was, when I was fourteen. I was just totally, totally taken by that album. It was life-changing for me."

At this point, *Hunky Dory* was unreleased, although it enjoyed a proper showcase on John Peel's *In Concert* on BBC Radio 1 on June 3, 1971, at the Corporation's Paris Studios. According to the Bernie Andrews and Jeff Griffin-penned *Bowie at the Beeb* (Virgin 2000) liner notes, the band with special guests included

David, Mick, Trevor, Woody, Mark Carr-Pritchard, Geoffrey Alexander, Dana Gillespie and George Underwood. The songs featured on the programme were: 'Queen Bitch', 'Bombers', 'Supermen', 'Looking for a Friend', 'Almost Grown', 'Oh! You Pretty Things', 'Kooks', 'Song for Bob Dylan', 'Andy Warhol' and 'It Ain't Easy'. Some judicious editing was required and this time it was 'Oh! You Pretty Things' that did not make the transmission on June 20.

That summer, as David continued to write the songs for the up-coming album centred around his latest alter-ego, Ziggy Stardust, Mick devoted his extra time to producing David's former girlfriend, Dana Gillespie. He and David co-produced her version of 'Andy Warhol', which was allegedly written for her to sing. They also co-produced the track called 'Mother Don't Be Frightened' which earned Mick his first commissioned 'string arrangement' job. Seizing this as an opportunity to labour in the studio, Mick used the skills he had recently learned from working at Tony Visconti's side.

The Edwards and Zanetta book *Stardust: The David Bowie Story* covers the business practices of Tony Defries in detail. Here is a synopsis of one of Tony's most infamous deals which involved the voluptuous Dana Gillespie: Tony Defries who was quite confident that if he shopped David and Dana together, he might score one, if not both of them, a deal. When he had exhausted his efforts trying to get them signed in England, he set his sights on America. Meanwhile, he convinced David to sign to his newly formed (music producing, publishing, booking and management) company called the Gem Group. Gem promised him a six-year recording contract or, in other words, a future. Mick thought this promised him a future too. In addition to the recording contract, David also signed a lifetime management agreement with Tony.

Their musical careers were resting in the hands of Tony as he knocked on every label door in New York City. Defries would spend the next several months shopping around a promo album he had made which consisted of tracks by David on one side and by Dana on the other. Only 500 copies were pressed of this unique album, and due to the very different mixes/versions it is highly sought after. The band was preparing to go back to Trident to add finishing touches to *Hunky Dory* and record the songs that had been prepared for *Ziggy Stardust*. Mick's recording career seemed full of possibility.

Meanwhile, Mick and the boys were enjoying themselves. It was August, 1971 and Andy Warhol's show *Pork* had arrived in London. Warhol's latest artistic extravaganza (a play based on conversation tapes recorded at The Factory) was gaining huge attention much like everything else the Pop Art icon created. In an attempt to avoid the censors, the theatre placed advance adverts in the newspapers, such as the one in *Stardust* that read, "Warning. This play has explicit sexual content and offensive language. If you are likely to be disturbed, do not attend." With such advance publicity, The Roundhouse had a sell-out run with *Pork*. No one could be kept away.

The cast of Warhol superstars consisted of Tony Zanetta (who played Andy Warhol), Cherry Vanilla (who played Pork) and Leee Black Childers who was the production manager of the show. Other characters were Wayne (now Jayne) County, Gerri Miller, Jamie de Carlo Andrews and director Tony Ingrassia. These first three would soon play a major role in the mammoth publicity machine that would introduce Mick to the American eye.

Leee Black Childers fondly remembers the *Pork* era and, along with Cherry Vanilla, he would always go out to rock clubs after rehearsals. It's during this time that Leee and Cherry discovered the advantages of posing as writers/photographers for an American magazine called *Circus*. This enabled them to get the "royal treatment" at the clubs and rock-shows, but in reality they didn't work for a magazine at all, they were just great actors. These experiences would benefit them later when with MainMan. They would both pore over the music press to see who was playing. Leee spotted a poster with a picture of David Bowie in a dress, advertising a show at a place called The Country Club. He quickly convinced Cherry and Wayne that it might be worth investigating. Leee describes this club as "a garage behind a shopping centre. This wasn't a mall or anything like we have in America. This was four little stores in a row with a big garage (The Country Club) behind it."

There were only about thirty people there and though the New Yorkers were treated well, they were a little surprised to find David wasn't wearing a dress. "He was wearing big floppy pants with a silk shirt," Leee remembers, "and a huge hat. Then there was Mick Ronson." It didn't take Cherry long to notice Mick as she nudged Leee in the ribs and said 'Who's he?' Leee adds, "We had gone to see David but there was this beautiful blonde standing there." They were both very curious about Mick but Leee explains, "He was very, very shy with us because we were there on behalf of Andy Warhol, so we were, in many ways, quite scary to him." In addition to meeting David and Mick, this was the same night that the *Pork* cast met Angie Bowie and Dana Gillespie. "The whole extended family," as Leee puts it.

The outrageous manners of the *Pork* gang were revealed when David introduced them from the stage. "Cherry stood up and popped one of her tits out and waved it around for the audience to see," tells Leee. "All of that kind of stuff really wasn't Mick. That wasn't the way he was and it really embarrassed him. If he could've blushed under that snow white Hull skin he probably would have."

Cherry describes the night as "a small club situation, it was all very informal. David was playing an acoustic guitar, Mick was playing electric guitar and Rick Wakeman was playing the piano. Being from the Warhol crowd, we felt we had the right to walk right up and introduce ourselves. We invited them to come see the play and they brought David's new manager Tony Defries. After that, we went out with them socially to The Sombrero, a little gay dance club in London (where Bowie had previously met Freddi Burretti)."

At The Sombrero, Cherry and Leee wondered if Mick Ronson was gay. "He would dance with Cherry," explains Leee, "but he didn't dance with me. To me, that was sort of an indication that he probably wasn't gay and that he was just there because he was with David."

Cherry had developed quite a crush on Mick but didn't take it too seriously because he was just so "cute and sweet." She does admit that she might have scared him a little bit. "Mick was so shy when we first met that he could barely speak and even when he did he had such a thick Hull accent. It was hard to understand him, as an American, so I had to keep asking him to repeat himself and we just giggled a lot. Of course, I was practically attacking him sexually because Bowie had Angie and Mick was the guitarist and he was just a little darling! He would always laugh and not take me too seriously, but in a way he loved it because I don't think that girls had really paid so much attention to him up until that point."

It wouldn't be long before Tony Defries would utilise these underground superstars to launch his endeavours in New York. Cherry: "We went back to America after socialising all summer with the Bowies and Ronson. Tony kept contacting Tony Zanetta, Leee Black Childers and myself on how he should market Bowie in the States. It was very informal in the US. We were all hanging out at Max's with magazine writers and we went to clubs and concert halls where we knew the promoters so we'd get in backstage and so on. It wasn't yet set up like a business. Tony was picking our brains. We were just giving him the information as New York rock 'n' roll fans. However, it did get to be more and more formal as it went along. Each time Tony would come to America, we would get more involved in forming a management team, which is eventually what happened."

Back at Haddon Hall, the guys were having their share of both tough and cherished times. Trevor Bolder laughs as he remembers this incident: "We were all sleeping on the balcony. Mick was doing some string arrangements for a band called Milkwood (The New Seekers' spin-off band) so he would spend all day writing. On this particular weekend, he had to have these finished on a Sunday night so he could go in the studio on Monday morning and put them down. David's mum was coming in on the Sunday morning and Mick spoke to her on Saturday night and said, 'When you come in, can you wake me up? I have to get all these string arrangements finished.' So when she arrived on the Sunday morning, she immediately walked upstairs to the balcony and starts shouting at Mick, 'Wake up, Wake up!' Mick jumped out of the bed screaming, 'I'm late for the session! I'm late for the session!' He must have been dreaming about work because he thought it was Monday morning. He was stark bollock-naked running at David's mum! It was quite a sight. I think he scared her to death."

Mick's work with Milkwood proved beneficial, in spite of that embarrassing incident. He did make the session on time and arranged the B-side of their first single. According to Ronson archivist Sven Gusevik, Laurie Heath was a member of The New Seekers at that time and he played Mick a demo of a song he'd written called 'This Is for You'. Mick would later record this song for his second solo album.

In September, Bowie's band officially began recording *The Rise and Fall of Ziggy Stardust and the Spiders from Mars* at Trident Studios. They had originally laid down 'It Ain't Easy' at the *Hunky Dory* sessions but, as history has it, it found its spot as the last track on side one of the *Ziggy Stardust* album. Work continued a few days later, with the recording of 'Shadowman', which remains 'officially' unreleased.

During this time, Tony announced that he had secured a recording contract with RCA Records. Mick, David and Angela were obviously thrilled beyond belief and excitedly prepared for their trip to New York to formally sign the contract. Angie Bowie knew it was 'show time' and wisely insisted that everyone looked magnificent for the visit to RCA. Clothing designer Freddi Burretti of the aforementioned fictitious band Arnold Corns was brought back to work, as the trio shaped their images into what's been referred to as 'the *Hunky Dory* look' (Authors' Note: this is (late) September 1971, nine months before the actual release of *Ziggy* and the short haircut that came with it. At this point in the story, *Hunky Dory* is two months away from release and Bowie is still sporting the long hair, floppy hat and baggy pants associated with the *The Man Who Sold the World/Hunky Dory* era).

The New York experience was a success in more ways than one. RCA's Dennis Katz had arranged a generous deal for David. It was also on this trip that Mick and David would have the opportunity to meet Iggy Pop, Lou Reed and Andy Warhol, which ultimately secured them a special spot in the New York scene.

Annette Peacock, a pioneer of the synthesizer (a prototype was given to her in 1968 by Bob Moog) had made quite a name for herself within the avant garde and jazz communities. One of Mick's musical idols, she explains how she first crossed paths with him: "There was a young A&R guy at RCA called

Bob Ringe (Dennis Katz's assistant) who wanted to hip up the image of the company. So he signed David Bowie, Lou Reed and me. While we were in the studio recording my album (*I'm The One*) I noticed that two extraordinary, charismatic men appeared in the control room. I insist on closed sessions, so I asked Bob to request that they leave. Later, he told me that it was David Bowie and Mick Ronson. They were both a very, very special kind of person with a extraordinary environment and atmosphere that they carried with them."

Mick immediately recognised Annette's unique style and talent, could see she had a really solid band and that her songs were fresh and original. Her vocals were extreme, dramatic and emotional and her use of electronics in jazz-rock fusion was highly innovative. This is a fine example of Mick's talent for recognizing the musical expression of others. This virtue would later provide him with an endless supply of work as a solo artist, session man and producer.

On October 14, 1971, girlfriend Denise Irvin gave birth to Mick's first child, a son named Nicholas. He was born at Kingston upon Hull Royal Infirmary. Being so close in age, he was the perfect playmate for little Joey "Zowie" Bowie, David and Angela's son born May 28, 1971.

As they awaited the release of *Hunky Dory*, the band continued recording *Ziggy Stardust* songs. Plenty were recorded, while others were started (three known tracks from the September sessions) and never finished. Overall, the band recorded some twenty tracks in addition to the actual eleven that made the final cut of the album. *The Ziggy Companion* website notes that the November sessions (lasting two weeks) included the recordings of 'Star', 'Hang On to Yourself', 'Moonage Daydream', 'Five Years', 'Soul Love', 'Lady Stardust' and (unreleased until 1990) 'Sweet Head'. According to David Quantick's Beatles book,

Revolution, the piano that Mick played in the studio was the same one used for the original recording of 'Hey Jude'.

Meanwhile, out on the West Coast, Rodney Bingenheimer and friends had created a heap of hype about Bowie's fabulous recording deal with RCA. This rumour mill provided enough fuel to crank the engines needed to properly launch *Hunky Dory*. The album was finally released at the end of the year, in both America and Europe. Tony Defries immediately drafted in Zanetta and Vanilla, delivering them boxes of *Hunky Dory* albums to give to all of their influential friends. Geographically, all the bases were covered.

After the New Year, the recording of *Ziggy Stardust* continued. This January session delivered three of the cuts that would make the album: 'Starman', 'Rock 'n' Roll Suicide' and 'Suffragette City'. Mick, uncertain of his future only nine months ago after leaving Hull, now felt confident that they had just recorded possibly their finest work to date. If he had any doubts, he need look no further than over the balcony at Haddon Hall to see trails of eager journalists lining up downstairs for their chance to be entertained by the Bowies.

Woody has his own thoughts on the period: "Honestly, I think *Hunky Dory* was a bit too 'songwriter-like'. The eventual sound that we ended up with on *Ziggy Stardust* had more of a group sound. Although it was still Bowie, it was more of a group thing. That's really what he needed. Mick was instrumental in much of that because he was able to take Bowie's chord sequences and put it into a rock thing. Whereas Bowie probably would not have been able to do that at the time. After *Hunky Dory* it was like, 'Yeah, it's good!' We knew it was going to work. 'Changes' was put out as a single in January 1972 and was the first to enjoy a lot of airplay, which was encouraging. Then as soon as we recorded *Ziggy*, it was like 'Shit, this is it!' There were no doubts in anybody's mind.

Trevor Bolder has similar opinions: "When we had finished the *Hunky Dory* album, I really liked it, but it didn't feel particularly special, not like it was going to be a big-selling album. That did happen with *Ziggy Stardust* though. When we finished that album, everybody knew something was going to happen. Especially when we heard 'Moonage Daydream' coming out of the speakers after it was mixed. There was something magical starting to happen."

Mick Ronson's future wife and local hairdresser, Suzi Fussey, created her own sort of magic: "I used to do David Bowie's mother's hair in a local salon and she would always tell me about her son David. He used to walk down Beckenham High Street with a dress on next to his wife who was dressed as a guy and he'd have his little baby, Zowie. I started doing his wife's hair. Angela was quite the personality. She would be very willing to experiment with colour and different cuts and styles. After that, she'd invited me to go to her house to do a perm for her. I went up there and she'd forgotten about the perm but David was there and I got to meet him. David asked me 'What would you do to my hair?' At the time, everyone had very long hair, T. Rex was all the rage. I said, 'Well, I'd cut it off because everyone has long hair and it would be a really good idea if you had short hair.' So, in my opinion, between the three of us we invented that Ziggy look. I eventually ended up going on the road (America, Europe and Japan) with them, meeting Mick and doing his hair. That's how I started with them."

Tony Defries was one of many who approved of the shocking haircut and the image it portrayed. It suited Ziggy's spaceman character perfectly and portrayed a persona that Tony felt was exquisitely marketable. He immediately offered Suzi a job as the band's hair stylist/personal assistant. As plans began to unfold for their UK tour, the rest of Bowie's band was encouraged to glamorise their image. A band labelled the 'Spiders From Mars' was certainly deserving of an acute image, but the rest of the group's fashion-sense took longer to evolve than David's.

Mick's sister Maggi remembers the infancy of the change: "As the Bowie thing started progressing, Mick used to wear these shirts with the frilly bits down the front. He had a white one and another colour, but I'm sure they were for women. They just didn't sell men's shirts like that. There was a lot of clothing on the scene then. The music was always great but the clothes always stuck in my mind as well."

Woody remembers it as something of a joke: "You have to understand, we had been just T-shirts, ripped jeans and sneakers, you know? I suppose we had been into a bit of the flamboyant thing playing hard rock, but it would only be snakeskin boots or similar. I might wear moccasins and an Indian head-dress or something, but it wouldn't be the whole glitter thing. So, when we got into wearing the stuff on *Ziggy*, it was very much a case of "you must be joking?"

It wasn't just their clothing that had to be worked on in preparation for the recording, as Woody explains: "A lot of the neighbours were old-age pensioners. We had to soundproof the basement and we did this to the cellar ourselves. That was where we rehearsed for *Ziggy*. It was a room about twelve foot by six foot, we just crammed ourselves in there, shut the door and you couldn't hear anything (outside)." Simultaneously, concert rehearsals began over at The Royal Ballroom on Tottenham High Road.

On the home front, Haddon Hall had become a haven of activity. "Angie would invite some of the *Vogue* and the 'in' fashion magazine models to come down and visit," recalls Woody. "Mick and I would wake up in the morning, look down and there would be like eight gorgeous females undressed and we would be like, 'Bloody hell!' You have to understand we were Northern boys!"

Meanwhile, David had announced, "I'm gay!" to *Melody Maker* on January 22, 1972, thus creating a large wave of headlines that swamped the music world and exponentially escalated interest in him and the band. David's new image had already gained intense interest within the gay community and this announcement validated that curiosity. A *Gay News* article published later in the summer found Peter Holmes implying that once David becomes as popular as he deserves, "that'll give gay rock a potent spokesman." Gay or straight, male or female, most of the audience accepted his bold declaration. Music was moving forward and rapidly. The new generation of 1970s kids were avidly embracing the glamorous new trails that Bowie and his band were blazing.

Suzi Ronson remembers how "David wanted Mick to pretend that he was gay. He wanted Mick to announce that they were this bisexual bureau. Mick got really, really, *really* cross and said, 'No fuckin' way!' He stormed off. I think he went back up to Hull. David had to talk him into coming back down to London. It was never asked of him again."

Woody shares a similar story; "Mick actually left one day. In fact, it was the day when David asked him to put on the gold suit. He just used too many swear words to repeat. He packed his case and was at the station. He said 'You must be joking, I'm not going out like that.' Bowie asked me to go and sort him out, 'We need him back.' I went to the station and sat on the platform with Mick and talked. He came back and eventually he got into it. If we had been not as naive we probably would have never done all that. There was a lot of youthful and naive determination to make it."

The combination of their great songs, determination and controversial androgynous image had scored the band a fair amount of radio and press. The band did sessions for the *Sound of the Seventies* radio show with Bob Harris and also performed for the UK's hot television programme at the time, *The Old Grey Whistle Test* (recorded and screened February 8). The songs performed were, 'Oh! You Pretty Things', 'Queen Bitch' and 'Five Years'. 'Oh! You Pretty Things' did not air with the other two songs. Instead, it would remain in the vault for another decade, first appearing on UK television, in 1982.

Bob Harris had known David for years but he doesn't recall meeting Mick until he compered the first part of the *Ziggy Stardust* tour. "Mick and David very much played off one another. I thought that Mick was vitally important to the way everything sounded. His guitar work and his presence was an integral part of it and, without that, it just wouldn't have worked in the same way."

The Old Grey Whistle Test was broadcast from a very small studio, as Bob explains: "It was really small, like a living room size. Getting a band and all the amplification and everything else in was a major problem. Usually the bands would record a backing track, which we would use in the studio, and then the vocalist would sing live. Due to the environment, it wasn't the sort of place where a band could just completely let go. So, it was very much a case of filming David as the frontman and some other shots of the band. What you didn't get in that studio was a sense of the chemistry between David and Mick, which I thought was the focal point of everything. The other Spiders were great but it wasn't like they were up front with David in the way that Mick often was."

On February 10, the first major UK tour started at The Toby Jug, Tolworth, London. "Even though we were already booked in small places like pubs and whatever," as Woody remembers, 'it wasn't a matter of 'I wonder if they'll like us?' or

'How will we go down tonight?' Everybody knew it was good and that made a difference."

The Clash/Big Audio Dynamite guitarist Mick Jones was a huge fan of the band. "We knew it as a *band,* not so much David Bowie. Ziggy Stardust And The Spiders From Mars were a real band," he says with conviction. The media and the fans immediately labelled the group, referring to David as Ziggy, Mick as Ronno and the band (most often including Mick) as The Spiders during the course of the tour.

The show was brilliantly staged. The introduction music was Beethoven's Ninth Symphony adapted from the controversial film, *A Clockwork Orange*, which fittingly added to the drama of the concerts. The tour stomped through every university and town hall that would open its doors and the kids embraced it en masse. Mick was finally having the dual opportunity to play for a living and share his intense expression on the guitar to yearning ears, in the process influencing countless future bands.

Fortunately, photographer-journalist Mick Rock came into the picture just in time to capture this magical era on film: "Ronno was the metal, macho counterpart to Ziggy's multi-sexual pose. He was the electric power as well as the musical arranger. From the outset, Ronno's star shone brightly. He was never simply a sideman; he was Ziggy's pal and anchor. He understood Ziggy and could structure the interpretation of his music. Without Ronno, Ziggy would never have braved the heat of the attention he inspired. Without Ronno he could never have achieved the transmutation," says Mick Rock in his 1984 book *Ziggy Stardust*.

Ronno had a glamorous, monstrous, gangster attitude on stage, yet off it he remained free of any ego, acting as if he were just another bloke from Hull. Suzi Ronson explains: "More than anything I think, he was just *so* nice. That was the first impression I got of him. Him on stage, him with that guitar, how could you not get turned on by that? He was the hottest guitar player in London. He was the hottest guitar player I ever knew. Definitely very talented and yet he had this other inner quality, he was a very spiritual person. It was attractive to find those two elements together. When Mick was on stage he was like an evil doll with his make-up and his hair and the facial expressions. Then, when he came off, he was just a real nice lad."

Ex-Dramarama bassist Chris Carter (who has spent many years hosting some of Los Angeles' hottest radio shows) is a long time fan of Ronson's. Chris explains how this contrasted with the records: "When you saw Mick live, it was a completely different thing. He was much more raw and you really didn't see the finesse that you heard on the albums." Leee Black Childers agrees: "Mick had his own approach as to how to play guitar. His was very energetic, very forceful, so much of a difference to what he was, really."

As the band continued to tour, Tony Defries was delivering *The Rise and Fall of Ziggy Stardust and the Spiders from Mars* acetate to RCA Records in New York. 'Starman' backed with 'Suffragette City' would be released in the UK as the single on April 28. Promotions continued throughout the summer with television appearances on ITV's *Lift Off With Ayshea* (screened June 15) and *Top of the Pops* (screened July 5). Radio support continued with the broadcast of the *Sound of the Seventies* Radio 1 show. The BBC airwaves (*Top Gear*, *Johnny Walker*, etc) remained kind to them throughout the duration of the tour.

When referring to the BBC sessions in general, Woody comments, "Because it was BBC equipment, you didn't have a lot of facilities. You have adequate facilities but you don't have a surplus of effects or a surplus of time to spend on it. I think that those were the only times that what we really sounded like was recorded. Both Trevor and I prefer those sessions to the albums. On the albums, a lot of the energy that we had was mixed out of it. You would only know about it by actually hearing the backing tracks of the album itself before it was mixed. A lot of the guts were taken out. Even on *Ziggy*, it was cleaned up and streamlined, produced and squashed really. It still worked even though all that was done to it, but it was better before."

Meanwhile, with the release of *Ziggy* imminent, Mick and David spent some time in the studio working with England's accomplished yet nearly-defunct Mott the Hoople. Mott's drummer, Dale 'Buffin' Griffin, recalls how it came about: "It was Overend Watts, the bass player of the group who first noticed Mick Ronson and David Bowie. He was always raving on to us about *The Man Who Sold the World* album. He had a copy of it, which he played in the group car when we were going to gigs. He was saying what a great guitarist Mick was, how he didn't play like anybody else and had a great style of his own. It was Watts who got us involved with David, after the group split up over an unpleasant nadir in our career in Switzerland. We all came back to England, he rang up Bowie and asked if there was a job going. There wasn't, of course, but Bowie said 'Why? What's happened?' Then the offer of help came."

David wrote 'All the Young Dudes' and gave it to Mott the Hoople's singer-songwriter Ian Hunter in the hope of resurrecting the band. Ian knew instantly that it was a hit and graciously accepted. Ultimately, it would end up as the title of their forthcoming album, which David had also offered to produce. These *Dudes* sessions would result in Mick's third meeting with Ian Hunter, the man who would eventually become Mick's best friend and musical partner. Ian recalls those initial meetings with Mick: "I just liked him because we were both products of the George Orwell School of growin' up. We sort of thought the same way and had the same problems. 'He's a workin' class lad', I remember thinking.

I think the first time I met him was at dinner. We all sat on the floor around these big round tables of this Indian restaurant. I think it was on Kensington High Street. Mick was there and I struck up a conversation with him. The next time I saw him, he was coming out of a meeting with David and was very upset for some reason. I met him again when writing the string part for this song called 'Sea Diver', which was on the *All the Young Dudes* album. I said to him 'How much do you want?' and he said 'Twenty quid'. He actually wrote the arrangement out on the proverbial fag packet and it was very good. I told him I wanted it Randy Newman-ish. I'd heard this song 'I Think It's Going To Rain Today' and I liked the arrangement. I think he based it on that. Mick wasn't around when we did the *Dudes* album. David was there producing and playing sax, but I never saw Mick."

Mott's drummer, Buffin, tells it this way: "For 'Sea Diver' Mick wrote the brass and string arrangement and conducted the players. I hadn't met Mick before we did the session. Obviously he was very busy, because there were quite a few brass and string players and that's expensive. You have to get the whole thing down quickly so he was under a lot of pressure, but it was very interesting to watch him doing it because it's not normally the guitarist in any group – or the guitarist in David Bowie's group – that does arrangements, strings, brass and conducts as well. An arranger or conductor will normally be in their mid-years, in their forties or fifties. For this young chap to be doing that work was quite unusual."

On June 6, 1972, *The Rise and Fall of Ziggy Stardust and the Spiders from Mars* was released in the USA and Europe. Mick played an integral part in this influential album, contributing guitar, piano and vocals. The radio broadcasts and touring were complementary to the release, fulfilling the promise of 'Ziggy Is Coming' which had been so often publicised by Tony Defries. The public could finally embrace the fully marketed package: the publicity, the tour and now the record. If you were especially lucky, you received a *Ziggy Stardust* shopping bag at the point of purchase. These rare bags were one of the promotional tools used to create a buzz around the album's release.

The album would have a lasting impact on millions of people's lives. "It was like listening to music in the future," says Rodney Bingenheimer. Def Leppard guitarist Phil Collen admits, "I really got into it from the *Ziggy Stardust* album. That's around when I started playing guitar. That whole glam thing, being a kid, you got wrapped up in it." Song four on side one specifically fuelled the fire in the soon-to-be-huge rockers Def Leppard. Singer Joe Elliott explains more: "The first time I ever heard Mick Ronson was on 'Starman'. It was released as a single in England in 1972, just before the *Ziggy* album came out. I wasn't really aware that it was Ronson; it was more Bowie at the time. As Bowie's career took off and he became huge, it transpired that Ronson was a focal point, slightly off centre, as it were. I just loved his guitar playing."

Slaughter And The Dogs' guitarist Mick Rossi was also changed: "'Starman' made me want to be a guitar player. Watching that whole period of music at the time was really exciting." Rich Kids and ex-Sex Pistols bassist Glen Matlock agrees: "'Starman' was the one, that made me want to be a spaceman. It really was good. Different. It was like the real beginning of glam rock. It was kind of pop and still glam rock but it was also great in a more serious way at the same time."

The Rich Kids guitarist Steve New casts his vote for 'Moonage Daydream'. "It was that track, that solo, that was the one. That song still has an impact on me. I really wasn't a Bowie fan, but I got into him because of Ronson's guitar playing. There's loads of great guitar on *Ziggy Stardust*, but 'Moonage Daydream' is just one of the all-time greatest guitar tracks ever. I was in me mum's living room when I first heard that solo. It sounded to me like it was millions of notes but it's actually only a couple. It was really from the soul. At the time, I had been into Cream and Hendrix and it had the same effect on me that 'Voodoo Chile (Slight Return)' did. It was like it was coming from somewhere else. I hope to God that I will leave this planet having done something like that. It's every guitarist's dream to put down a solo like that and Mick did it. For him, it probably wasn't much hard work at all, he was probably just feeling good at the time."

"Mick was always distinctive and you would always know it was him," says Chrissie Hynde. "He never got into any cliché, playing too fast. He was economical and just had these great sounds and these fantastic riffs. He really was one of the great, great rock guitar players."

"It's about connecting," says Annette Peacock. "Anything that Mick did was approached from a place of real integrity. He had wonderful instincts and ability. That's what makes a musician great. From the perspective of the listener, he seemed to make a direct pathway from his heart to yours. A real connection. Everything else is irrelevant when that connection is made with that passion, the passion of his sound. In a sense, he had a classic rock sound, in its intensity, but he always went for the passion. I told him it was angst. He was like the maestro, the king of angst. He had this incredible melodic sense and his solos and riffs were always distinctive with definitive melodies. That is an unbeatable combination. You very seldom get that where somebody can do both those kind of things, the energy and musicality at the same time. Passionate musicality is very, very rare."

The audience was passionate too. The shows' attendances had increased due to the release of the album and David seemed to be mastering the art of entertaining. Each gig had intensified in time for Mick Rock to capture on film one of the most infamous stage stunts of rock history at the June 17, Oxford Town Hall show. The camera's eye absorbed an image of Ziggy performing his now infamous and legendary guitar-fellatio act with Ronno. Mick Rock notes in his aforementioned book that "nobody tells me that this is going to happen and everything about it has a magic sense of spontaneity. I just happen to be at the side of the stage in the right position at the right time. It becomes a classic rock 'n' roll gesture, like Hendrix setting his guitar on fire or Pete Townshend smashing his guitar." The show was on a Saturday night and by Monday afternoon (thanks to Defries) this photograph was printed as a full page spread in *Melody Maker* as a 'Thank You' to the fans. This image rocked the boat on both sides of the Atlantic, creating enormous interest in the duo.

As the tour progressed, they were cramming the venues to capacity. It's been noted that 1,000 people were turned away at the door of their Croydon Greyhound performance. In addition, the *Top of the Pops* television broadcast (July 5) hit like lightning, as Ziggy and Mick appeared in every living room across England. Ziggy had electrified his audience by singing with his arm around Mick's neck, a bold and shocking gesture for the time. Preserved on video by collectors, this image still remains one of the most treasured video moments in Mick's musical career.

Echoes of the previous night's 'Starman' performance buzzed in the streets of the UK the following morning. Up and down the country, an entire generation of future rock stars were inspired by that exact television moment. Bowie's androgynous beauty entranced future stars such as Boy George and Ian McCulloch, who knew their destiny from that moment on. David and Mick's blend of asexuality and laddishness struck a chord in the psyche of Britain's youth like no other band since The Beatles. The single landed in the Top Ten two weeks later.

On July 8, the group played at The Royal Festival Hall on the South Bank of the Thames, in aid of *Friends of the Earth* who were raising funds for the 'Save the Whale' cause. This show remains special because it featured the first UK appearance of Lou Reed, who was the special guest that evening. Ironically, Mott the Hoople was lined up to play support but in the end chose not to play. Later that week, US journalists were flown in to review the Friars, Aylesbury show. Tony Defries seized this as a perfect chance to whip up a media blitz in America, prior to their scheduled arrival in September.

Ian Hunter reflects on the *Ziggy* show he witnessed: "When I saw them on stage, I wouldn't watch David so much as I would watch Mick, because it made more sense to me. I could see that he was human. David was kind of strange. He wasn't really a rocker. I was a rocker and I preferred rockers. So I would gravitate towards Mick. I thought he was fabulous."

Though the band wasn't accustomed to rehearsing that much, they spent the first two weeks of August doing just that. Trevor explains: "We did *Ziggy* then we went into rehearsals in a place called Stratford. We rehearsed the show in a small theatre for about ten days. That's before *Ziggy* had even made it. We went out and played pubs after rehearsing and then it took off." The band continued by touring and preparing for the anticipated shows at The Rainbow and the upcoming USA tour.

Meanwhile, American hipsters Iggy Pop and Lou Reed were in London recording their new albums. Iggy and The Stooges recorded *Raw Power* at the CBS studios and were newly under the wing of Tony Defries. Mick's involvement with Iggy was social only (and minimal) whereas, David would (later) mix *Raw Power.*

They did, however, work jointly with Lou Reed. They began working on Lou's upcoming album, *Transformer*, landing Mick and David back at Trident Studios. Mick saw the opportunity to work with Lou Reed, formerly with the Velvet Underground and a NYC legend, as a privilege. Yet the feeling was mutual, as Lou himself explains: "Ronno was a great player and a great arranger, as well as a wonderful person. It was a joy to work with him, although, it did take me weeks to understand his Hull accent!" Mick's craftsmanship had ensured that he'd contributed to yet another of 1972's most memorable records.

All the songs on *Transformer* were written by Lou Reed (although 'Wagon Wheel' has been rumoured to have been written by Bowie) and recorded in August. The album was co-produced by David and Mick. Ronno also directly contributed to its sound by helping Lou with arrangements, taking on the string and bass arrangements himself. He also played guitar, piano and recorders and lent his voice to the vocal backing tracks. He also assisted David, Lou and Ken Scott in the mixing of the album. A December 2001 DVD aptly titled *Classic Albums Transformer* provides a unique insight into the process behind this recording. It includes a track-by-track look at the album, featuring interviews conducted with Mick and others involved with the project.

Both shows at The Rainbow Theatre sold out. They were extravagantly staged, featuring Lindsay Kemp and mime company plus backing singers the Astronettes. Mick Rock filmed the August 19, afternoon rehearsal, part of which was used for the promotional video for (the upcoming single) 'John I'm Only Dancing'.

A handful of shows later, the finale of that epochal first

UK tour took place on September 7, at the Top Rank Suite, Hanley, Stoke-On-Trent. CBS released Mott the Hoople's *All the Young Dudes* album the following day. 'Dudes' had been issued as the first single, on July 28 and held its position at #3 on the UK charts (Top 30 in USA) for some time. It was the latest, greatest single on the radio and thirty years later, it's still ranked highly by critics and fans. It's fair to say that Mick couldn't possibly have realised at that point how many times he would play this anthem throughout his lifetime. One thing was for certain, if "Boogaloo dudes/carry the news", then Mick Ronson was destined to deliver.

CHAPTER 5

HE WAS THE NAZZ
WITH GOD-GIVEN ASS

In America, Tony Defries had his own plan to carry the news. He established MainMan, a division of Gem, to cement the chances of Ziggy and the Spiders conquering the USA. Official headquarters were set up in New York City and staff quickly organised. New York City movers and shakers Tony Zanetta, Leee Black Childers and Cherry Vanilla were officially added to the payroll.

"MainMan grew out of a sort of social-artistic meeting," says Cherry. Everyone was given a title: Cherry would be the Secretary; Leee would be Vice-President; and Tony Zanetta the President. "They were fairly empty titles really, because Tony Defries ran everything. He gave us titles so that we would feel important enough to follow his directive," explains Leee. "It was like back in High School when you used to have clubs and everybody would elect a President, Vice President, Secretary and Treasurer. Well, of course, the Treasurer was Tony Defries."

Tony Zanetta (AKA Zee) and Leee went on tour with the band in the beginning while Cherry was left to set up the office. Cherry had actually come from a structured office background (as a radio/TV producer) before she became an actress: "I got the filing cabinets and typewriters together and (eventually) hired people but initially I answered the phones, tried to get bookings, typed contracts, I even got Bowie and Ronson's pants to the cleaners. At the beginning, I did whatever had to be done."

Taking the pants to the cleaners may seem like a mundane task to most people but given the importance of the band's image, it was a crucial element that could not be overlooked. In fact, with Suzi Fussey officially employed by MainMan, the band's image in America would become more exaggerated than ever. The hair colours were getting brighter and the make-up becoming heavier, in spite of initial reservations from bassist Trevor. "At first, it felt very strange but we got used to it. When David had initially put the idea across, it was that we were going to look like the droogs in *A Clockwork Orange*. That was the idea with the boots and the suits. Everybody thought that we looked like the guys out of *Star Trek*, which was completely wrong. When we had to put the make-up on, Bowie convinced us that it made your face look better under the lights. We went along with that one as well. Then everybody started wearing make-up. We didn't wear make-up to the extent that a lot of the bands did, like The Sweet and Gary Glitter and all of that, but we did get used to it. So long as you were playing to twenty thousand people, you didn't really care what anybody said or thought."

Mick agreed with Trevor about the make-up. Later in life, Ronson would tell writer Tony Parsons that "the make-up and all that wasn't a brand new idea. It wasn't as though it had never been done before. Elvis used to slap on a bit of make-up."

THE SPIDER WITH THE PLATINUM HAIR

By this stage, Mick's earlier protestations to Bowie about any perceived sexual ambiguity appear to have subsided. "Mick didn't have any problem with the sexual perception that the audience might be putting on him," opines Leee. "I think he was perfectly comfortable with it. He never showed any signs otherwise. He would put on the flashy stuff that Freddi Burretti designed or that Suzi made up for him. He knew he was in show business and he knew who he was."

In an attempt to capture more of the 'album' sound on stage, a pianist was sought out to tour with the band. New York jazz musician Mike Garson had contributed to Annette Peacock's *I'm The One* album. At her suggestion, Defries contacted the pianist who was then living in Brooklyn. Concerned that Mike wasn't interested in working with them, David contacted Annette (who had established her own relationship with MainMan by this point), asking if she might exercise some influence or give his band an endorsement.

Annette explains: "I called up Mike immediately and vouched for the credibility and musicality of the situation and the people involved." Mike had previously spent his time teaching one or two days a week so that he could have the rest of the week to practice the piano and play his jazz gigs. Having as many as ten students a day, Mike realized he was getting burnt out on teaching and was ready for a change. That morning, he had actually just announced to one of his students that, "I'd love to go out with a famous rock band." Strangely, Tony Defries called him nine hours later.

Mike Garson recounts it thus: "I went into Manhattan to RCA at the studios where they were rehearsing. I walked in there and I saw Mick, this really angelic, stunning guy. He had the most gorgeous hair. The colour was unbelievable. He wore these wild, tight pedal-pusher style pants. It was like a fantasy world, because I was this jazz musician who had come in my dungarees. I looked through the window into the recording studio where these three other guys – David, Trevor and Woody – were all wearing different coloured hair and wild outfits too. Mick was the one that greeted me right by the piano. He was going to be conducting the audition. It was fascinating because they obviously knew he was the most senior musician of the bunch. He was very, very warm and made me feel very comfortable. I felt a kinship and instant connection with him.

I go over to the piano and Mick shows me the chords to the song called 'Changes'. He said, 'What would you do with something like this?' I looked at the first six or seven bars of the song, sat down at the piano and played it. About seven seconds later, he stopped me and said, 'That's it, perfect.' I knew then that this was going to be a lot of fun. That was my first encounter with Mick.

It never dropped from that level. We shared a very high mutual respect for each other. We performed two different things, but because he could play the piano, he had a respect for how I played. He knew that this was all I did and that I'd worked my whole life towards this one endeavour."

Mike passed the audition with flying colours. He was given a list of songs to learn quickly, as the tour would soon be in full motion. The band was scheduled to open its American dates in Cleveland, Ohio on September 22. They would charter a bus from New York to Cleveland, to accommodate David's nervousness about flying. The practical consequence of this terra firma transport was that Ziggy and the Spiders experienced America at ground level, which provoked David to write new material. Their travels across the country are directly responsible for the inspiration of many songs featured on the forthcoming *Aladdin Sane* album (Aladdin Sane being another part of Ziggy, a reflection of his time in America).

THE SPIDER WITH THE PLATINUM HAIR

Cleveland was an appropriate place from which to launch the tour because of its supportive radio base and enthusiastic fans. Radio station WMMS played a huge part in turning Cleveland on to Ziggy and the Spiders. Denny Sanders (music director) and Billy Bass (programme director) were daring enough to spin records that were being largely ignored by rival radio programmes. They would play *Hunky Dory* and *Ziggy Stardust* tracks repeatedly, breaking down airwave barriers in order to introduce Northeast Ohio to the new brave sounds of British Glam.

The Cleveland 1972 concerts are often misrepresented when referred to by fans and music historians. The repeated confusion stems from the actual site of the venue. Public Auditorium (aka Public Hall) and Music Hall are in the same building. Music Hall is the smaller of the two halls and a large stage curtain divides both venues. Clearly, the September 22 show took place at The Cleveland Music Hall and if you were there, you were one of the privileged. It's looked upon as a landmark show in the history of Ziggy and the Spiders.

George Bertovich of Checkered Records in Canton, Ohio, was at this American debut: "I worked at Record Revolution in downtown Cleveland and it was the first time we ever closed the store for a concert. There was such a buzz. I can't even compare it to anything since. There was something about it! There was all this hype, the band was supposedly flying over and he (Ziggy) was going to boat it over." It wasn't just the show itself that was attracting attention. RCA hosted an after-show press party at the Hollanden House which was also the talk of the town, fuelling the already heated curiosity of a fascinated Cleveland. The return shows in November were already being feverishly anticipated.

The Plain Dealer's legendary music writer, Jane Scott reveals more about the excitement generated that evening in her original review of the show: "More than one hundred young persons swarmed outside of Public Music Hall, unable to buy tickets. Tickets sold out within days of a simple announcement in newspapers and on radio. Police escorted three suspected pot users from the hall and chased away ten youths who had climbed up the side of the building, trying to get in through an upper window." Cleveland has always been known for over-zealous fans and this reported 'break in' confirms that devotion. Jane notably mentions the performances of both 'Lady Stardust' and a cover of The Beatles' 'This Boy'. Both of these numbers would eventually be dropped from the band's set list.

One week later, Jane described the seismic repercussions from the previous Friday night's Music Hall show. Obviously, Bowie was the centre of the media's eye but Jane wrote, "Other fans talk about guitarist Mick Ronson, bass player Trevor Bolder and drummer Woody Woodmansey, and rave about 'Five Years', 'Lady Stardust' and 'Suffragette City'."

While en route to Tennessee, 'The Jean Genie' was developed from an impromptu tour bus jam. The second show of the tour in Elvis' hometown Memphis sold out, providing a timely boost to the band's confidence ahead of their debut in the Big Apple. "The first time we ever played in New York was at Carnegie Hall. It was incredible," remembers Trevor.

Annette Peacock enjoyed the shows: "I saw them at New York and several concerts in LA. I was busy dancing in the aisles like everybody else. Cherry Vanilla and I were sitting in the audience and she said to me, 'Ah, it's so great, too bad David doesn't have an ass.' I said, 'Yeah, yeah, but check Mick out.' Mick had the greatest derriere in the business. He was just so great looking. It was such a trip."

After more shows, the band returned to New York to record their upcoming single 'The Jean Genie'. They had a six-day break before the next show in Chicago, allowing Mick sufficient time to travel to Toronto to assist a band that RCA's Bob Ringe was working with at the time, The Pure Prairie League. Bob had approached Mick about getting involved in some session work. He was producing their second album titled *Bustin' Out*, scheduled for release later that year. The band, led by Craig Fuller, had started recording in June, so by this point their album was nearly finished. Mick was happy to oblige and agreed to lend a hand.

Joseph F. Laredo explains in the liner notes of The Pure Prairie League's *Greatest Hits* that, "in an inspired decision, David Bowie's collaborator Mick Ronson was recruited to provide string arrangements that greatly enhanced such efforts as 'Boulder Skies' and 'Call Me, Tell Me'. *Bustin' Out* featured The Pure Prairie League's most enduring signature hit in 'Amie', which wouldn't break as a single until three years later. 'Amie', featuring Mick on backing vocals and bass guitar, helped push *Bustin' Out* to #34 on the album charts. Laredo claims that, "most critics and fans would agree, that this album was The Pure Prairie League's finest hour."

The Spiders continued to invade cities such as Detroit, St. Louis, Kansas City and Santa Monica. The latter is worth noting because a second show was added to meet the demand of the Californian fans. Furthermore, this October 20 show was recorded, making this the band's first live American radio broadcast.

Santa Monica has been bootlegged a number of times as well as being officially released in 1994, via MainMan Productions. These authorised versions were put out by Griffin Music (USA) and Golden Years (Europe) and licensed to Trident Music International. Though these digital versions are no longer available, they merit a mention because all these years later there is still great interest in them. During the promotional stages of the Griffin release, there were also promo videos distributed of the live performance of 'Ziggy Stardust'.

The *Santa Monica* live recording perfectly captures the raw intensity of the Ziggy show. It also preserved some less-than-perfect backing vocals by Mick. 'Five Years' for example, is one of Mick's less successful moments; however on numbers like 'Space Oddity', he proves he can handle the harmonising with David. Good or bad, Ronno enhanced Ziggy's own vocals. Their shared harmonies were a necessary element in the verbal delivery of Ziggy's message. It would be a skill that Mick would hone as time went on.

Rodney Bingenheimer remembers their visit to Santa Monica: "Mick and David came to my club (English Disco on Sunset Strip) and, of course, David did some mime stuff on the dance floor. Mick was meeting all the chicks and then saying to me, 'You were right' (in reference to Rodney's prediction at Trident Studios a year earlier of future Stateside success for Mick). David wore this waist jacket with a fur collar, but not real fur. It was a black plastic jacket I think, with tight pants. Mick wore an open shirt."

While on tour, Leee's responsibilities entailed making sure the band stayed on the road, that each show was properly set up, including checking the equipment and stage, to ensure Ziggy and the Spiders were properly displayed. The MainMan team had their work cut out for them but they had also quickly mastered the art of spending. They were instructed to act like superstars, in turn creating the illusion of superstardom. Tony's aggressive business skills put him in a position that enabled his employees and artists to get away with just about anything.

"Defries talked RCA into booking all of the hotels and everything on the tour," explains Cherry. "Instead of the band having any money (nobody had cash), everything had to be charged. Tony Defries told us to charge everything (including meals) to the hotel bill. When it came time to check out, we made sure that the whole band was already on their way to the next town. Then whoever - me, Leee or Zee - would check out last and insist that RCA was picking up all of the bill. The hotel would try and refuse, claiming RCA were not paying for all of the extras. Then we would call Tony, who would call RCA saying, 'I've got my people out there, stuck in this hotel and you want them to do the next gig and it's been announced, it's in the press, it's sold out and if you don't clear this hotel bill....' He was juggling money and he was brilliant at it.

You could charge everything! You know, beauty salons and spas and boutiques. On that first tour, I don't know if Mick was that much of a spender, but everybody was, especially the ones from England. They were buying everything at the hotel, jewellery, cameras, whatever and charging it to the RCA bill. It got to be a little outrageous and crazy but it all worked."

The show's set list consisted of several numbers from the *Ziggy Stardust* album, which was a real crowd-pleaser. Suzi Ronson remembers 'Moonage Daydream' as one of the stand-out live tracks. "Oh, that guitar solo! It always use to drive me nuts, especially live." Other songs were featured from earlier albums including the heavy guitar-driven 'Width of a Circle' and a sassy version of 'Queen Bitch', which always demanded applause.

Ziggy and the Spiders loved their audience, as Leee recalls: "Ronno cared about the kids. He loved rock 'n' roll and he just wanted them to feel it. To feel it in their bones, if only for one night, you know? That's what he was out there for." Mike Garson also commends Mick's attitude: "He was a special person in that he cared about you. He cared about people and he was interested in people. It's unusual, because most artists are very wrapped up in themselves. Certainly he was concerned about the music and his career, he had this other thing that was way beyond what you would expect from a lead guitarist. He just had this care and concern for others. It was his compassion as a person and his passion for his music that set him apart and it manifested itself through his instrument. He was my favourite guitarist almost instantly. I've played with a lot of great guitar players but his melodic concept and the way he saw tones and motion from the guitar, plus the love that he had for it… he's still the guy that moved me the most."

The band had some time off between Santa Monica and San Francisco, as David was busy mixing Iggy Pop's *Raw Power* and Leee was setting up MainMan's West Coast division as per Tony Defries' orders. While in Frisco, Mick Rock shot the promo video for 'Jean Genie' (featuring MainMan employee, the gorgeous Cyrinda Foxe) creating one of music's most glamorous videos, which combined a 1960s sensibility with a Warhol-esque spoonful of Pop Art. As the tour progressed, American music magazine *Rolling Stone* showered the band with publicity, putting Ziggy on the cover of their November issue.

In Phoenix, Arizona, there were more pressing, albeit superficial issues, for Mick. "He went swimming and his hair turned green", remembers Leee. "He had such fair skin and here we are in Arizona, right? He's English and he had no idea that the sun is deadly. There he was running around in his little bikini swimming gear and turning bright red. Then, what does he do? He dives right in the pool. His hair had just been bleached a beautiful silver, a fabulous colour that Suzi had perfected. The swimming pool was so full of chlorine that the next day, I had a red and green guitarist. Bright green hair and bright red skin."

The group continued the tour, heading south-east towards Florida then eventually north again, aiming towards Ohio.

En route, the band recorded more tracks for the *Aladdin Sane* album.

Meanwhile back in the UK, the new single 'Jean Genie', backed with 'Ziggy Stardust', peaked at #2. The US single 'Jean Genie', backed with 'Hang Onto Yourself' didn't fare as well on the chart, in spite of the tour and the recently re-issued *Space Oddity* and *The Man Who Sold the World* albums. Incidentally, both albums were re-issued with recreated cover artwork depicting Ziggy.

On November 25 and 26, Ziggy and the Spiders returned to Cleveland for two more nights at Public Hall. These shows provide a wealth of cherished memories for some of those in attendance. Ohio native Chrissie Hynde recalls, "I was about 21 years old. My girlfriend Sue was actually in a band at the time, but I'd never gone to someone's soundcheck and I didn't really know what they were all about. We drove to Cleveland and stood outside in the afternoon. They were playing 'Five Years' and it was just mind-blowing for me. I still remember the sweater I was wearing.

"We were just mesmerized. They came out and one of their security guards started talking to us and said, 'Why don't you come on up to the hotel suite?' For me, it was the biggest moment of my life. We went up there and afterwards we drove them to a restaurant. It was a major, major day in my life."

The next night Chrissie and Sue went to the show and managed to say hello to Mick. "We weren't groupies or anything. I was extremely naive and wouldn't have even known what a groupie was. Somehow we managed to get into a backstage after-show party, which wasn't too difficult in those days. I was too scared (in a fond way) of Bowie, but Mick was very personable and we struck up a conversation.

Mick was one of the nicest men I've ever met. Certainly one of the best-looking and one of the great guitar players. It was a pretty devastating combination. You didn't expect someone like that to be such a sweet person, you were so scared of people like that, or I was, you know? I was so in awe of great guitar players. I won't get into technicalities, but Mick was the only player that I think could actually sound like Jeff Beck, who was also unrivalled technically, stylistically and everything. He always kept it really rocked up, he had certain Beck-isms, which can only be taken as a compliment."

Music connoisseur and collector, JohnO (a devoted fan of David's for over twenty five years) recalled the atmosphere that evening: "When we got to the Hall, the outside of the building was covered with posters of *The Man Who Sold the World* (the kicking cover found on the reissued *The Man Who Sold the World* album) with "SOLD OUT" slashed across all of them. There must have been thirty or so, they went all down the street and around the corner. There were people lining up and it was pretty exciting. (For their stage entrance) out came Ziggy Stardust, with strobe lights and Mick Ronson!" JohnO's simple but sincere statement is one of many accounts that prove Mick's presence burnt a lasting impression on those in the audience.

The band then worked their way over to the neighbouring state of Pennsylvania for the Pittsburgh and Philadelphia concerts. Philly would close the first leg of the USA tour, capping off three blazing, sold out nights (November 30 and December 1, 2) at the legendary Tower Theatre. The tour had been a huge success so a press conference and reception party were held for the band on their arrival back in New York. The band also recorded 'Saturday' and 'The Prettiest Star' while still in the city.

Impeccably timed, RCA released Lou Reed's *Transformer* album on December 8, while the band prepared for their return home to Haddon Hall. The excitement generated by the Ziggy and the Spiders tour could now continue with this latest Bowie/Ronson-endorsed album to fawn over. Lou Reed's gender bending *Transformer* systematically became Ziggy's American step-brother and that alone set the stage for every teenager to have a glamorous Christmas 1972.

Cherry Vanilla salutes *Transformer*: "To this day, people think of that as a kind of ultimate Lou Reed album. Even though it was an effort with Bowie and Ronson's contributions, it was more than that, it was a collaboration." Mick's sister Maggi has this to say: "I would imagine that *Transformer* probably gave Mick a lot of satisfaction because he did so much on it. He had quite a lot of input but never went around blowing his own trumpet. As a fourteen-year-old, I felt very grown up, listening to Lou Reed and Annette Peacock's *I'm The One*. That used to make me feel very independent."

The year 1972 delivered some of the most memorable records of the decade during which time glam rock carved itself an important niche in music history. Fellow glamster, Cockney Rebel's Steve Harley, shares this comment about Mick's accomplishments in 1972: "Mick's work on *Ziggy Stardust* and Lou Reed's *Transformer* is simply the best of its genre. Full of tenderness, beauty and sympathy."

Ziggy Stardust and the Spiders returned home with a two-night stand at London's Rainbow Theatre. Kevin Cann's *David Bowie Chronology* notes that the second night was on Christmas Eve and the audience were encouraged to bring a toy for a child in need. A large quantity of presents was subsequently delivered to the Dr. Barnardo's homes in London on Christmas Day (Bowie's father having worked for this charity). They wrapped up the enormously successful year with a closing show in Manchester.

Maggi Ronson remembers that final gig, which was

preceded by her very first flight. "Angie took me on the plane up to Manchester which was a bit of a thrill. Afterwards, we were backstage (the stage just revolved around) and we had a bit of a party. There were very flamboyant people around, all the beautiful people, outrageously dressed in these wonderful clothes and amazing coloured hair. They used to put me in Bowie's clothes then. I remember wearing the suit that he had on *Ziggy Stardust*, that he wears in the telephone box. They also did my hair. I was still young then, so it was a thrilling time."

Bowie and the Spiders went back out on the road during the first week of January 1973 in Glasgow, Edinburgh, Newcastle and Preston. The reaction from the fans was sheer pandemonium. Cherry Vanilla recalls the scenes: "I never got tired of seeing or hearing them play and I worked for them! We never did sit down. We would all be up there, me, Angie, Leee and Zanetta. We were so full of positive energy, so high on it. We had done this whole thing with our heart and soul. We had believed in David Bowie and the Spiders from Mars. We were out to prove to the world that we were right about them. We could see it happening, we were so excited for them and for us, in that we were all a part of it. Our hard work was paying off. Our hunches and instincts were right."

As with The Rainbow gigs at the end of 1972, the latest set list had been shortened, losing the acoustic section and concentrating on the harder rocking material. To set the tone for the evening, the shows opened with a manic cover of the Rolling Stones classic 'Let's Spend The Night Together'. Bowie's provocative mid-song rap (and Ronson's dive-bombing guitar runs that accompany it) put the audience in the palm of their hands from the first number. Mick's mother says, "Michael was so delighted to even be in the picture and the concerts were out of this world. Bowie was wonderful on stage, the show of all shows!"

On January 17, the band made a television appearance on BBC's *Russell Harty Plus*. David was interviewed and performed a solo acoustic rendition of Jacques Brel's 'My Death'. Then the Spiders appeared (all dolled up in their glittery finest) and mimed to a pre-recorded backing track of the up-coming 'Drive-In Saturday' single. The appearance certainly played a part in the success of that single in England, where it reached #3 in the charts after its release in April.

It was time to finish off the new album, so the band entered Trident studios on January 20. They recorded some new tracks and assembled tapes from their previous sessions in America. Several songs from David's past were re-recorded including, 'The Prettiest Star', 'John, I'm Only Dancing', and (it's rumoured) 'Conversation Piece', but only 'The Prettiest Star' would make the actual album. Another song recorded for the next album, *Aladdin Sane*, but left in the can, was the Spiders' rendition of 'All the Young Dudes'. Glam Rock's 'National Anthem' would, however, be featured on the next UK tour in a memorable medley, sandwiched between 'The Wild-Eyed Boy from Freecloud' and 'Oh! You Pretty Things'.

According to Annette Peacock, Bowie approached her about contributing synthesizer to the new album, but she declined. "I was getting pulled in many different directions. Mick was advising me not to work with David. He seemed to want me to hold on to what I was and not to be incorporated into the Bowie kind of thing. He seemed to be very concerned about that. At any rate, I wasn't that interested in working with David. Although I was a huge fan and respected what they were doing, I was interested in doing the avant-garde jazz thing."

With Annette's refusal, David turned to Mike Garson to provide him with a touch of the 'avant-garde jazz thing' that a couple of the tracks required. Mike says, "The *Aladdin Sane* sessions had the biggest impact for me, because that's where the piano had the largest contribution. Mick had a lot to do with the creation of that album, there's just no question about it. The stacking of the guitar parts, the arrangements, he was right in there. He was very astute and clever to help guide me through what to play. Of course, the final production of me playing the solos on 'Lady Grinning Soul' and 'Aladdin Sane' did come from the old mastermind, David, but on the mechanics, in the studio and in rehearsals, Mick was taking charge. He was always very respectful and continually asked for my feedback and suggestions." In 2003, Mike Garson was still recording and gigging with Bowie's band, making him one of the latter's most enduring collaborators.

Mick is credited with co-arranging the album with David and co-mixing with Ken Scott. His musical contributions, however, are a little more vague. "Played by David Bowie & Mick Ronson, with T.J. Bolder on Bass & Woody Woodmansey on Drums. Represented exclusively by MainMan", reads the credit. Mick contributed acoustic and electric guitars as well as piano and backing vocals to the tracks.

As a whole, the album had a much harder, rocking edge than the more controlled and polished sound of *The Rise and Fall of Ziggy Stardust and the Spiders from Mars. Aladdin Sane* was, in fact, a fractured reflection on Ziggy's time in America, and therefore required a desperate, chaotic edge, which Mick had no trouble at all in supplying. The album's opening cut, 'Watch That Man', tips its hat to the sound which the Rolling Stones perfected on *Exile On Main Street,* the bar room piano, honking sax, female backing vocals and ripping guitar work that would make Keith Richards proud. The Stones were also saluted on the album with the cover of 'Let's Spend The Night Together' and a reference to Jagger in the lyrics of 'Drive-In Saturday'.

Other highlights are Mick's guitar work on the rhythmic 'Panic In Detroit' and the screaming leads featured on 'Cracked Actor'. The album ends, however, on a reflective note with 'Lady Grinning Soul'. In *Rolling Stone's* review of the album, they called the song 'beautifully arranged' and noted that 'Ronson's guitar, both six-string and twelve, elsewhere so muscular, is here, except for some faulty intonation on the acoustic solo, very poetic.'

By January 24, the album was complete and they were soon off to New York for what was called 'US Tour II', for which it was decided to bring along additional musicians. Bowie told Charles Shaar Murray in the January 27, 1973 issue of *New Musical Express*, "I would like to get one thing straight: it's not an additional Spider. The Spiders are still Trevor, Mick and Woody. We've just got in some back-up men on tenor saxes and piano and voices. I read in some of the papers that the Spiders were expanding - no way. It's three Spiders, back-up musicians and me." In addition to Mike Garson on piano, Bowie's old mate John 'Hutch' Hutchinson was on second guitar, Ken Fordham and Brian Wilshaw handled sax and flutes, and Geoffrey MacCormack added backing vocals and percussion.

Behind the scenes, however, trouble was brewing with the Spiders, as Woody remembers: "In America, there were a lot of magazines that wanted to interview the Spiders and they wouldn't let us do that. It was like 'we don't want you to do interviews' and 'we don't want you doing this and don't do that.'" The greater blow came when Woody learned from Garson that he was making "four times what I was on," which led to his questioning the additional musicians. When Woody and Trevor found out that they were also making more, an immediate mutiny was at hand. "It didn't sit too well," says

Woody. He remembers that it ended up in "a big fight with everyone in one hotel room."

Woody and Trevor confronted Defries. They informed him that unless they received a pay rise, they would not be doing the tour. "He agreed and the tour went on," recounts Woody. "It got fairly heavy throughout that period. I suppose because it had started out as a group thing. It was Ziggy and the Spiders until it became really big, and then it became Bowie and somebody else in the background." Leee Black Childers feels that "Trevor and Woody weren't shown any respect, they were treated like they may as well have been roadies. David showed Ronno a little more respect because he knew how much he needed him."

All the tension made the Spiders consider other options. "We started looking at how we were going to secure our futures," explains Woody. "Mick knew Lou Reed's manager well. He told us, 'I can go and get you a deal tomorrow if you want one.' So he went to CBS and they said, 'We'll give you $100,000 tomorrow morning if you come down at 10am. All you have to do is sign, then we'll do a proper deal.' We thought that was pretty good, but Tony Defries found out about it and hit the roof."

Away from this tension, Bowie's touring machine was beautifully oiled. The Bowie entourage headed over to RCA Studios in New York on February 6, for a week of tour rehearsals. In addition to polishing up live versions of the new songs from *Aladdin Sane*, the Spiders had to memorize their stage cues as well. Woody says, "All the stuff was worked out right down to where each individual would stand for the beginning of the number and what would occur during it. It was all totally worked out, like a theatre company."

Since the new Aladdin Sane character was fractured and schizophrenic, Bowie decided to portray him onstage with heavy make-up and multiple costume changes. Japanese fashion designer Kansai Yamamoto came to New York to present Bowie with some fabulous new costumes. They were designed around Noh and Kabuki theatre and were able to be dramatically torn apart, revealing another outfit underneath. David loved the designs so much that Kansai was given the task of creating nine more costumes for the tour.

The opening show was held on Valentine's Day 1973, at Radio City Music Hall in New York. In addition to a sell-out crowd of 6,200 fans, many celebrities put in appearances including Truman Capote, Salvador Dali, Johnny Winter and Todd Rundgren. Woody remembers an incident from that day's sound-check: "We had another guitarist on with us, I can't remember why. This guy could play like three hundred notes a second. He was doing this and it was impressive when we were jamming along at the soundcheck. There were about four rows of journalists and photographers watching. Then Mick just strolls in, walked on the stage, plugged in and just hit one note. It wasn't that it was Mick, it was just that his one note did more than everything this guy was doing, whose fingers were bleeding and fingernails were bouncing all over the place. All the heads just turned and watched Mick and that was that. He had that ability, yet he didn't really see that as anything special."

The show once again opened with Walter Carlos' music from *A Clockwork Orange*, this time accompanied by a film of a trip through outer space. Then a single spotlight landed on Bowie, who was hanging in a round steel cage, fifty feet above the stage. Slowly the cage began its descent as Mick's power chords echoed through the venue. Stephen Davis reviewed the show for *Rolling Stone,* and noted that, "it was truly an amazing sight: Bowie, who won't fly in planes or ascend above a certain level in buildings, coolly gazing at his adoring fans, while his band, The Spiders From Mars, augmented by six additional musicians on horns and percussion, cranked into 'Hang Onto Yourself'."

Frankie LaRocka, (future drummer for the David Johansen Group) attended the show and says, "Mick definitely stood out for me. The way he looked and the pure brute strength that he played with. During the amazing solo at the end of 'Moonage Daydream' the hair stood up on the back of my neck, I was pinned to my seat. The amps were screaming bloody murder. I thought the speakers were going to fly out of the amps, it was so forceful."

The first part of the concert ended with an acoustic version of 'My Death', followed by a brief intermission. The second set began with Bowie and the Spiders dramatically rising up from a large trap door. The financial squabbles and tensions were still in the air and Woody remembers that, "we just stood there right at the front of the stage and the four of us came up and it was really good. What people didn't know, is that we were cursing each other while it was going on." The second set went down a storm with the crowd, despite featuring nine numbers from the as-yet-unreleased *Aladdin Sane* album. After finishing off with 'Suffragette City', complete with smoke and strobe lights, the band finally left the stage.

They returned for an encore of 'Rock 'n' Roll Suicide' at the conclusion of which a fan leaped onto the stage and embraced Bowie. He collapsed and was carried from the stage. Rumours quickly sprang up that gunshots rang out in the hall and fans were convinced Bowie had been murdered. Backstage, Bowie was diagnosed with exhaustion and slept twelve hours straight. It all made for a juicy story and yet more invaluable publicity.

On February 16, the band was off to Philadelphia, where they were performing seven sold out shows in five days. The more sparse attendance on many dates of the preceding Ziggy

Stardust tour was not repeated during 'US Tour II'. Due to Bowie's and the Spiders' rising popularity, it was becoming necessary to perform a matinee show on almost every date of the tour. These extra gigs quickly sold out as well.

During the tour, a real incident between Trevor and Mick became incorporated into the act. Trevor recalls: "In the middle of 'Width of a Circle', there used to be a fight scene between me and Mick with a flashing strobe light. That actually started out as a real fight. He was doing something onstage and he annoyed me, so I took a swing at him with my bass and he ducked. He swung back at me, and in the end we finished up with this routine. Then we used to do it every night. We used to nod at each other, 'All right, I'm going to swing now, I'll nod and you duck', but the strobes would be going so fast you couldn't see the nod. We used to get cut as well. Quite a few times I got cut by the ends of his strings. He'd catch me and cut my face, or I'd catch him across the back of the head or something." Audiences loved the 'fight scene' and so did the band. Mike Garson use to leave his piano bench for a better view. "There was no piano in that tune, so I'd go out into the audience and watch it. It was the coolest thing."

Mick's antics with Bowie were a central part of the show. There was something magical about the combination of Ziggy and Ronno. Joe Elliott of Def Leppard likens it to "what you get between Jagger and Richards, and maybe Tyler and Perry." Glam legend Steve Harley goes one step further, declaring that "no better foil to a great frontman has ever existed. Bowie and Mick were the dream ticket to pop superstardom." Mike Garson feels that, "History, I think, will really know the true magic of those two faces and that guitar, the things they would do. The whole act, the whole thing, it was pure magic. It was electric every night." Mick talked about his role in the show to Kevin Cann, in an interview conducted at the Hammersmith

Odeon in 1992. "David would be more delicate and a little more woman-like, and I was kind of like, stomping along on the side there, a bit more like a... I can't really say bricklayer, but that's kind of what I mean."

Leee Black Childers saw two different sides to Mick on the road. "When he was sitting on the couch in a hotel suite he would be really quiet and shy, but you put him on a stage in the same town and string a guitar on him and he became very aggressive. His guitar was really an extension of who he was. You could feel it and so too could the audience." Cherry Vanilla agrees: "Sweetness is the first thing I always think of with Mick. Even though there was all this 'gay' publicity and the raunchy lyrics, fashion and the 'Oh, I'm so wicked' aspect, Mick added sweetness. Even done up in Spiders From Mars gear, he was always the sweet one, a sweet boy. Yet, at the same time, he could be so tough, so Hull."

After the triumphant string of shows in Philadelphia, the tour hit Nashville, Memphis, Detroit and Chicago, before heading to the west coast. The US tour ended in California with sold-out shows at The Long Beach Auditorium in LA and a final concert at The Hollywood Palladium on March 12, 1973. No one knew it at the time, but these shows turned out to be the last US concerts from Ziggy Stardust and the Spiders From Mars.

From LA, David set sail for the tour's next destination, Japan, while the rest of the touring party flew back to England for a rest before these Far Eastern shows. Interest in Bowie and the Spiders had been growing in Japan, with 'Starman' becoming a huge hit there. *The Rise and Fall of Ziggy Stardust and the Spiders from Mars* was a success as well, enjoying a two-year run on the Japanese charts.

The Japanese concerts turned out to be wildly successful.

Bowie, presuming that the audience didn't understand a word of English, turned to the lessons he'd learned from mime expert Lindsay Kemp and put his whole body into acting out the songs onstage. In homage to the Japanese sumo wrestler tradition, he took to performing some of the shows in a jewelled athletic support, which led to some classic images of Ziggy and Ronno captured by Japanese photographer Sukita.

Mick and the band also enjoyed the Japanese culture, attending some traditional theatre and sightseeing at a number of different historical locations. It was certainly an eye-opening trip for the lads from Hull. Woody says that, "we were all the things that you dream of when you're a young kid. When you first start in music you think, 'I'll be able to do that' and 'I'll be able to go there' and 'I'll get this and I'll get that'. We got all of that to a degree, because it was like a travelling circus freak show. You couldn't help but get pulled into it and carried along with it. Although we were the ones doing it, we also ended up being the spectators of it really."

In the midst of the Japanese tour, several recordings were issued back in England. Firstly, on April 6, the 'Drive-In Saturday' single was issued and peaked at #3 in the charts. Then the *Aladdin Sane* album arrived on April 13. It had advance orders of 150,000, the biggest in the UK since the Beatles era. Even though the album didn't win over the critics in the same way *The Rise and Fall of Ziggy Stardust and the Spiders from Mars* had, it didn't matter. The record quickly reached #1 in the UK album charts (Bowie's first #1 album), and #17 in the US. Also on the same day, RCA quietly re-issued the 'John, I'm Only Dancing' single, replacing the original version with the far punchier take recorded at the *Aladdin Sane* sessions. Unfortunately, it was issued without the information that this was indeed a new recording, and since the same catalogue number was used, the release passed largely unnoticed.

On April 20, the band performed their last show in Tokyo. Egged on by Angela Bowie and Tony Zanetta, the Japanese fans almost caused a riot when they rushed the stage. The band was forced to perform three encores, culminating in a version of Chuck Berry's 'Round and Round'. Angela and Zanetta had to leave Japan immediately following the concert to avoid arrest, heading to Honolulu instead of London to throw off the enraged police. While the rest of the entourage flew back to England, Bowie took the long way home, first sailing to Russia, and then boarding the Trans-Siberian Express for a week long trip through the USSR. Bowie arrived home on May 4 and the next day threw what turned out to be the final party at Haddon Hall. Groups of fans had started camping outside at regular intervals, so it was considered wise to move on. Mick and the Spiders, along with Lindsay Kemp, Tony Visconti and his then-wife Mary Hopkin, Freddi Burretti, Ken Scott, and other friends, attended the huge bash. Three days later, the band holed up in central London, rehearsing for what turned out to be their final British tour.

The eight-week tour of the UK was set to begin at the Earls Court stadium in London on May 12. This was to be the first time the venue was used for a rock concert, and the largest gathering (18,000) of UK rock fans at that time. Cherry Vanilla remembers an incident that occurred that day: "By this time, I was the official PR lady and didn't have to do the other chores anymore. Bowie didn't want to do a lot of press, so I was kind of editing what he was going to do. This guy who was writing one article assured me that it was going to be great coverage, front page and all this kind of stuff. I agreed and he got an interview with Bowie. They were soundchecking over at Earls Court when the paper came out. There was nothing on the first page, but inside there was this third of a page, a not-very-favorable advance review. I had promised that all this very positive and big and front-page stuff was going to come out of it. I had to walk up the aisle of Earls Court, everybody was waiting to see the paper. Bowie and Ronno came over to the edge of the stage, and I was practically crying because I was so freaked out.

I had to show them and take the blame. I was really expecting Bowie to freak out and fire me on the spot. I couldn't control the media, but he'd given up two hours of his time for this interview. David had a flash of anger at me, like I would have myself, truly, if the same thing had happened to me. For a brief moment, he gave me a terrible look that cut through me, but then he said, 'You know what? Just forget it. It doesn't matter, it really doesn't, don't worry about it.'

Then there was sweet Ronno. 'Oh Kathy, don't worry, it's great' he said, giving me a hug and saying, 'it doesn't matter', just being his wonderful supportive self. He always called me 'Kathy' because my real name was Kathleen. Everyone else on the tour called me Cherry or Vanilla, but he always called me 'Kathy' with that Hull accent. It was a great moment with both of them.

Fortunately, there was a nice ending to the story. I was so upset that I hadn't even looked at the writer's name on that piece. It transpired that this was an early edition and what was coming out later was a special edition. About an hour later, the special hit the streets and there was Bowie's picture on the front! It was all huge and fabulous, with a favorable article too. It's funny, because Bowie could have fired me on the spot or been very mean or nasty. He wasn't. They both could have, because Ronno, well, it was on his behalf too. In the end I was triumphant – and so were they."

Ironically, things didn't turn out so smoothly at the concert. The sound equipment proved to be inadequate for this size of venue and the poor stage visibility caused fans to surge out of control, rushing the stage for a better view. With fights breaking out and people being crushed, the gig had to be stopped and the band left the stage while order was restored. Defries saw to it that another show already scheduled at the venue was immediately cancelled.

Future Def Leppard guitarist Phil Collen saw the show and it made a huge impact on him. "Mum and Dad took me there. Everyone was completely done up, the stripe on the face and glitter everywhere. It was just wild. This fairy-tale story behind the songs was something you could really relate to. For a teenager just getting into music, it was very instrumental in influencing me, a real positive effect. Every guitar player would play standard chords, but Mick would play a root note and just sustain it. His use of wah-wah as well and he never got in the way of the voice, which is very important. A lot of guitar players miss that point completely. There was always that great professionalism about it."

The Earls Court show was fortunately the only disaster on what turned out to be a massively successful tour. As the dates wound their way through England and Scotland, a pattern developed with soundcheck at 5:00pm, the matinee show at 7:00pm and the second show at 9:00pm. This gruelling pace was maintained to keep up with the increasing and seemingly insatiable demand for tickets. There was no question about it: this was the hottest band in England.

Mick reacted to the fame with his usual restraint. Former girlfriend Sandra Goodare remembers that, "Mick never changed at all, except that he began to drink. That's the only difference I ever saw in him. I don't mean he was a drunken slob, he was so kind and nice to everybody. He was totally unpretentious and totally unswayed by it." David Ronson says, "Obviously, it's not right to say it wouldn't affect you in some way. I don't think you could be human for it not to, but the truth with Michael is that it never actually changed him as such. That's what he wanted to do in life, so he obviously had to go with the flow, but he never changed as a person. He was always still Michael."

Trevor Bolder explains that, "I just sat back and enjoyed it really, rolled along with it. Mick had more pressure on him than us, because he was the Keith Richards to Bowie's Jagger, if you like. The only thing that I hated about being that famous and that big in England was that you couldn't go out on the streets. There was always kids hanging around. You'd have to sneak out through a back road from where you lived. I enjoyed the playing and being in a big band touring the world, it was a position I'd always wanted to be in. It was quite incredible."

Inevitably, fame had its negative repercussions. Many people were less than thrilled with Mick's role in the bisexual world of Ziggy. At one point, a car Mick had purchased for his family was vandalized with paint. Maggi says, "A lot of people were jealous, saying 'Ronson's a poof' and all that kind of stuff. The pressure was on quite a bit. I used to just go along with the flow a bit and get a few drinks down at the pub."

Mick made sure to include his family at several of the shows on tour, putting them up in hotels whenever necessary. Maggi says, "He used to include us in all of his things. He always stayed very close to us." Minnie Ronson agrees: "When we stayed in hotels, Michael was always making sure everything was all right. We didn't mix with Bowie a lot because he was very distant and kept to himself with Angie. Michael observed everybody, he never left anybody out."

Fans who couldn't get enough of Bowie and the Spiders travelled all over England to see as many shows as possible. Mick Jones of The Clash reveals that, "when Ziggy Stardust and the Spiders from Mars used to play in England, they were one of the groups I used to follow around. I would jump on trains and hide in the toilets when the ticket inspector came round. I'd just jump off before the final destination and climb over the fence. I'd try and get into the show for nothing, sometimes it worked, sometimes it didn't." Ronson was impressed with the determination and dedication of the fans and made sure he took care of them. His brother David Ronson relates that, "he was always there for the fans that used to hang outside the hotels. He would always take the time out for them. If these people were out on the hotel steps, he would often actually pay for hotel accommodation for these people. He always had a warm heart."

In June, in the midst of the tour, RCA decided to try their luck issuing a single from the two-year-old *Hunky Dory* album. It worked. 'Life on Mars?' (complete with Mick's stunning arrangement) further solidified their success, becoming a huge hit and climbing to #3 on the British charts. Penned in part as a parody of Sinatra's 'My Way', the song needed 'big' strings to match the original and Ronson's creative instinct was perfect in its tone.

On the surface things seemed to be perfect, but behind the scenes major problems were about to come to a head. RCA Records were refusing to foot the bill for a proposed 'US Tour III', which would consist of thirty eight gigs in high profile venues around the United States. After seeing the bills that the MainMan organization ran up on previous tours, their hesitation was perhaps understandable. They wanted Defries to scale down the tour, just as they had done on the second US tour, with gigs only performed in areas where record sales were strongest. Defries, always with an eye for the biggest and grandest, turned them down. There was only one thing left for Ziggy Stardust and the Spiders From Mars - early retirement.

Defries decided that David would retire from the concert

stage while he considered his next move and Mick would be given the chance at a solo career. In Suzi Ronson's opinion, "it was very wrong, the way that they broke up that band. David had done Ziggy to death right along with Mick in a way. If he had done it further, he felt that Ziggy might be all that he was ever going to be (especially) if he'd done one more American tour for example. So the management company decided that if David isn't going to do it, well then Mick, it's your turn to be out there. In a way, that was so unfair because Mick had been right along with David. David just needed some time off to re-generate and think about what he needed to do next. I think Mick also needed some time off." Recalling the events leading up to the end of the Spiders, Mick told Kevin Cann, "It was just something that had to happen, it was always going to happen. I knew that it would eventually."

Ziggy Stardust And The Spiders From Mars ended in grand style at the Hammersmith Odeon in London on July 3, 1973. D.A. Pennabaker, the man responsible for *Monterey Pop* and the Bob Dylan documentary *Don't Look Back*, was to be filming the evening's show for posterity. In addition, the RCA mobile unit was there to record the concert, with the intention of releasing a live double album. To add to the excitement, Mick's musical hero, Jeff Beck, would be joining the Spiders for a couple of numbers.

The band roared through the set with the force of a locomotive train and Bowie, knowing that this was the end, was positively electrifying. At the end of 'White Light/White Heat', Bowie announced Jeff Beck to the already delirious audience. Mick began the 'Jean Genie' riff and after he and Jeff traded solos, the tune wandered into the Beatles classic 'Love Me Do', as the audience went berserk. Jeff then stuck around for a cover of Chuck Berry's 'Round and Round'. Mike Garson remembers the occasion: "They were great together. I mean,

Jeff is a great, great guitar player. Like I said, Mick moved me more, did and does, you know? Of course, Jeff had a certain influence on him and Mick had a lot of respect for Jeff, so you could feel that on the stage. They were just back and forth, it was just a great, great jam. Wonderful. It's hard to emphasize the emotion that Mick was able to put through his guitar. I didn't get that from lots of people over the years, at that level. I never got it in rock as much as I got it from Mick. I got it from some people in the jazz world over the years, but never the way I got it from him in rock. He actually penetrated more with his feeling and intention, more than even jazz musicians that I worked with who are obviously phenomenally trained musicians and a whole other level of expertise but still, I never got any more than I got from Mick."

After Beck left the stage, Bowie dropped the bombshell. "Everybody... this has been one of the greatest tours of our lives. I would like to thank the band. I would like to thank our road crew. I would like to thank our lighting people. Of all of the shows on this tour, this particular show will remain with us the longest, because not only is it... not only is it the last show of the tour, but it's the last show that we'll ever do. Thank you." The band, in shock, performed the final number 'Rock 'n' Roll Suicide' in a highly emotional manner. The final, perfect touch occurred when a fan leapt onstage during the song's closing notes to hug Ziggy, only to be pulled off by security. It couldn't have been planned better.

Garson states that, "none of us knew what David was actually going to say at the Hammersmith when we played that concert. I think we were all in shock in our own individual heads and minds so nobody really took notice of how anyone else was feeling. Collectively, we were a little thrown off."

Especially the other Spiders. Woody says, "I didn't know and Trevor didn't know, but Mick did. There were a lot of different things going on during the last two tours we did. One of the things that we had verbally sort of agreed on with Bowie was that we would help him get up to the top and then we would be doing our own stuff. That was because the three of us had been playing together quite a long time before joining Bowie. We were quite close as friends, you know?"

Trevor says, "Mick knew what was happening, he knew David was going to announce it. He already had his solo career planned. David had told him and quite a few other people knew as well. The only people he didn't tell were Woody and me. I think they didn't know what our reaction would have been if we'd have found out. The reaction would have been we wouldn't have turned up for the gig!"

An hour's worth of footage from this pivotal event was edited into a special for American television in 1974, but the film and audio recordings of the show ended up being shelved. It wasn't until 1983 that Bowie would release a film and double album of the concert, but the results were a little disappointing. In addition to perhaps unnecessary vocal and instrumental overdubs and edits, the watered-down remix squelches the true firepower of the Spiders. Another drawback is that Beck's performance is missing, therefore those versions of 'Jean Genie/Love Me Do' and 'Round And Round' remain officially unreleased to this day. Most fans prefer the sound of the famous bootleg *His Master's Voice* that was made from the television special. It includes the 'Jean Genie/Love Me Do' jam, the entire farewell speech and a cover insert featuring Ziggy and Ronno.

The next day, July 4, 1973, as Americans celebrated their Independence Day, every glam kid in England was in mourning. To gain maximum publicity, MainMan turned the shock news into a media event. An official announcement was made that the upcoming US tour was cancelled and that Bowie may never tour again. A retirement party was held at the Café Royal in Regent Street with a star-studded guest list including Paul and Linda McCartney, Keith Moon, Lulu, Tony Curtis, Peter Cook, Dudley Moore, Cat Stevens, Ringo and Maureen Starr, Mick and Bianca Jagger, Jeff Beck, Lou Reed, Barbara Streisand, Ryan O'Neal, Sonny Bono, Elliot Gould, Britt Ekland and Dr. John, who supplied the live music for the evening. The press lapped it up and photos of the party appeared in all the major music magazines around the globe. As news of Ziggy's retirement filtered into the United States, Rodney Bingenheimer says, "I wasn't too happy about that and neither were the patrons of my club."

The past year had been a wild ride for Ziggy and the Spiders, summed up best by Trevor Bolder: "It went from taking the Ziggy thing through London pubs to finishing it off by playing seven weeks in England, two sold-out shows a night. We got three nights off in seven weeks. Starting off from nothing to being huge. That whole thing was incredible and it was very short. Maybe that was a good thing in some respects, because the memory of it is better than if we'd stayed together for a really long time and got bored. Since it finished so quickly, it made it into a big legendary project that everybody talks about. Most of it was great fun."

It was truly the end of a golden, glittery era.

CHAPTER 6

SOLO ON 10TH AVENUE

With Bowie's performing career temporarily on ice, it was time to put other plans in motion. Bowie would record an album of cover songs while he considered his next move, while Mick prepared for his promised shot at solo stardom. First though, there was the matter of the other Spiders.

Trevor and Woody were sure that they would be continuing with Bowie, but that wasn't the plan. They were to be replaced by Jack Bruce (ex-Cream) and Aynsley Dunbar, but when Bruce declined it was decided to keep Trevor on board. Trevor recalls how Woody was given the news: "Woody got married and somebody rang him up on his wedding day and told him he was fired. Knowing that he was getting married that day, it was just complete spite. I went to see David at his hotel and created a bit of hell with him. Mick told me to keep my mouth shut or I wouldn't be working, because David would get rid of me as well. David had actually said to me, 'If you don't like it, you can clear off and we'll get another bass player as well.'

When everything had calmed down, David said to me, 'Come over here, I've got some songs to play you,' and he played me all the songs he was going to do on *Pin Ups*."

Pin Ups was to be a tribute to the 1964–1967 period of British rock, a time when The Kinks, The Who, The Yardbirds and The Pretty Things were the hot bands in clubs such as The Marquee. Mick was more than familiar with the twelve numbers selected to appear on the album. As a member of The Mariners, The Crestas and The Rats, he had performed most of these songs in clubs back in the old days. He must have been excited at the mere thought of recreating Jeff Beck's solo in 'Shapes of Things', one of his favourites.

Having grown tired of Trident Studios, Bowie was looking for a more exotic place to record. Marc Bolan highly recommended the Chateau d'Herouville in France, where he had recorded his own masterpiece, *The Slider*. With their destination decided upon, the Bowie entourage left Victoria Station on July 9, 1973, to travel to Paris. In addition to Mick on guitar, piano and backing vocals, the band featured Trevor on bass, Mike Garson on piano, Aynsley Dunbar on drums, Ken Fordham on sax and Geoffrey MacCormack on backing vocals.

The recording sessions began on July 10 and lasted until the end of the month. Mike Garson: "They were fun sessions. I didn't know any of those songs, so they could have been written by anybody. They could have been David's songs, I had never heard the originals. I was just enjoying Mick's playing, he was just doing his thing, more great Mick Ronson. To me it was just another record to play on that I could contribute my style to. Great album by the way." Trevor felt differently: "It was really bad, the band thing had gone then. Once you pull any member out of a band, it changes. It was sad not having Woody there."

Looking back on the album in a 1988 interview with Jan van der Plas for Holland's *Music Maker* magazine, Mick named *Pin Ups* his favourite of the Bowie albums he worked on. "That album was great to do, because the songs were our favourites when we were teenagers. I started to play guitar because of Duane Eddy, and shortly after that you got The Beatles, The Stones, The Yardbirds. The best music is the music that gets you so excited that you want to pick up and learn to play an instrument by yourself. With *Pin Ups* we got to record all those songs ourselves."

Several visitors arrived during the recording sessions, including journalists eager for the scoop on Bowie's future plans. One guest was Lulu, who Bowie had met at the Café Royal party. They had discussed the possibility of working together and Bowie invited her to the sessions in France. Once she arrived, Mick and David worked up new arrangements for 'The Man Who Sold the World' and 'Watch That Man', and backing tracks with the band were quickly recorded. Not only were the Lulu tracks and *Pin Ups* album completed at these sessions, but a host of other cover versions by American artists like the Velvet Underground and Bruce Springsteen were also recorded for a proposed *Pin Ups II*, an idea that never actually made it to fruition.

After the sessions were completed, Mick joined David, the band, and MainMan staff for a holiday at a rented villa in Rome. It was there that romance finally blossomed for Mick and Suzi Fussey. "When The Spiders broke up," Suzi recalls, "I went and started working with Mick. We kind of got together there, in Italy. That's when we started being romantic." Suzy and Mick's new relationship got the blessing from the MainMan camp immediately, as Cherry Vanilla remembers "Suzi was perfect for Mick. It was fairytale time, you know? Our little Camelot, it was lovely."

Another visitor on the Roman holiday was Mick's sister Maggi. "In Rome he sent me home with a bunch of clothes and I was like, 'I can't wear that!' He gave me these fur coats, Donny Osmond hats, different coloured boots and checkered dresses, which was quite different to what other people were wearing. I could wear it in Rome and I could wear it in London, but I couldn't wear it in Hull!"

After a few days, Bowie went back to England to oversee the final mixing of *Pin Ups*, while Mick and the band travelled back to France to begin work on his first solo album, *Slaughter On 10th Avenue*. Leee Black Childers was there and recalls the atmosphere at the French studio: "The Chateau D'Herouville is where George Sands and Frederic Chopin once lived, therefore it's a very historic place. It wasn't heated or anything like that. It was still like an old fashioned chateau. All the tiles on the floor were not cemented down, so it would go clatter, clatter, clatter as you walked down the hall. We would eat in a big dining room with a long table and ate whatever we were given. Generally it was pretty simple fare, but the advantage to recording was that the studio part was right there. If you got inspired at three o'clock in the morning, you could get up, plug things in and do some recording. We were living there as opposed to booking time like you would have to do in New York or Hollywood. It wasn't a wild time at all, it was a very quiet time, really."

Leee recalls Suzi's new role as Mick's personal assistant: "She was kind of there to be the nurse maid. She would make sure everyone was OK. And she did, she was very good at that. She was very motherly. Ronno really concentrated on his work. He was really very private. He would be in his room, he would be reading or sometimes listening to music. Mostly he was concentrating on what he was going to do the next time they went into the studio. When they were in the studio, they worked very hard, all of them. They would sit around, drink beer and then get inspired and go into the studio at three in the morning. They would play in there until eight in the morning, or until Suzi came to them and said, 'OK boys, you've got to eat!'"

The easy-going atmosphere at the Chateau made the sessions pleasurable for everyone. Trevor says, "I enjoyed doing *Slaughter On 10th Avenue* with him. I played all the brass on it as well. We had real good fun actually, it was quite a laugh. We had a good time doing that album because David wasn't there and Mick's a lot more open and friendly. I'd known him for such a long time it was like two mates making an album together."

The songs Mick chose to record came from a few different sources. Two of the songs originated from Annette Peacock's *I'm the One* album. One was written by Annette, the other was a cover of an old Elvis Presley song ('I'm The One' and 'Love Me Tender'). Annette remembers "I recorded 'Love Me Tender' on *I'm the One* and Mick covered that version and arrangement on *Slaughter On 10th Avenue*. Mick did tell me that he and David were playing it in all the hotel rooms and the musicians in the band, the Spiders, were all playing it. He'd even got the Polydor release which was difficult to get. Of course, I was really touched and flattered. I would guess that it was probably the imagination and the energy of my music that intrigued Mick. It had a lot of raw rock 'n' roll abandon, kind of 'do or die', on the downbeat, attitude. Plus, none of the takes were over-dubbed, it was all done live in one take. I think David and Mick recorded in layers and were very careful. They had a different approach so I think from a musician's point of view, he would've enjoyed (my method). Also, I think it has that sound, that same kind of intensity and passion that Mick gets when he plays. He just goes for it completely in that same kind of way. We did have that in common, a real commitment to the moment, the present, what's happening now. He's the master of all that."

Mike Garson remembers that, "Mick was a big fan of Annette Peacock's stuff. We did that song 'I'm The One' which I had also recorded with her. She was a good friend of mine. So Mick paid his respects to her. I mean, she was not well known to the world the way these guys were."

Mick co-wrote two of the songs ('Only After Dark' and 'Pleasure Man') with Scott Richardson. Scott was the lead vocalist in SRC, a Detroit band who had released several records on Capitol. Scott had been brought into the MainMan fold by Angela, and quickly became friends with Bowie. After Ziggy's retirement, Mick toyed with the idea of forming a band called Fallen Angels with Scott on vocals, Mick on guitar, Trevor on bass and Aynsley Dunbar on drums. Scott backed out when Defries asked for a share of the band's profits he couldn't agree to, so it was over before it began. Too bad, as these two songs confirm the band had potential.

Bowie himself donated 'Growing Up And I'm Fine' (which would have sounded fabulous on *Hunky Dory*) and wrote lyrics for two other songs. 'Hey Ma Get Papa' was written to music Mick had previously composed and is the only song to carry a Bowie/Ronson songwriting credit. 'Music Is Lethal' was an Italian song by Lucio Battisti. Mick heard the song in Rome and immediately wanted to record it for his album. The only problem was the original lyric couldn't be accurately translated into English, so Mick asked David to write some suitably dramatic words.

The title cut, a cover of the Richard Rogers classic, is to this day one of Mick's greatest achievements. Mike Garson remembers the recording session: "I had sort of known that track, because it was a modern day, classical piano piece that was written in the 1940s or 1950s. I had played a little bit of it when I was twelve or thirteen. Anyway, Mick decided to use that song but do his own arrangement. We worked on the piano part from midnight to six in the morning. He just wanted me to get it perfect. Normally, I do my tracks in one or two takes and I'm in and out and that's that. Somehow, he really wanted it right, so he just kept doing take after take, refining it repeatedly. He was a very good producer, something I remember very, very, clearly. I haven't heard that track in twenty-five years but at the time I remember loving it. I also loved his directions to me and how he allowed me to contribute so much." With the bulk of recording for this debut solo project finished, Mick travelled back to England. *Slaughter On 10th Avenue* just needed finishing touches and a final mix, which would be done at Trident Studios.

While they were away recording, Ziggy-mania was still at full throttle in England. *Aladdin Sane* was #1 on the charts and the previous four albums were all in the UK Top Fifty, where they would remain for ten weeks. This impressive feat was a first in the British charts. Bowie's popularity was so white hot in the UK that even a September 1973 re-issue of 'The Laughing Gnome' (a joke number recorded in 1967 for Deram Records) sold 250,000 copies and reached #6 on the charts. Its success delayed the release of the new single, 'Sorrow', by a couple of weeks. When it finally appeared on October 12, it was another hit, peaking at #3.

In the States, it was a different story: sales were good but not phenomenal. RCA complained to Defries that they could not sell *Pin Ups* without a tour. A solution came in the form of an offer from the American television network, NBC. They wanted David to appear on their weekly rock show *The Midnight Special*. The show had premiered in February of 1973 and was a huge success. It would obviously be the perfect vehicle to promote the album and give Ziggy a fitting American send-off.

David decided to call the programme *The 1980 Floor Show*, a pun on one of his new songs, '1984'. In the spirit of the *Pin Ups* album, the filming took place over three nights (October 18, 19, 20) at The Marquee. Much to its management's dismay, The Marquee would be given a face-lift to give it the impression of a futuristic cabaret. Random members of the David Bowie Fan Club were given the chance to attend, along with select members of the press. MainMan staff mingled with the crowd over the three-day event, delighting the press and the fans with their outrageous behaviour. Cherry Vanilla says, "*The 1980 Floor Show* was a little burlesque or something. It was one of those weird little wonderful things that worked very well, but could have been a disaster. Marianne Faithfull was stoned and in a nun's costume and Amanda Lear, the transsexual, was hostess. It could have been really bad, but it was fabulous!"

Bowie brought along the *Pin Ups* band for the occasion, supplemented by Mark Carr-Pritchard on second guitar. Also on hand for backing vocals and percussion were The Astronettes (Geoffrey MacCormack, Jason Guess & Ava Cherry) a vocal trio that Bowie was set to produce an album for. Mike Garson remembers the experience: "That was a great show. It was very intense and tense and also exciting. There seemed to be loads of waiting and waiting and waiting. Bowie had some wild hands made for him which were really bizarre." In addition to new costumes for Bowie, Freddi Burretti had designed a stunning all-white outfit for Mick to wear that made him look 100 per cent rock star.

The highlights of the show were the two numbers performed as 'duets' with Mick. 'Space Oddity' (with the two of them blending their vocals effortlessly) recalled simpler times from the early Ziggy shows, while 'The Jean Genie' featured Ronno and

Ziggy playing off each other to maximum effect. Even though Mick broke a string during his enthusiastic solo, it was still a powerful performance. Trevor Bolder says that "during *The 1980 Floor Show* you had David, who was now acting like the big rock 'n' roll star. A man you couldn't get near to who used to drive you to gigs at pubs. Now you couldn't even get to talk to him. Then you had Mick who was all dressed in white and he was going off to do his solo venture and be the star. Then you had me in the background dressed in black with the rest of the band. You've got all these other musicians playing and it's not the Spiders anymore. It was finished then really, that was it." Mick wouldn't perform live with David Bowie again for ten years.

Pin Ups was issued on October 19, the second day of filming at The Marquee. It had advance orders of over 150,000 in the UK and immediately went to #1. Once again the critics were not overly enthusiastic with their reviews, but most generally praised Mick's role in the recordings. Greg Shaw reviewed the album for *Rolling Stone* (in the December, 20, 1973 issue) and noted that while well-equipped to cover the material "with Mick Ronson's obvious brilliance in the genre, as evidenced by his one-man Yardbirdmania on 'The Jean Genie'", the album was an overall disappointment. Iggy Pop reviewed *Pin Ups* for *Phonograph* magazine and declared that the album "sounds damn good. Mick Ronson is getting a better sound than ever. I mean, he's getting one of the best rock 'n' roll rhythm guitar sounds on this album I've heard in two or three years. I really like what he's playing too, especially on 'Rosalyn', 'I Wish You Would', 'I Can't Explain' and 'Anyway, Anyhow, Anywhere'. It's simple and to the point, with a lot of authority, which is how I like to hear a guitar."

In the midst of finishing off *Slaughter On 10th Avenue*, Mick invited his sister Maggi to the studio once more. Maggi had informed her mother Minnie that she was ready to move out and get a place with some friends. "That afternoon, when I was in the office where I worked, I got a phone call from Michael in London saying, 'Would you like to come down and live with me?' So I knew she'd been on the phone with him, but of course I said, 'Yes, I'd love to'. I think it was just before I was seventeen when I came down to London. I got straight off the train and went up to Trident studios where they were doing *Slaughter On 10th Avenue*."

It wasn't long before Mick enlisted his sister to handle some background vocals on the record. "I was in the studio and he said, 'Oh, do you want to sing on 'Love Me Tender'?' Putting the headphones on, singing into a microphone and hearing it back through the headphones just felt really weird to me. So, they put a speaker in the studio, into the recording box with me, so I could just hear the track back, which was great. It was really good. Hanging out and listening to everything on the big speakers and basically just living in the studio for weeks. Going around the corner to the sandwich shop, it was just a totally different way of life, the studio life. You get totally removed from what's going on in the world. It was a whole way of living."

There was one final session with Bowie at Trident in November of 1973. Bowie came up with the idea of adapting George Orwell's *Nineteen Eighty Four* into a musical. He had already written several songs for the project, before permission was denied by Orwell's widow. A medley of '1984/Dodo' is one of the songs recorded for the project that features Mick on lead guitar. Eventually, Bowie used some of the material for his *Diamond Dogs* album, but this version remained in the vaults until 1990 when it was issued on Ryko's *Sound And Vision* Bowie box set.

Mick and David began to drift apart after this, with both men moving in different directions. Contact between the two was minimal over the years, as Suzi recalls, "David and Mick were very close while working together, but after Hammersmith rarely saw each other and did not remain in contact."

Also around this time, Mick was offered some studio work with Al Stewart. Mick told Sven Gusevik in the fanzine *Ronson Ablaze!* #3 that, "Al Stewart was just one recording session and it didn't work out too well. He asked me to play like Tim Renwick, and I said, 'He lives around the corner so phone him. Here's his telephone number.' So I left!"

The rest of the year was spent in preparation for Mick's first solo album and tour. Mick had discussed his concept for the album with Charles Shaar Murray in an interview for the September 29, *NME*. "It's about two people falling in love. At the moment, the story's about a guy. He's a layabout - just sort of bums around the streets. He sees this chick and falls in love with her, just wants to be with her. She's a dancer in a night club and a prostitute. She falls in love with him as well, and in the end she wants to quit and go with him. But her pimp boyfriend finds out. She comes out of the club one night and he shoots her. And I'm left alone without her."

Cherry Vanilla was the head of MainMan's short-lived video division and was given the opportunity to bring this vision to life. "Originally, what happened was Leee had it in his mind to shoot the back cover on the 10th Avenue street corner in Manhattan. He wanted to have the whole shot of the corner. He asked us about how to light up the whole corner with big movie lights. That's what got us on to thinking, 'Well, why don't we shoot a film?' I produced it and Macs McCarey directed it."

"It was done in a real bar on 10th Avenue," recalls Leee. "The people who ran the bar and the bartender all participated, and it's funny because no one got paid. There were all of these people in there, we're moving in these cameras and disrupting their lives for an entire evening and no one even mentioned about getting paid, either for the use of the location or for themselves for being in the film. It was just magic. It wasn't only the bar but the people who lived in the apartments upstairs. We just invaded their apartment and said, 'We need this window so that Alice can be looking out of your apartment,' and they just said, 'OK'. There were giant lights all over 10th Avenue and film crews everywhere. That's one of the nice things about New York, they just let it happen."

Cherry remembers that, "everyone volunteered. We told them to dress in vintage or something that would look vintage or waterfront. We fed them all, gave them all free drinks at the bar, lit up the whole street corner and had it all wet down. We had Mick do that voice-over and I played one of the hookers. It was like a party, all of our friends were there. I knew how to do things very economically. My thing at the time was, 'Tony, it's costing nothing'. We filmed that whole Ronson full-length video on 16mm film and carved a sixty-second and a thirty-second commercial out of it. Leee Black Childers got his back cover photo out of it. We had a cast of thousands and a limo for Mick and Suzi. We did the whole thing for $3000. Everything, the whole nine, including the editing right down to the answer print to show Defries."

MainMan planned a huge promotional push for the album and needed new publicity photos of Mick. "Mick was alright being photographed," explains Leee, "because once again, we get back to show business. It was his job. He didn't really pose. I mean all of us, everyone on the Bowie tours for example, were in love with him and thought he was the most beautiful thing on earth. He knew that's what we were saying. So in that respect he would get a little shy when I was photographing him. He would do his job though. He'd take off his shirt, he would do his cute little smile. It wasn't like a lot of stars whom I've photographed. For example, Rod Stewart immediately thinks 'This is good!' as soon as the camera is turned on him. Mick was never like that. I would have to be like, 'Take off your shirt, Mick, unzip your pants, Mick' and he would just do it. He never ever didn't do anything that I told him. Yet, never, to my knowledge, did he think of himself as beautiful which of course he was."

The publicity photos were only part of a campaign for Mick that included an official Mick Ronson Fan Club, magazine adverts, buttons, a promotional interview flexi-disc, T-shirts, stickers, posters and the *piece de resistance*, huge billboards of the album cover in New York and Los Angeles. It had to be more than a little overwhelming for the quiet boy from Hull. It certainly was for the press, who could smell the hype a mile away. It was all leading up to Mick's debut concerts on February 22 and 23, at The Rainbow Theatre in London. Mick's band consisted of Trevor Bolder on bass, Mike Garson on piano, Richie Dharma on drums and Mark Carr-Pritchard on second guitar. Joining them was a five-piece horn section, The Thunderthighs on backing vocals *and* The London Symphony Orchestra.

The whole Ronson family attended that opening concert. Mick's mother says, "I think he freaked out a bit, because he wasn't a frontman. He was shy. Also there was an orchestra with him. What a big thing, going from being a side-man for Bowie, to being a frontman with an orchestra." Brother David (who was only eleven-years-old at the time) recalls, "I was extremely proud and it was quite mind-boggling. Obviously being a young lad myself, being in the position to see such things and experience such things was awesome, really impressive."

In addition to all of the other pressures, the concerts were being filmed and recorded. Cherry Vanilla remembers that, "We brought this whole crew from the States, there were six cameras on the concert. It cost $60,000. We filmed the whole show and then went up to Hull and did films of Suzi and Mick dancing, and little cafes in his hometown and everything. Michael Kamen came and told me at one point that Tony Defries gave him the twenty-four-track tapes from the concert to tape over, because he didn't feel they were worth anything. I hope that wasn't true. The problem was that Mick was so nervous that it wasn't really a great concert. It was too much. He shouldn't have done it with The London Symphony Orchestra. It just added to his nervousness. It could've worked, I suppose, if Mick had done it a few more times, but he decided that he wasn't going to do that again, so maybe that's why Tony didn't think the film was worth anything. There were moments that had to be worth something, I know. I was like, 'Film everything!' but Tony thought I was getting carried away. That was the end of the film company."

The press were not convinced about Ronson's solo attributes. Most agreed that The Rainbow shows were a disappointment and that the orchestra was an unnecessary distraction. Michael Watts reviewed the shows for the March 3, 1974 issue of *Melody Maker* and concluded that, "Ronson was the victim of a massive hype." He certainly had a valid point when he concluded that "considering all the effort being expended, it was dumb not to release the album before the gig so as to get the audience accustomed to it." The 'Love Me Tender/Only After Dark' single had been released shortly before the shows and made little impact. When the album did arrive on March 1, 1974, it managed a Top Ten placing on the British charts. Also out in March was the Lulu single which Mick had co-produced with Bowie, 'The Man Who Sold the World'. It quickly became a #3 British smash, putting Lulu back in the spotlight in Britain. Mick attended a reception held for Lulu to celebrate the record's release at Les Ambassadeurs in London.

Mick's first and only UK solo tour got underway in April. This time without the orchestra. The shows consisted of material from *Slaughter On 10th Avenue*, along with covers of The Pure Prairie League ('Leave My Heart Alone'), Joe Cocker ('Something to Say'), and Donovan ('Music Makers'). Mick's cover of 'Moonage Daydream' was clearly the audience's favourite. The band have mixed feelings about the tour. Trevor says, "working with Mick on that tour was a breath of fresh air. It was great fun." By contrast, Mike Garson remembers, "there was a certain sadness and frustration that we were fighting upstream."

The rest of the tour was received with mixed reviews from the press. Chrissie Hynde reviewed the April 19, Hammersmith show for the *NME* and noted that, "The kids are going bananas. The band is tight and Ronson's in control this time – unlike the Rainbow gig when he looked about as lost as some wino who'd wandered in off the street. He's not even trying to be sexy (although he is anyway). I mean, here's a guy who befriends anybody who'll give him the time of day. He doesn't have to try to do anything. Nobody, but nobody dislikes Ronson – and that's his calling card."

Mick Rossi of Slaughter and the Dogs recalls that, "the first time I saw Mick perform was in Manchester, at The Free Trade Hall on the *Slaughter On 10th Avenue* tour. I bunked off school to go and get tickets for that. I got caught, but it was worth it. We rushed the stage when he was doing 'Only After Dark' and I shouted out 'Ronno!' and he made eye contact with me and put his thumb up. That was so cool." After the show, Mick Rossi and his friend were in hot pursuit of the band. "You know how fans run after the limos? Well, we were running after his coach and it stopped. It was very strange, and this was about a mile after all the other fans had dropped off. The coach just stopped and the doors opened, it was like something out of the *Twilight Zone*. It was so freaky, they just let us on. I thought I was dreaming. He took us back to the hotel and Trevor Bolder and Mike Garson and all the people that were working on the tour were there. I was just staring at him all night, basically. Wherever he was, I was just staring at him like a little kid. We were planning to sleep on the station, me and my buddy, and go back the next day. Mick said, 'You don't have to do that,' and he booked us a room. Of course, we didn't sleep all night. We kept saying 'We're here with Ronno! We're here with Ronno!'"

Maggi: "It was a good tour and I felt for Michael through everything because I knew how anxious he was to prove himself. There were a lot of people expecting a lot of things from him because of being with Bowie, so my heart went out to him. I was very aware that if people were being critical or if he'd read any negative write ups then that would hurt him. He hadn't got over that point and it was still very important to him then."

Suzi feels that, "Mick was slung out there before he was ready. Mick has always worked better with somebody else. I think he missed having that other key person. He's not very vocal. He always used to have a hard time expressing exactly what he meant. He would look at you and think you'd understand, but he had a hard time vocalizing what he was really feeling. Yet, with the guitar he could tell you anything he wanted."

Cherry Vanilla agrees: "I feel Tony Defries pushed Ronson in the wrong direction. Ronson was fantastic as second fiddle, as the guitarist, as the rock guitarist. He was perfect. Defries tried to put the same treatment onto Ronson that he did onto Bowie. To make him a pop star in the only way he knew how. Whereas, I think Ronson would have been better taking the route of writing arrangements and movie soundtracks and not trying to be the flashy pop star, because his persona was just too much of a real person. He was too sweet. Not that Ronson wasn't dramatic and great on stage, I mean, look at the things he did with Bowie. Given time and understanding and patience he probably could have done his whole solo career in a bigger way, but I think he liked being in partnerships. He enjoyed that."

Mick talked about the solo tour with Kevin Cann: "While I was on the road and started to play that material, I began to think to myself, 'Is this right for me? Why am I doing this? I don't really feel that comfortable doing this, it's not really 100 per cent me.' I was starting to feel very uncomfortable within myself. I knew that other people would spot that in the audience and I didn't want that. I initially felt that doubt in rehearsals really, I was thinking, 'Hey, wait a minute. I can't wait to finish this.' I just couldn't wait to get it over with. Everything kind of happened in such a rush, I just got very confused. It just all happened so quickly that I didn't have time to work it out or why I was doing it."

'Slaughter On 10th Avenue' was issued as the second single from the album in England, backed by a live version of The Pure Prairie League's 'Leave My Heart Alone'. It failed to cause much of a stir. The *Slaughter On 10th Avenue* album didn't register much sales activity in the States and a subsequent proposed US tour was dropped. It seemed that a backlash to the hype was inevitable. Mick was ready to abandon his solo career there and then.

CHAPTER 7

ONE OF
THE BOYS

MainMan was, by now, a big concern. As well as Mick's own solo plans, Defries was heavily involved in David Bowie's *Diamond Dogs* and Dana Gillespie's *Weren't Born A Man* projects. Plans for Mick's second solo album were also underway, which he reluctantly agreed to record for RCA.

"There was a big machine (MainMan) working at that particular time. We had a lot of employees, a lot of money was going out every week and Tony Defries was someone to pick it up, he just kept on going with it," says Suzi Ronson. "We were all so young. You didn't think about saying 'We're not going to do this!' We just thought, 'Oh well, I suppose we better do it,' you know? We didn't know anything."

In April, Mick teamed up with Bob Sargeant, who had previously found his own spot as a denizen of Britain's progressive rock scene. Mick earned a 'recorder' credit and assisted Bob, producing four songs on his album *First Starring*

Role. In turn, Bob co-wrote the title track for Mick's upcoming second solo album entitled *Play Don't Worry*.

Two months later, Mick joined Dana Gillespie in the studio while she recorded tracks for her RCA follow-up *Ain't Gonna Play No Second Fiddle*. Mick produced two tracks ('Never Knew' and 'Lavender Hill') but they were not released until 1994.

The *Play Don't Worry* sessions began in July, 1974. Although most of these tracks feature different musicians, the album retains its cohesiveness. Recorded and mixed at The Chateau near Paris and a studio in the south of France, as well as Trident Studios and Scorpio Sound, London, it reflects Mick's commitment to make the best of his solo profile.

Mick took on huge responsibilities for this album, including arranging, conducting and producing all of the tracks. The strange brew of songs he selected to record demonstrated his ability to transform other composer's work into a musical sculpture of his own. He stepped up and took on the challenge of writing his own lyrics for the first time, something he hadn't done on his debut solo album. In addition, he plays no less than eight of the instruments on the album including, guitars, piano, bass, drums, harmonicas, clavinet, recorder and synthesizer.

Back in Hull, he received full support from his family, but they knew that he was drinking from a big cup of courage. David believes, "it was a very bold move to actually go out and try something different. He experimented and was brave enough to take that on."

Maggi contributed to both of her brother's solo albums and remembers the *Play Don't Worry* sessions as "good fun". At the same time she says, "I think he was even more concerned about that album than he was with *Slaughter*. It always kind of stopped my enjoyment of it in a way, because I was so worried about how it was going to be received and if it wasn't well-received, I just felt it was going to be disastrous for him."

Mick's band of gypsies included Beverly Baxter, Miquel Brown, Trevor Bolder, Jeff Daly, Richie Dharma, Aynsley Dunbar, Paul Francis, Mike Garson, Ian Hunter and the Microns, Neil Kernon, John Mealing, Sid Sax and Vicky Silva. Together, they would help Mick weave a total of ten songs.

The first single from the album, 'Billy Porter', (delayed and selected for release in January, 1975) was penned by Mick and opens the long player brilliantly. It remains, without argument, one of his finer solo achievements. Campbell Divine quotes Mick in his *All the Young Dudes* biography regarding the song's conception: 'We'd had this friend named Billy Porter and he told a lot of jokes, so the song was originally a joke song. Then, I was talking to Lou Reed and the lyrics became things Lou had told me about getting mugged in New York, plus the joke parts I'd already written."

Mick really took a hold of 'Billy Porter', balancing it with stellar sax by Jeff and ARP synth work from Neal. The 'silly, willy Billy Porter' backing vocals against the sound of the air-raid sirens work brilliantly. This smashing single was complemented by the cover of Annette Peacock's 'Seven Days'. Most B-sides of the 1970s were capable of catching the listener a little off-guard when first flipping the record. Repeated turns of this seven-inch revealed a deeper side of the guy who wrote the brilliant A-side.

"I was so flattered and pleased and surprised that he would cover 'Seven Days', says Annette. "I really couldn't exercise any objectivity about it. So, it's difficult for me to sit back and have a judgement about it and criticize it, when I'm coming from that place of surprise." An alternate version of 'Seven Days' exists that runs to six minutes and is featured as a bonus track on the *Snapper* CD (a 1997 re-issue of *Play Don't Worry*).

It's considerably different, with its improvisational two minute jazz-fuelled piano frenzy finale. Mick had now managed to salute Annette's songwriting on both of his solo releases, clearly highlighting his admiration for her work.

Next up on the album were the crashing chords of 'Angel No. 9' exploding from the speakers. This track was written by Craig Fuller (of The Pure Prairie League) and is the longest song on the album, featuring *the* guitar solo of all guitar solos. This melodic whirlwind of riffage successfully magnifies the 'space face' aura that Mick mastered during his years with Bowie. Mick's rendition of this country/rock number transforms it into a triumphant, rocked-up anthem that's quite capable of taking the listener to another dimension.

Richie Dharma, one of five musicians earning a drumming credit, notably makes his entrance on 'Angel No. 9'. Maggi shares this: "Mick was really pleased with Richie, he really liked his drumming." Bass credits go to the unwavering Trevor and backing vocals are thanks to the ladies, Vicky, Beverly and Miquel.

Several of the original vinyl album's tracks are elongated on the re-issued CD. Twenty years later the digital version of 'Angel No. 9' reveals an audible yet whispered 'you bet' from Mick at the closing of the track. This extra ten seconds was a fascinating discovery to fans that had engaged themselves in memorizing every lick of the vinyl version decades ago.

Mike Garson's unique contribution is very evident on 'This Is for You'. This song features both lovely piano and some genuinely amazing arrangements. Songwriter Laurie Heath had played Mick the demo of 'This Is for You' during their endeavour with Milkwood a few years earlier. On this album, Mick makes it his own, crooning the open-letter lyrics tenderly, as if they were his own.

Revered as a rock 'n' roll classic and one of the best live

songs ever written, Mick chose to present here his version of the Velvet Underground's 'White Light/White Heat'. Bowie had given Mick their recorded backing track (a cast off from the *Pin Ups* sessions) over which Mick put his own vocal down. Hundreds of bands have covered 'White Light/White Heat', but most of them fail to fuel it with the attitude it commands. It's just one of *those* songs. It requires thick-skinned vocals, chaotic guitar and frenzied feedback at the finish. Most fans would agree, if it lacks any of these three, it's instantly disqualified. Mick had no problem with these pre-requisites. In fact, it was destined to succeed, with the adrenaline-charged Mike, Trevor and Aynsley backing him brilliantly.

The second side of the album opens with 'Play Don't Worry', the co-written Sargeant number mentioned earlier. This serves as another example of Mick's talent for orchestration. Tastefully done, he includes the clavinet for this one.

'Hazy Days', fades in perfectly. Penned by Mick, the lyrics paint a "high in the sky" reflection that's tainted with regret. They imply that there is no choice but to leave, yet the 'la la la' melody begs to differ. "I'm sorry that I left this way/I simply couldn't stay/Your ideals would always drive me crazy/Hazy, crazy, lazy points of view" was a four-minute recorded rhapsody.

"Ian Hunter was around during *Play Don't Worry*. They had sort of been friends for a while because they had done *All the Young Dudes,*" says Maggi. 'Girl Can't Help It' was written by Bobby Troup but is widely known as a Little Richard rocker. During the actual session, as Jeff was putting the sax solo on, Maggi came up with the name The Microns. "I thought that was quite good, backing vocals by The Microns. So, we just went in, me, Suzi and Ian and put the vocals on to 'Girl Can't Help It'. We had a good night. I really enjoyed it."

THE SPIDER WITH THE PLATINUM HAIR

Like 'Music Is Lethal' from the first solo album, 'The Empty Bed' ('Io Me Ne Andrei') was an Italian song that Mick heard, loved and wanted to cover. Baglioni/Coggio originally wrote it, but this time Mick wrote the English lyric himself. It is a definitive sad song and exhibits a challenging range of vocals from Mick. Apparently, the original co-author Baglioni was very flattered by Ronson's version. Sid Sax leads the strings, while all the other instrumentation is credited to Mick.

The final song on the album, 'Woman', was written by Adam Taylor and recorded by The Pure Prairie League for their debut album released in March of 1972. Obviously, the band had made an impact on Mick and he found success in rockin' up their country-rooted melodies. This is the second of three songs he would record under their influence.

The press enjoyed the album and were suitably positive. Ron Ross in *Circus* magazine wrote, "As was to be expected, the arrangements and production are masterful. Ronson's original material is much improved, and so is his voice, which has found a comfortable range and become more expressive. Best of all, there is a lot more guitar-laden rock 'n' roll to start a raver's blood rushing and Ronno rocks on with much less self-consciousness and more obvious enjoyment." Steven Rosen in *Guitar Player* was even more succinct: "The title track expresses a typically Ronsonian optimism and faith."

Mick had spent the past year of his life restructuring and evolving into his solo career. Meanwhile, Ian Hunter was doing the same with Mott the Hoople. Lead guitarist Mick Ralphs had left to form Bad Company with Paul Rodgers in August of 1973. The following month, ex-Spooky Tooth guitarist Luther Grosvenor (Ariel Bender) was recruited but only lasted one year, leaving in September 1974.

Mott the Hoople were renowned as a great live band and

had gained themselves a loyal following, including Mick Jones. "I was a fanatical fan of Mott the Hoople. I would go to school the next day and my ears would be ringing and I couldn't hear anything. I was a fan of the original band. The time that we followed them around, they were the most decent people to their fans. It taught me a lot back then. They used to let us in for nothing and invite us back. Mick Ralphs was a big influence on me. One time at the Dagenham Roundhouse, he was right over the other side of the bar. I had my pint and he had his drink and he sort of acknowledged me and went 'cheers'. I poured my whole pint down my front."

Mott the Hoople was an awesome band, but with the loss of Mick Ralphs and then the departure of Ariel Bender, the guitarist position was once again wide open. Media rumours had already mooted that Ronson would be joining the Rolling Stones (replacing Mick Taylor) but these whispers were soon quashed as Mick accepted an invitation to join Mott the Hoople. This decision would be life-changing for Mick, as it cemented his long-standing and close friendship with Ian Hunter.

Mick retained his deal with RCA records while Mott the Hoople were still very much Columbia (CBS) recording artists. Mick genuinely wanted to fit in and for the band to work. Maggi remembers that Mick was more comfortable at this point in time. "I think it took a lot of pressure off him. Those two albums were very stressful for him." Simply put, it was a relief for Mick to be in a band again. Mott the Hoople were equally relieved hearing that Mick would be their new guitarist.

Ian Hunter remembers it thus: "There was a girl named Anya (Wilson) who worked as a publicist for Bowie. She used to say, 'You should get a hold of Mick'. This was after David had done this pseudo-retirement thing. Then Mick Rock was saying to me, 'You should get a hold of Mick, he's sitting up there on his own and he's doing nothing.' Mick Ralphs had left and we had Luther, who was great on the stage but he wasn't creative, or at least he wasn't with Mott. Mick appealed to me because I knew the amount of arranging he had put into the Bowie stuff. I knew he had made a big contribution to that music and I thought maybe he could do the same for us. Maybe, he could even write a bit."

"Ian was of course over the moon and I was very pleased too as I was a great admirer of Bowie's," says Mott the Hoople keyboardist Morgan Fisher. "I think my musical work just prior to Mott and certainly since then, shows that I have perhaps a wider view than your average rocker. I had always admired the modern tendencies in Bowie's work (and did in his later work too) so it was quite a thrill to feel that influence coming into Mott. I had great hopes for the future."

Drummer Buffin felt the same: "I can't tell you how thrilled we were when we heard that Mick Ronson would be joining. It was like an electric shock, like fifty Christmases had come at once with fifty Santa Clauses and piles and piles of presents. We were just overjoyed, because we really thought it was the end of the group and then suddenly you hear Mick Ronson has been cleared to join. We were just flattened. It was just fantastic, absolutely fantastic. We thought, well, this is it, what a group!

Mott had gone through something of a decline because we hadn't really done anything since our Broadway shows (Mott the Hoople had sold out a week of concerts in New York and were the first rock band to play on Broadway, shows which were recorded for a live LP). We really needed something to bring us back with a bang and who better than one of the best guitarists in the world? Unless you're a complete maniac, you want the press and the television and the radio and the record buyers and the concert-goers to be thinking 'Wow! Mott the Hoople is with Mick Ronson. We want to see that, we want to talk to them, we want to put them on our television show, we want to have them on our concert stage!'"

Very quickly the guys pulled themselves together as a band. Buffin shares this story about the scene: "It was quite a rush to get it together. For that reason really, there wasn't a good bit of time to socialise. We went around to Mick's home a few times, this enormous flat in Kensington by the Albert Hall. It's near where Winston Churchill used to live, so it was a very posh area. It was very odd because there were a lot of hangers-on there, strange people who knitted and made clothes and cut hair and did various things. I think most of us found it quite off-putting because you don't normally go home and find this little tribe of people, like Father Christmas elves. So, that was a bit weird."

Morgan remembers those visits vividly and somewhat differently: "The first time I went to Mick's sumptuous apartment, Suzi was there, of course, and all sorts of bright-eyed Bowie-ish people with various colours of hair. The atmosphere was bright and fresh. I felt that this is where it's all happening, this is the cutting edge - cool! While I was there, I had my hair cut drastically short for the first time in years, with encouragement from all present. Pete 'Overend' Watts (bass guitar) and Buffin soon did the same although not on that same day. So Mick made an immediate difference to our haircuts! Generally, it felt like Mott was getting spruced up and dragged, un-protesting, into the modern world."

Though his contribution in the studio with Mott was minimal, two tracks are essential in the scheme of things and result in a case of quality not quantity. 'Saturday Gigs' was the title of the upcoming single (featuring Mick's overdubs) and was scheduled for release on October 18. Mick also recorded one original with the band titled 'Lounge Lizard', which remained in the vaults until *The Ballad Of Mott* CD was released in 1993.

Morgan describes the initial vibe as "good, fresh and challenging. I think the recordings were great. I felt there was great potential there." In agreement, Buffin says that, "Ronson was great in the studio because he was very at home in that situation. He knew how things worked and how to do things; he knew how to get where he needed to go. Technically, he was a great guitarist but emotionally as well, he had a great feel, he wasn't just technique."

Morgan was very impressed: "Mick brought an all-round musical approach, looking at a song as a whole, not just as a vehicle for some fun guitar playing. Mick also sang well and played other instruments, so he could get a feel for what all the members were trying to do. In terms of guitar sounds and playing, he tried to give each song what it needed and create new sounds for that purpose. I think his guitar solo on 'Saturday Gigs' took three days. He experimented with changing the tape speed while he was recording and so on, doing things which are now available at the flick of a switch due to digital technology. I liked that because I was into doing similar things, trying to use a tape recorder as a sample, etc."

"Oh, yes, he did that," confirms Buffin, but "it sort of worked and it sort of didn't. It just felt like he needed a tremolo arm, but of course he was playing a Gibson Les Paul that didn't have a tremolo arm. So, he did it by slowing the tape down and then speeding it up, or vice versa. Of course, technology wasn't that wonderful in those days, so it was quite difficult to do. That's the only thing we really got to see him do. Of course, the engineer kept telling us 'oh, oh, it was a fantastic session, Mick's overdub guitar session, best thing I've ever seen' and we were just saying 'Yeah, well, we wish we had seen it.'"

Buffin feels that the situation within the studio was irritating because they weren't allowed to go to the sessions when Mick recorded his guitar parts. "We were banned, they just banned us from the sessions. Later, the story was that we just couldn't be bothered to go, which is just not true. I know Watts and I, and I'm sure Morgan as well, wanted to see him play. Overend Watts was particularly a great fan of Ronson's guitar playing. But we were not allowed to be there and were pretty annoyed about that.

'The Saturday Kids' as it is on the anthology (*All the Young Dudes* Box Set) has nothing to do with Mick. It's 'Saturday Gigs' on CD Two that has all of Mick's work on it. And yes, a fair bit of that. We heard some of the things. We heard the main solo, we were there when that was put down, but for a lot of the other stuff, as I say, we weren't allowed in the studio, nor were we allowed to be there when he was mixing that song." Buffin admits that the sessions are ancient history now and the mix is fine, but at the time he resented being excluded. Mott the Hoople was meant to be a democracy and he felt this semi-private session seemingly jeopardized that feeling of unity.

'Saturday Gigs' was a song where Mick's sense of drama and power could enjoy some expression. "What he did on 'Saturday Gigs' was very powerful, especially as it was a new song and he could add more to it, as I did, with my synthesizer interlude in the middle," says Morgan. "It was the most experimental Mott recording I'd experienced and I was very fulfilled by it, from creating the almost classical piano intro to fiddling around for hours with my VCS3 synth and composing an orchestra-like middle section." The version that Morgan is referring to can be found on the *Ballad Of Mott: A Retrospective*.

"'Lounge Lizard' was another cup of tea. It happened really quickly and easily and I thought, 'This is Mick's Lou Reed side, where he gets down and dirty.' It was nice to see his wide range," says Morgan. Dirty defines the music well, Buffin explains: "The way we did it, was just a dirty, messy, rock song like say, The Faces were doing at that time. It was just meant as… not a jam but a semi-sort of boot-along that didn't mean a great deal." It's an outright rocker that is a gem in Mott the Hoople's treasure-chest of songs.

CBS had plans to release *Mott the Hoople Live*, recorded at The Uris Theatre, Broadway, New York on May 9, 1974, and the Hammersmith Odeon in London on December 14, 1973. This, combined with Mick's arrival, a new single and a planned tour earned them VIP treatment from their publicist, the late Tony Brainsby. He prepared a press release after hosting an impressive conference at the Grosvenor House Hotel in London. The press release states the following:

Earlier this week, Mott the Hoople announced that guitarist Ariel Bender was leaving the band in order to pursue a solo career. Ian Hunter introduced Mott's new member, guitarist Mick Ronson, who has been rehearsing with the band for the past few weeks.

Mick Ronson's first public appearance with the band will be in Sweden on October 10, when Mott commence their European tour. He makes his British debut in November when Mott embarks on an extensive British tour.

The posh hotel provided the perfect scenery for Leee (still employed by MainMan) and Mott *Live* cover photographer Dagmar to capture Ian and Mick in a playful mood. Taking pictures on the terrace turned out to be great fun and brought out the best in everybody. "That was a good photo session," recalls Leee. "Mick did have a lot of humour, you know? I have a picture of Mick grabbing Ian's tit. He had a whole lot more humour when he was with Ian than he did when he was with David. He was able to show his own personality a little more and was encouraged to do so by Ian, very wisely, because then that added to the show."

Prior to this European tour, the new Mott line-up recorded an un-screened slot for BBC TV's *Top of the Pops*, performing the new single, 'Saturday Gigs'. Buffin remembers that, "because they weren't sure whether the record was going to go up or down, they didn't record us during the time when they film the main show. So, we were just in an empty studio with four or five cameramen and no audience, nothing. They just recorded it that way. I hadn't been given a microphone. I sang the chorus; the voice on 'Saturday Gigs' chorus is me. When we would watch *Top of the Pops*, we would always laugh because there was usually a drummer at the back, singing along to a song he hadn't really sung on, just mouthing away. I wasn't going to be one of those drummers, so I wanted a microphone. I couldn't get one and I kicked up a stink about it. That was put down as me being jealous of Mick having a microphone and me not having one. All I wanted was a microphone.

I also complained about the direction, because they weren't showing any shots of Morgan or me, which I didn't think was right. We always had that argument at *Top of the Pops*. They're the worst camera directors in the world. They're the kind of people who, just as the rhythm guitar is playing will cut to the keyboard player; if there is a lead guitar playing, they'll cut to the bass player. They really don't know what they're shooting.

Every time, we've been to *Top of the Pops* we had the same thing. Great big riles with the directors about the camera shots except this time, that was turned around as me being jealous of Mick getting more shots than I was. It had nothing to do with Mick. He was there, yes, but it wasn't directed at him, it was directed at the man who was telling the camera man what to do." Clearly, this wasn't an ideal atmosphere for the session, highlighting a discomfort within the band that slowly burned throughout the duration of the revamped Mott the Hoople.

The new Mott the Hoople continued preparing to embark

on their European tour, encompassing Sweden, Denmark, Germany, Switzerland, Liechtenstein, France and Holland. The tour started on October 10 and ended on November 3, 1974. "It all happened very fast and we had to rehearse quite quickly," says Buffin. "Mick had to learn all of the Mott the Hoople numbers and we learned three or four songs that were his, that came from his album or that he had done on stage as part of his solo act." Out of the songs rehearsed, only two of them were actually performed live, 'Angel No. 9' and 'The Girl Can't Help It'. In addition, the new single 'Saturday Gigs' and 'Lounge Lizard' were added to the already sizzling Mott the Hoople set list.

Sadly, the tour with Mick would prove to be the breaking point for Mott the Hoople. Management and record company politics, poor communication, ego, pride, and sheer exhaustion were all contributing factors in the poison that affected its members.

Ian and Buffin share similar memories of the tour. However, they come from two different perspectives. The scandalous, stressful and emotional wounds they suffered have long since healed, but some of the scars seemingly remain. Morgan was also affected of course. His memories from the tour are more centered on the music and how Mick changed that aspect. Pete chooses to remain silent on the subject but the following anecdotes from Ian, Buffin and Morgan provide interesting theories as to why Mick's joining the group changed everything.

"His joining Mott had a disastrous effect, it really did. I just never thought what happened would happen. He joined and it was difficult, because he was with RCA and Tony Defries and we had Fred Heller and were with Columbia," says Ian. "It really was difficult, I mean two limos would turn up, one for him and one for us. So, there was this kind of separation thing. Mick was out for what he could get, Tony was out for what he could get and that was in everybody's interest. It made a lot of sense; Defries could use the Mott publicity to promote Mick because his second album was just coming out. I understood that and I could take that. What I hadn't figured on was that the rest of Mott got real resentful about the way they saw Defries and possibly Mick using the Mott situation for his own ends. On the other hand, I was knee-deep with Mick and I knew that he was genuine, I knew that he and Suzi were alright."

Buffin admits there was definitely some tension: "There was one occasion where the RCA rep was a very young, vivacious woman. Overend always had an eye for the ladies, so he thought, 'I think I might go in Mick's car,' because our limo was packed with people, we were just jam-packed like sardines in there. So, Pete (Overend) went over to the limo and sat in and was talking to this RCA girl. She said, 'You're not with Mick's group,' and another guy said, 'but he's in Mott the Hoople.' She said, 'No, no, you're not with RCA. You must go to the other car.' He got thrown out of the car and we were all just laughing but deep down we couldn't understand why Mick had allowed that, I still don't really. That just seemed a bit strange. It was suggested that we were jealous he had a limo. That didn't matter at all; it was obvious that was going to happen because RCA weren't going to not send a limo for Mick Ronson if CBS were sending a limo for Mott the Hoople. They weren't going to be outdone by CBS Records."

Ian explains: "The trouble was that Defries more or less hypnotized them, he was a pretty hypnotic kind of bloke in those days. He did it to me a few times, you had to sort of go home and think about it."

"I think Mick lived a cashless life," Buffin says. "They just lived on credit cards. Everything was charged and that seemed strange to us, because we made about £75 a week, which was about $110 in those days. That was our princely payment for the week. We tried to get Mick to take the £75, but he just wouldn't for some reason, which we could never figure out. We thought at least he would have some cash in his pocket. If he's going to be in the group he's due to have a payment from the group. That was strange, because had it been me, living a cashless existence, I would have liked to have a few nice crinkly pounds in my pocket, but there you go." Perhaps Buffin was unaware of the nature of Mick's agreement with Tony Defries. Tony negotiated with Mott the Hoople's management that Mick would do the tour for nothing – only expenses – but would want to be able to promote his own solo record with RCA.

"Going on the road was horrible," says Ian. "It was a long time ago but I don't see why I should lie about it. It was awful. I was a wreck. Mick was all right because he was sitting over there in his camp. He had his limo, record company and his album. Me and Mick were all right, but we had this other thing to contend with. I mean, when you went down to breakfast people took the furthest possible table away from you. All the time they were thinking that we didn't want to know them and we were thinking that they didn't want to know us. A very strange set of affairs it was. I thought I knew the Motts well enough after all of those years that they would automatically figure out what was going on, but it had the opposite effect."

Buffin describes it this way: "On the tour, we didn't really get to see much of Mick at all. We didn't have a great deal of cash. So, when we were touring, particularly in Europe, the hotels tended to be very expensive. If you stay in an American hotel, it is very reasonable if you want to have a coffee shop meal or something like that. You'll get a good meal at a reasonable price and we could afford America just about, but Europe was very expensive. Scandinavia in particular. We couldn't afford to eat where Mick and Ian were eating with Trudi Hunter and Suzi. There became a 'them and us' situation. It was them in the posh restaurant in the hotel and the rest of us had to go out into the streets looking for some cheap workman's cafe to eat in. So, we became like the underclass, which got, very, very, very, irritating."

Overall, the band (excluding Ian) felt as if they didn't know Mick at all. They had been in the group with him, playing on the road and still they never could seem to communicate with him. "I would sometimes see Mick," recounts Buffin, "and think 'There's Mick right? I'll go to and talk to him' and he would look at me like the devil was approaching and would make any excuse to get away and never talk. He looked frightened when he didn't want to talk and he would always seem to run to Ian, like, 'This nasty boy has been trying to talk to me,'" says Buffin. "Everything that I've ever heard about Mick from people who worked with him, is what a great guy he was, how friendly he was, all really nice, positive things and that's how he always seemed but something was happening."

Buffin defines it thus: "It felt like asset stripping. That's what it felt like." By contrast, Ian says, "I just thought that the rest of the band knew, like I knew, what was going on. I thought that we could strengthen this, but the band never went with me, they went against me. We did not need that because we were weak and we were tired. I was doing all the writing, I was doing the press and all of that kind of stuff and then they lumbered me with the responsibility of handling this. I mean, trying to work it out with Mick and Defries and trying to work it out with them, it was too much."

In spite of the band's internal wreckage, Mick appeared content just playing the gigs. Leee Black Childers explains that, "after the shows with Mott, Ian would go into hours of analysing the show, how it had gone and it was driving me crazy, you know? See, Mick and David, to give David credit, never did that." Mick retained that same spirit while in Mott the Hoople. "He was like 'when the show is over – the show is over' and he reverted back to Hull and would laugh and talk. I never heard him discuss the show or argue about anything. He would just sit there and be really cool and then go up to bed.

He never did anything scandalous. He never tied a groupie up and put bologna all over her and stuck her on the elevator and sent her to the lobby, you know?" says Leee. Shamelessly, Mick was concentrating on the music. Morgan Fisher explains that "Mick was taking care of his solo career at the same time as being a member of Mott. I think he was musically fulfilled by his solo work, but it seemed that he enjoyed climbing into what was a pretty successful vehicle so he could go out and play live much more than if he'd concentrated on just his solo career.

Mick brought a sense of style and class to the shows, always immaculately dressed and coiffured, thanks to Suzi. He was very friendly to the audience; he loved shaking hands with people in the front row. He was also very committed and determined to playing one hundred per cent at every show."

By contrast, Morgan describes a certain tension backstage before the shows, which was quite different to Mott's heady, drunken, partying days with Ariel. "Mick would psyche himself up before the gig and sometimes he'd explode with anger at Suzi for, say, losing a hairbrush. I felt a little sorry for her being dressed-down like that in front of us, but he thought she loved him so much she would put up with it." Suzi did love Mick and in spite of the occasional outburst, it was obvious that they were very much in love.

In spite of all these tensions, all the members were excited by the revised set list and enjoyed playing the new material. "It was great," says Buffin. "I think we did 'White Light/White Heat' (if indeed, 'White Light/White Heat' was rehearsed it failed to make the actual live set) and we did 'The Girl Can't Help It' which was quite fun to do and 'Angel No. 9'. It was quite a song, but we never quite got the arrangement right. It didn't seem natural somehow, but I guess we only played it about eight or nine times all together on the road, so that's not a lot really, to get used to a reasonably complex song. It felt pretty good on stage. It's always difficult to tell, but you always felt that whatever Mick was doing, it was solid and well-played and convincing."

Morgan adds, "I guess the song list was mainly up to Ian and Mick, but approved by all of us. I enjoyed Mick's songs as it was a pleasant change from Mott stuff, more musical in a way, more challenging."

Eighteen gigs later, they found themselves in Paris, scheduled to play their show at The Olympia. "It was odd, I didn't suspect much at all," says Morgan when questioned about this notorious date. "I was impressed by arriving at Charles de Gaulle, an amazing futurist-style airport. Mick was met by two very attractive and sophisticated record company ladies (probably from RCA France) who presented him with a very expensive bottle of Cognac, one of those bottles that looks like it's frosted. I think Tony Defries was there too, in a mink coat, smoking a huge cigar. Generally, the feeling was, 'This is gay Paris' and we're doing it in style!"

Ian remembers doing Olympia in Paris and recalls the discussion with Defries after the show. "He said to me, 'You should be thinking of doing something better than this.' I said, 'Why? We just had about fifteen encores, it couldn't have gone down any better.' His answer was, 'Well, yes, but that's what always happens.'"

On November 5, Mick was interviewed by Bob Harris on

THE SPIDER WITH THE PLATINUM HAIR

The Old Grey Whistle Test, talking positively about his position in Mott the Hoople. Mick, looking especially well-groomed, expressed his excitement about contributing to the songwriting.

A complete UK tour had been scheduled, but during the one-week break, Ian went abroad, travelling to the USA for business. All the while, questions arose within the remainder of the group. Buffin recalls, "In hindsight, once that tour was over, we're thinking, 'Why did they stay, just that little tight knit group just the two of them? Mick and Ian and the two wives and what could've they been talking about all that time? It does seem that's what was on the agenda, dumping the band, to just going off and doing their own thing. I don't think Mick was any part of that. Thinking back over it, I think Mick just found himself in the middle of this situation.

I'll be honest, I bore a grudge against Mick Ronson for quite some time but having examined it and having more information since then, it's obvious that he was an innocent party in the whole scheme. At the time, I was very frustrated. In fact, I might have felt rather darker thoughts about him before, but now I just feel that he was the unwilling partner to this scenario that was going on in the background. I think that's why he was kept out of our way. I've never been in a group where there was that sort of situation where somebody in the group was not available to speak. It's just very weird and it's a great shame because I think that there could have been a really good band there but it just wasn't allowed to happen because some people had other ideas."

In November, while still in the USA, Ian suffered from physical and mental exhaustion. As a result, he had a breakdown, which required him to re-evaluate his situation. Heeding the doctor's advice, Ian chose to rest, putting the band in the position of having to re-schedule dates, many of which were already sold out. It was reported that Mott the Hoople would complete the tour and still proceed with their plans of recording a new album after the New Year. However, this did not prevent the rumour mill swinging into action. Word on the street was spreading that Mott the Hoople had disbanded and by December 28, the rumours became reality when the break-up was officially declared in the media.

In turn, the band was forced to cancel the remainder of the tour dates and let go of their proposed album plans. Ian and Mick had left Mott the Hoople and were both currently in the States. Ian explains: "I had been in the hospital for a while and when I came out I was in Bobby Colomby's house, the drummer from Blood Sweat and Tears. Mick came there. He left England after me. He left Mott after me! He left about a week after me. We didn't plan it. It just sort of happened."

Mick explained to Kevin Cann in a 1984 *Starzone* interview that, "Mott the Hoople was really just something else to do, but I like Ian, really more than I liked the band. It was Ian that I did it for; the band talked me into joining them, which was just for about three weeks. I got disillusioned real fast. It was partly my fault I suppose, it just didn't gel. Ian was also getting tired of that situation too, so it was a good excuse to work together. He asked me if I would do an album with him if he left Mott and I said, 'Sure' and that was it."

Morgan explains that, 'in those days I, for one, was a heavy drinker, which does not do a great deal for one's clarity. In a sense, I was naive and if I'd been a bit more on my toes I might have persuaded Ian and Mick to take me with them to the USA, but the way it happened was so fast and surprising. Ian was in the USA when we got the call that he was sick and we had to cancel the rest of the tour. I'll let the other musicians speak for themselves, but I just wanted to get things up and running again as soon as possible. It seemed like the best thing, grab a new singer and keep going as Mott. It turned out to be musically rewarding as a player/arranger, but in terms of good songs, well, Ian's your man. If I'd had more guts, I might have jumped on a plane to New York and said, 'Take me with ya'. Basically, I felt very much in the middle of the Ian/Mick versus Pete/Buffin split and I took the easy way out."

Buffin closes his Mott recollections by saying, "It's a matter of great regret to Morgan, Overend and myself that it didn't happen, that it all went so badly astray. We really weren't the bad guys like we've been made out to be."

Buffin, Morgan and Overend carried on for several years recording and touring in various forms (as Mott and British Lions) as their deal enabled them to start fresh with a brand new slate (Ian's solo deal was cross-collateralized). The new Mott provided the fans with a very interesting body of work that has recently been digitally restored by Angel Air Records and Columbia's Rewind in England.

After resting and regrouping, Ian returned to England to begin recording his debut album titled *Ian Hunter*, at Air Studios, London, in January 1975. Former Rats bassist Geoff Appleby, drummer Dennis Elliott and pianist Pete Arnesen were brought in to contribute to the project. The role of lead guitarist, organ, mellotron, mouth organ, bass guitar and collaborator credits went to his new partner in crime, Mick Ronson.

During the recording of the *Ian Hunter* sessions, RCA finally released Mick's *Play Don't Worry* album in February 1975. With the added exposure from his recent involvement with Mott the Hoople, his second solo album, which had been shelved for months, seemed aptly timed. However, sales didn't live up to expectations.

Photographer Clive Arrowsmith captured the infamous image featured on the gatefold cover. Mick is frozen in motion under superb lighting, playing the Gibson, looking sensational.

Four images are used throughout, portraying Mick as an angelic, heroic guitarist, appendix scar and all. Steve New of Rich Kids laughs, "What about that appendix scar?! I thought it was really sweet that Mick kept that in there. I know that sounds completely ignorant but it really was sweet." Ronson historians oddly consider that if a fan mentions the "scar" (tongue in cheek) it somehow measures their devotion to the album. Silly as it may seem, that scar managed to push some sensitivity buttons, accelerating one's desire to get it on the turntable.

Mixed reviews of the album followed, yet for many it was the logical successor to his *Slaughter On 10th Avenue* debut. It's not that the records are similar in theme or vision, but they complement one another, giving the listener that necessary dose of solo follow-up.

Annette Peacock says, "I wished he'd have done even more solo work. I thought he had a potentially brilliant career in that direction. The big thing about Mick was that he didn't like his singing. The sound of his guitar alone, that's all he would've needed." Suzi agrees, "*Slaughter On 10th Avenue* is pretty good. With *Play Don't Worry*, I think we were struggling a bit. There is some good stuff on there though, some great guitar work. Mick never had a problem playing guitar; he had a problem with lyrics. I think that it's more apparent there."

Steve New feels that, "Mick never wanted to be a frontman. As far as going out and sort of pretending to people that he was larger than life or some sort of space alien from another planet, that just wasn't him. I don't think he could bullshit people to get their money or whatever, which is what so many pop stars are about."

Mick's two solo albums didn't change the face of music. However, they definitely left an impact on many. Most notably, they proved capable of breaking down time and cultural barriers by influencing one of Japan's hottest rock bands, The Yellow

Monkey. Bass player Youichi Hirose admits, "About the time we were forming this band (Tokyo in 1989), I got a cassette tape from vocalist/guitarist Kazuya Yoshii of both Mick's solo albums. It really opened my eyes. It taught me to appreciate music on a deeper, heightened level - each track, each take, every rehearsal."

Both of Mick's solo albums have stood the test of time and still receive their share of compliments. Morgan Fisher says, "I enjoyed Mick's first two solo albums, very creative and wide-ranging in terms of musical styles." To a degree, Mick had accomplished the challenge of his solo career. He had also confidently primed himself to carry the axe for Ian Hunter's solo debut and, loaded with ambition and a newfound direction, he looked forward to the boundless possibilities that this new partnership promised.

CHAPTER 8

WHERE DO YOU GO WHEN YOU'VE GOT SOMEWHERE TO RUN?

Ian and Mick were set to embark on a two-week UK tour, beginning on March 19, 1975. CBS Records had scheduled Ian Hunter's self-titled debut for March 28. Ian gives Mick the credit for pushing him forward: "Mick was just great to be with. You never knew which way he was going to go. He always had a different slant on things. It was his idea to go in and do that first song together when we did. He said, 'You should go in now because your emotions are upside down and that's the best time to go in and make a record.' So that's what we did.

Mick was at the top of his game. He had been hanging out with Visconti and Mick would ask him all these questions while working on Bowie's records. Visconti would explain things to him, so he was learning about all the board equipment. By the time I went in with Mick, he knew virtually everything in there and was using it, he was extremely thorough. I enjoyed all the benefits of that. That was a real eye-opener for me.

After first working with David, who had a good knowledge of the studio, and then Mick. We had no knowledge so I learned a lot."

"With people like Bowie and Hunter, you're talking about strong personalities," says Joe Elliott. "I wouldn't say ego, but strong personalities that may not take to somebody saying, 'I don't think that bridge in that song is very good', unless they really believed in the person that was saying it. Having seen what Mick had done with Bowie, Ian did believe in him."

Bassist Geoff Appleby remembers, "The whole experience was brilliant and great fun. The magic between Ian and Mick was in their communication, the respect for each other, but most of all with their love and friendship. I loved working with Mick, he's the best guitarist I've ever worked with and one of the best friends I've ever worked with."

The *Ian Hunter* album notes divide the songs into Parts versus Sides, setting a stage for the nine tracks that graced the recording. Mick provided all of the arrangements while he and Ian co-produced the entire record together.

Part One featured, 'Once Bitten Twice Shy', the album's first single, which was released on April 4, 1975. A signature "'ello" from Ian greets the listener, as a hypnotic drum beat and guitar groove provide the perfect background for Ian's sassy opening vocal. Ian and Mick are perfectly balanced, complementing each other on numbers such as 'Lounge Lizard' (a re-structured version of the Mott the Hoople song of the same title) and 'The Truth, the Whole Truth, Nuthin' but the Truth', to name just a few. One of the album's highlights is the beautifully crafted 'Boy'; this is Mick's first credited writing collaboration with Ian and remains a favourite amongst his fans. Overall, Ian and Mick had delivered a masterpiece debut that still holds, gripping the simple ground it was built on: quality songs - quality rock 'n' roll.

The album's striking packaging portrayed colourful cover art inspired by the infamous image *Bond of Union* by M.C. Escher. In addition, photographer Peter Lavery brilliantly captured a handsome-looking Hunter for the back cover. Sporting a hat and his trademark shades, Ian's look is so dead-on serious that it's irresistible. His look reeks of truth and of dare and seemingly whispers 'play me' to the more curious of folks.

"That was a good record," says Ian. "It went on for about six weeks at Air studios in London. I remember I smashed me hand through a pinball machine on the last night. Stitches, hospital, the lot. Then we went out and toured and people loved it."

Touring with Ian afforded Mick the licence to both showcase some of his solo work and allow him the opportunity to step in and out of the spotlight by choice. This seemed to be the ideal situation for Mick and for the audience, as Joe Elliott remembers: "The first time I saw Mick play live was in 1975, Sheffield City Hall, the Hunter/Ronson Tour. They played a mixture of stuff from Ian's album and off of Mick's two albums. They played a bunch of Mott the Hoople stuff as well. The highlights for me were Mick's 'Slaughter On 10th Avenue' and Ian's version of 'Boy', which went straight into 'Roll Away The Stone', that was superb. Mick wouldn't play 'Billy Porter', much to the annoyance of hundreds of people that were screaming out for it, because that was the current single at the time. It was difficult to see why at the time, but it's easy to see why in hindsight. It's not really a guitar-based song. It's a very difficult thing to do live."

'Angel No. 9', 'Growing Up And I'm Fine', 'White Light/ White Heat', 'Play Don't Worry' and 'The Girl Can't Help It' were also played during the tour. "It worked out great," says Ian. "I thought it was great and the people thought it was great. It was one of those bands you kind of liked even if they weren't very good." Incidentally, the pianist on the album, Pete Arnesen, was unable to tour so former Mott organist Blue Weaver came along instead.

Mick Rossi made a point of going to see Mick every time he played a show. "I would always turn up at the show and I got to kind of know some of the people on the crew and I got to know Michael." It was at this time that Rossi first met Ian Hunter: "We had stayed at the hotel and we were coming down for breakfast. I was so nervous and shy... still. These were my heroes. I was eating my breakfast and watching my manners and everything, trying to behave and not be a pig. Ian came down and went, 'Alright', and he took a bit of bacon off my plate with his hands. When he did that, I felt really at home, I could relax."

Obviously, the touring was enjoyable. Ian and Mick had proved themselves to be the perfect team and both their friendship and musicianship blossomed as a result. Morgan Fisher never saw the Hunter/Ronson band live but states, "I was glad to see Ian having such excellent musical support from Mick for his songs, as he was a writer more than a musician and needed someone to spark off. He had worked well with Mick Ralphs and here was someone who could take him into more mature, sophisticated territory. I'm glad he found such a good friend in Mick. We all need friends."

In support of the tour and album, the band was invited to appear on *The Old Grey Whistle Test* on April 11. "That was very memorable," says Geoff Appleby. "It was originally scheduled as a Hunter/Ronson set to promote Ian's solo album, but Ian had to shoot off to America, so we did it without him." Mick and the band pulled it off, playing 'Angel No. 9' and 'Play Don't Worry'.

Ian shot back to the USA. He was living in New York as an official citizen of the United States, so he had to leave Britain on April 3. Ian's manager, Fred Heller, had scheduled some dates in America for May and June, but this Stateside tour was cut short due to complications with the PA system and stirrings within the management camp. In spite of enthusiastic fans, there was an implication that the USA shows were a let down, which did little for the band's momentum. "We were such a likeable band. I saw no reason on earth why that band should fall. I had a great drummer, a real good bass player, we looked good, the material was coming, but it just got wrecked by management," says Ian.

Mick's quirky and nonchalant manner was often a source of almost comical frustration, as Ian explains: "I remember we did a video for 'Once Bitten Twice Shy'. We did it in one afternoon and it was brilliant. We were sitting in the Top Ten in England with 'Once Bitten', so we got on the plane to go back to do *Top of the Pops*, which would have taken it into the Top Five. We're got off the plane at Heathrow and Mick goes, 'Are you in the (Musicians') Union?' and I said, 'Well, of course I'm in the union, you can't go on television if you're not in the Union.' 'Ah...' he says. I said, 'How much did we just spend on that video, Ronson? We're first-class on the plane; we're going to do *Top of the Pops* and you're telling me that you're not in the union, right?' 'Well, I might not be, I'm not sure.' That was it: cancelled. That's just one of the thousands of similar stories. I could have killed him at least once a week!"

Mick was living in New York with Ian where the duo were writing and recording tracks for another new project. Sadly, their individual label and management circumstances took precedence and prevented them from pursuing their joint creative vision. Mick's contract had him committed to another solo album, even though RCA didn't appear that interested. Meanwhile, Ian's camp had other ideas for him. A deal which might accommodate them both could not be sealed.

THE SPIDER WITH THE PLATINUM HAIR

Ian told *Melody Maker* on June 14: "I'm not going to tell you that we're a couple of lovebirds sitting on a bench, but I'm saying that we're going to continue working together for as long as it suits us. At the moment we're fighting for a Hunter/Ronson album, but it's difficult. We want to get the name Hunter/Ronson known, but according to contracts, the next album will be a Mick Ronson album." As indicated, this never materialised and Mick, unable to find a home closer to the Hunters, moved into Manhattan.

Ian was frustrated with his lack of control over the situation, and felt that as long as Mick remained with MainMan, it would be impossible for them to work together. "I think in the first instance with Mott, I didn't mind but with the second instance with me and Mick I did mind. I thought that had a lot of potential. I've never really spoken to Defries since or forgiven him for that. He naturally has made overtures to speak to me from time to time, but I've refused to speak to him ever since, because I really did like the Hunter/Ronson band."

Hunter went on to create and record his own solo album, *All American Alien Boy*, which was a favourite of Mick's. Ian explains: "He always thought that album was the best one I ever did. That's typical Mick, because he wasn't even on it. Anybody else would tell you the ones that they played on were the best. Not Mick." The album featured stunning songwriting and a slew of talented musicians. Produced and arranged by Ian, it's not a surprise that Mick paid his mate such a deserving complement.

While Ian was composing his album, Mick spent the summer of 1975 soaking up the sounds of Manhattan, going to clubs and mixing with the locals. Crossing paths with singer/guitarist Bobby Neuwirth, he was invited to join his band. A subsequent meeting with one of Neuwirth's friends led to an even more exciting adventure. While at a club called The Other End, Mick met the one and only Robert Zimmerman, aka Bob Dylan. In the David Bowie magazine, *Starzone*, a 1984 interview by Kevin Cann reveals Mick's wonderful account of this first encounter with Dylan: "I just met him in a bar one night. I had just moved into New York. I was down in the village and Bob Dylan was just sitting in this bar playing a guitar with all these people crowded in. I sort of squeezed my way in but this bartender kept picking on me, telling me to move out of the way. So anyway, he threw me out and I got pretty mad at that point and threatened to go through the window and there was a whole commotion. Then Bob Dylan came out to see what was happening and said, 'Hey, do you wanna come with me for a drink?' So, I said, 'Alright' and we went off. We went down to this club and he just said, 'Right, do you want to come on the road with me?' So I said, 'Sure'. I went home thinking, 'Great, I'm going on the road with Bob Dylan.'" He wouldn't hear from Dylan again until a few months later.

Mick was surprised when he got the long-awaited phone call one Friday night. "Right, we start rehearsing on Sunday," Bob told Mick. "We went in and did like 150 numbers in ten hours, straight through," Ronson explained to writer Adam Block in a 1976 interview. "I thought there'd be a set of numbers and we'd try to get them right, but there were so many, there was no way. I was a bit worried but they gave me encouragement by not saying anything. If I'd been playing a few notes and everybody's eyes had gone to me, I would've died on the spot. But *everybody* was so easy-going. I'd look to T-Bone Burnett for chords and sometimes *he* wouldn't know."

Later, Mick told Kevin Cann, "I actually knew very little about Bob Dylan. The whole set up with that tour was very loose, it was chaotic. Arlo Guthrie came up and sang his songs, as did Leonard Cohen and Joni Mitchell. I was playing with all these people. The Dylan thing was really laid back; you just strolled on and off playing songs. I never knew what I was doing from night to night, what songs or even what key they would be in. One night 'Blowing In The Wind' would be in C, the next night it was in F! Not only that, he would play it twice as fast. Then he used to stop middle of a number suddenly, and then start again suddenly and you really had to watch him all the time. He was amazing, the whole thing was incredible." Plus, Mick will go down in history for his infamous quote about Dylan's voice: "I always thought he sounded just like Yogi Bear."

Dylan had invited more than a dozen artists (and loads of friends) to contribute to the sound and vision, so the stage was overflowing with extraordinary talent. His steady line-up was as follows; Joan Baez (vocals/guitar), Bobby Neuwirth (guitar), Scarlett Rivera (viola), T-Bone Burnett (guitar), Mick Ronson (guitar), Roger McGuinn (guitar), Steve Soles (guitar), David Mansfield (steel guitar, mandolin), Rob Stoner (bass), Howie Wyeth (drums, piano), Luther Rixx (drums) and Ronnie Blakely (vocal). There was seemingly enough spotlight to go around and, as the tour progressed, Mick made it a point to exhibit his musicianship (with fuzz box and all) within this circle of all-stars.

John Morthland reported to *Creem* magazine that, 'For me, Ronson was the high point of the show I saw, early in the tour, in Boston. He played stark, crystalline solo lines that ached and they sounded all the better for being counter-pointed against the sound of eight strumming folkie guitars. While my friends walked out jabbering about Dylan's white face, his new songs, his animation on-stage, I was gasping about how I didn't know Mick Ronson could play like that." Mick learned to be comfortable with whatever he was playing, "after (Dylan and) the Rolling Thunder, I had more faith in meself," Mick admitted.

The Dylan tour took place between October 1975 and May 1976 during which time the Rolling Thunder Revue band played fifty-plus shows. During two different breaks in the tour (December 9 – January 22) and (January 26 – April 17) Mick managed to squeeze in some very notable projects.

On December 13 and 14, Mick went into Sundragon Studios and recorded the solo songs that are now featured as bonus tracks on the *Play Don't Worry* CD release. 'Stone Love (Soul Love)', 'I'd Rather Be Me', 'Life on Mars?', 'Pain In The City' and 'Dogs (French Girl)' are all the result of this session. The last song they recorded was '28 Days Jam', a long instrumental (with no writing credit – presumably a band composition). Mick wanted to record an album the following year built around these demos and he planned to employ T-Bone Burnett as producer and have people like McGuinn and Stoner around to lend advice and support. These tracks were produced, arranged and conducted by Mick. John Slaven from the *Only After Dark* website points out that "'Dogs' and 'Life on Mars?' were credited to Mick Ronson, but were actually written by T-Bone Burnett and Roscoe West respectively." Further complicating things, the full title of 'Dogs (French Girl)' is 'Never Had A French Girl Outside Of France' and 'Life on Mars?' is actually titled 'Is There Life on Mars?'.

Mick spent Christmas in England, reuniting with some of his mates from Hull. Trevor and Woody were busy recording their own album at Trident Studios, tagging themselves appropriately as The Spiders From Mars. Self-titled and released with candy-apple red printed artwork, the full-sized, raised spider image on the cover had an enticing marketing appeal.

Vocalist Pete McDonald and guitarist Dave Black, formerly

of Kestrel (Newcastle-based Prog rockers) joined forces with Trevor and Woody, unleashing ten songs that swagger with more rock than stardust. The stardust that remains is thanks to Mike Garson's contributions, which are found throughout the recording, most notably on the ballad 'Stranger To My Door'. Trevor Bolder confirms "Mick did come to the studio once and played on a track with us. He played on a single that never got released called 'Roller'." Though the album was released with little fanfare, it proved to be an artistic and worthwhile endeavour, a traditional rock album that suited their aspirations. Worthy enough that Castle reissued *The Spiders From Mars* on CD in June 2000. Incidentally, Trevor later joined Uriah Heep and their version of the song 'Roller' turned up on the 1977 *Innocent Victim* album.

Mick returned to the States to team up with Dylan and the Rolling Thunder Revue for a second Hurricane Carter benefit concert on January 25th, Houston. The January date was a one-off show and the Revue took a break until April. During this time off Mick recorded with Roger McGuinn in Los Angeles for his upcoming May '76 solo project titled *Cardiff Rose,* a terrific achievement featuring thirty-six minutes of classic McGuinn, complemented by covers of Dylan and Joni Mitchell. He was assisted by writers such as Jacques Levy, Kris Kristofferson and Bobby Neuwirth, while Mick played acoustic guitar, electric guitar, recorder, accordion, piano, organ, autoharp, percussion and provided vocals. Rolling Thunder Revue mates David Mansfield, Rob Stoner, Howie Wyeth, combined with Timmy Schmit (vocals) and Kim Hitchcroft (saxophone) added up to a classic effort from McGuinn that was hugely under-rated.

"He was a very gifted musician in all areas," says Roger. "I really loved the way he treated 'Jolly Roger' and when he played 'Chestnut Mare', he made that horse fly!" Mick also produced the album and McGuinn comments: "I was delighted with how good a producer Mick was. I'd just been friends with him and hadn't guessed at his hidden talent for production. I was very pleased with the results." Suzi Ronson really enjoys this album too and agrees with Roger: "Mick did a great production on *Cardiff Rose*."

The backing band for the Rolling Thunder Revue were collectively known as Guam and they would often perform a one-hour show before Dylan joined them on stage. Ronson's solo in the Guam set was the aforementioned 'Is There Life on Mars?'. Ronson and McGuinn had seriously discussed the possibility of forming a band with Wyeth, Stoner and Mansfield and taking it on the road in support of *Cardiff Rose*. Talk of a Ronson/McGuinn album was also on the table with Mick planning to use some of the Sundragon material. The project would be called Thunderbyrd, named after Rolling Thunder and The Byrds, but as history proves, this did not happen.

When McGuinn is asked about 'Guam' he replies, "Guam was just the working name of the Rolling Thunder Revue band. We were going to get a record deal (Thunderbyrd) after the tour, but it didn't work out. So, we never worked together again other than on the *Cardiff Rose* project."

The glorious results of his touring with Dylan's Rolling Thunder Revue landed Mick a spot ('Maggie's Farm') on the official live album released in September of 1976, titled *Hard Rain*. A TV special with the same name followed, heavily featuring Mick during his performance with them in May at the Hughes Stadium, Fort Collins, Colorado. A Los Angeles super-jam performance with Mick, Roger McGuinn, Carmine Appice, Tim Bogert, Bo Diddley, Mark Steiner, Albert Lee and Barry Goldberg was also televised. Known as the *Bo Diddley Super Jam* it was filmed and broadcast at a later date, for NBC's *Midnight Special*. Songs taped included the Beck, Bogart and Appice number 'Lady', plus 'Not Fade Away', 'Hey Bo Diddley' and one unknown number. Known to have only aired in the USA, this episode has yet to surface on video.

Dylan had hired a crew of people to film the shows and the events (some staged) taking place during the course of the tour. Hours of back-stage, on-stage and off-stage antics were filmed for Dylan's movie, *Renaldo and Clara*. Eventually released as a four-hour film in 1978 (later edited down to two hours), it included no less than seventy songs. Mick is featured on twenty five of these in addition to his acted character role. Mick played the part of a concert security man who just so happens to hold the key to the after-life. The movie is funny and exaggerated, yet when juxtaposed with the live material, it's a bird's eye view of the Rolling Thunder Revue, providing hours of strange but entertaining footage.

The shoes that Mick wore during *Renaldo and Clara* are significant to Glen Matlock of the Sex Pistols. "I first met Mick when I was working in Malcolm McClaren's shop and he, Ian and Suzi came in. I was there by meself, it was during the week and there were these sort of pink loafers, these pink shoes in the window, which Mick wanted to go try on. So, I had to get all of these boxes down from the top, because he had really small feet. We finally found a pair by which time there were all these boxes all over the floor. I looked at him and he said, 'You're pissed off at me, aren't ya?' and I said, 'No, no, no,' and he said, 'Yeah, it's alright, I'll put 'em back.' So, there he is, up the ladder putting all the boxes back. You know that bit in the movie where he's the security guard? Well, he's wearing them shoes."

Suzi Ronson remembers the Dylan shows fondly: "We loved it. It was a real classy tour, we had the best time." Roger McGuinn feels the same: "Mick and I were great friends on the tour. We hung out every night, the band was big but it didn't seem that way when we played together. Mick was just a killer guitarist. It was a lot of fun playing with him." Mick had made some valuable friendships during the course of his involvement with Dylan. According to Roger, he was "a great guy on stage and off. He brought a sense to the Revue that wouldn't have been there without him."

Mick's association with Rolling Thunder directly earned him a credit on Kinky Friedman's 1976 *Lasso From El Paso* record. Kinky was one of the many special guests who joined in on Dylan's Rolling Thunder Revue tour. *Lasso From El Paso* opens with a live version of Kinky's 'Sold American', recorded in May 1976 at Colorado State University.

It's been said that Mick expressed a wish to produce America's teen idol David Cassidy (also known as Keith from the television series *The Partridge Family*) before he became involved with the Rolling Thunder Revue. David, in an attempt to shed his teen image after quitting the television show, had signed a three record contract with RCA making him a label mate with Mick.

David recorded *Gettin' It In The Street*, his third RCA album at Caribou Ranch Studios in Denver. Cassidy invited a variety of musicians to the sessions and had shown great interest in collaborating with Mick. A meeting at the ranch during the Rolling Thunder Tour of May 1976 finally provided them with this opportunity. David told writer Chris Charlesworth how, "Mick came up to the studios and played on a couple of tracks on the album (only one is known to exist) and he helped me a lot." Mick and David also discussed the possibilities of collaborating more in the near future.

Later, when Cassidy and his drummer, Ricky Fataar, passed through New York, Mick booked the studio time and the team spent a few weeks rehearsing at Studio Instrumental Rental (SIR). There was talk of Mick producing David's new album and allegedly a joint venture was mooted as a possibility, although both these ideas failed to evolve. Rumours of a tour were also on the New York grapevine, but these rehearsals turned out to be the full extent of their work together after those initial studio sessions in Denver. Incidentally, *Gettin' It In The Street* was initially only issued in Germany and Japan (November 1976) and didn't get released in America until years later, in 1979. The title track, often described as a "gritty" little rocker, features Mick on guitar and fared very well on the German charts, peaking at #12 in April, 1977.

Meanwhile, Mick's relationship with Tony Defries was breaking down. Barry Imhoff provided advice for Mick about his contract with Defries and having connections at Bearsville Studios, became Mick's new manager. After Cassidy and Fataar left, Mick continued to audition personnel at SIR for what would eventually be the Mick Ronson Band.

He first chose to record with an unknown New York singer named Mary Hogan (sessions unreleased), before finally deciding on an all male four-piece band. The band featured himself on lead guitar and vocal, Mick Barakan on guitar, Jay Davis on bass and Bobby Chen on drums. They made their live debut opening for Gentle Giant on Long Island, June 3, but Mick still remained on the move.

One month later, Mick jammed with the New York Dolls on July 4, at Max's Kansas City. Later, on 26 and 27 July he made an appearance at the Ocean Club in New York backing John Cale, Patti Smith, David Byrne (Talking Heads) and Alan Lanier (Blue Öyster Cult). Lou Reed showed up on the second night and Chris Spedding was also part of the line-up. Ronson continued to jam around New York, playing with new groups; Topaz and The Alpha Band, both consisting of old Rolling Thunder pals.

Mick also hooked up again with Michael Chapman. "I didn't see him for a long time and then in 1976 he played on an album of mine called *The Man Who Hated Mornings*," says Chapman (this album was released in the UK the following year). "I had spoken to him in America about coming over and doing it. I actually wanted him to produce and play on it but he couldn't get there for one reason or another. Then suddenly he turned up in the middle of the sessions with his Les Paul, the first Mesa Boogie amplifier I'd ever seen and a bottle of vodka."

Mick let the vodka get the better of him that afternoon. Michael recalls the session: "He was not in a good condition. He came into the studio and played all day and it was awful. He kept saying to me, 'What do you want me to play like?' and I said, 'Play like Mick Ronson, that's what I want you to play like.' It went on and on and on for hour after hour and he was playing all of this terrible stuff. It was just nothing, I could've done it better and I'm not a rock guitar player."

Then, when Chapman was just about ready to write the day off, "all of a sudden he just clicked into gear on one tune, 'I'm Sober Now'. He played a solo which is kind of a country solo and then instantly afterwards he double-tracked it perfectly in harmony. Then, he went back to playing shit again. That was the only track I kept Mick on because the rest of it just wasn't worth having. I think that was actually the last time I saw him."

CHAPTER 9

BURNING
SOUNDS

Back in the USA, having experienced such a varied itinerary of musical activities, Mick and Suzi settled themselves in upstate New York. In the early 1970s there was a post-Woodstock fall out and many artists had moved to the area after the original festival. Mick liked it so much he eventually ended up buying a house there.

David Bowie had also parted company with Defries so MainMan were scouting for a new superstar. They found their man in Valonia, Indiana, when a twenty-four year old John Mellencamp sent Defries a demo tape for review. Tony quickly secured a record deal with MCA and they proceeded to put together the *Chestnut Street Incident* album. Mick and several others were asked to appear on this album consisting of originals and covers. It's likely that David Mansfield (Rolling Thunder) invited Ronson to the session as Mick was under Imhoff's management by this time.

Chestnut Street Incident was released in the States in 1976 whereas the UK release didn't follow until years later in 1984. This album featured eleven songs, produced by Tony Defries and James JC Andrews. Snapper Music recently released the album on disc with two bonus tracks, both of which feature Mick: 'Hit The Road Jack' and 'I Need Somebody'. It was during these sessions that John and Mick formed a lasting friendship.

It wasn't long before Ronson found himself involved with the incredible Mael Brothers, otherwise known as Sparks. Allegedly, Ron and Russell Mael were looking for more of a "rock" sound for their upcoming album titled *Big Beat*. The brothers recruited Mick because "we had always loved Mick's guitar work on the early Bowie recordings," explains Russell Mael. "To us he was the quintessential example of the difference between British and American guitarists. British = good, American = sucky. Everyone in a certain ilk of band tries emulating the sound and aura of those Bowie recordings which owe a lot to Mick's guitar. Rather than emulating, we had an opportunity to go right to the source."

Sparks rehearsed for several weeks with Mick on the *Big Beat* album. According to Russell, "Mick's manner was more easy-going than we expected. He wasn't creepy or dictatorial in his approach to our material. He allowed us to be creepy and dictatorial, but with Mick's guitar parts being so special, there was no need for us to be. Mick the musician didn't let us down with the image we had of him from his work with Bowie. His guitar work was every bit as musician-ly, flashy and cool as we had expected. Certain pop musicians stand out above the crowd. Mick was one."

Unfortunately, these demos were never released and shelved. Sparks chose to release the version of *Big Beat* featuring the assistance of producer Rupert Holmes and guitarist Jeffrey Salen. Undoubtedly, the demos that the Maels possess capture some crunching guitar work from Mick. "At one point he was going to produce the album. At another, he was just going to play. Finally, he did neither, but left us with several Walkman quality rehearsal tapes that we covet," says Russell.

Mick's decision to mix in the very good company of the Mael brothers strengthened his ability to work in circumstances that required a heightened flexibility. It's since been revealed that Ronson declined an invite to join Sparks in favor of leading his own band.

Now based in Woodstock, Mick was determined to rekindle his own group (Barakan, Davis & Chen) based on the auditions he did earlier at SIR. He would spend the next few weeks composing and rehearsing at a rented house in Woodstock. Calling themselves The Mick Ronson Band, they recorded a number of demos including 'Angel No. 9'.

John Holbrook and Dennis Ferrante were both involved with the engineering of these songs, recorded across two different sessions, which Mick worked on at Bearsville. "I was working as a recording engineer and producer in those studios," says John. "One day, Mick appeared with this band he had put together. It was just a four-piece. Mick's manager at the time had arranged some deal where he could record some songs at the studio. So, they showed up and we started recording.

Mick was drinking quite a bit but he was very personable. Very easy to get on with and, as a player, the sound that was coming out was amazing. That kind of sound, that kind of approach, I don't think I'd ever heard it before. I had heard the Bowie records but to actually be in the studio recording it was a new experience. It was a pretty good vibe."

Karen Barakan (now wife of Mick 'Johnny Average' Hodgkinson) met Ronson during this period: "I was assistant manager at Bearsville Studio and my job was to take care of the artists. I was to make sure that they were set up in their households and everything, as well as all of their recording needs. It was wonderful to take care of these four beautiful, sweet guys. They were all very nice."

Karen's ex-husband, Mick Barakan (Shayne Fontayne), actually came to the USA looking for Mick. "He came to New York to find Ronson and met up with him there. While in England, Mick had said to him 'Oh, when you're in the States come and see me.' He took that as an invitation and came to visit. He met up with him in the city and that's when they formed The Mick Ronson Band, so they all came (to Bearsville) as the new, hot, English band."

Albert Grossman, who had managed both Janis Joplin and Bob Dylan, had a new studio, which was a real asset for Woodstock. It didn't take long for word to spread through the music community when artists were recording there. Karen explains: "Whenever anybody new came to town in those days, you always knew it. It's Bearsville, it's Woodstock, and we had a lot of visitors that were very, very famous. These stars would be there for two-to-three weeks, during which time they would frequent the local establishments, so everybody knew they were in town. You can imagine the word of mouth when these cute Englishmen suddenly descended on town."

The Bearsville environment was ideal for all of the musicians involved. Mick's liberal working methods allowed the band's artistic abilities to shine. Most of the tracks didn't pass the demo stage however, because the mixing was not finished before the group agreed to seven dates in the New York area, where they played with Rush, The James Gang, Black Oak Arkansas and Gentle Giant.

After a possible deal with Atlantic Records failed to prosper, Jay Davis left the group but the rest of the band continued to record, this time at Turtle Creek Barn, an annex to Bearsville. Bassist Burt Carey joined the group for these sessions, which resulted in four new recordings and a few additional takes of previously recorded songs. Ultimately, all of the Mick Ronson Band recordings were shelved, unfinished, due to the absence of a record deal and financial difficulty. These sessions were finally available to the public in 1999, when Burning Airlines released these tracks as a limited edition, two CD set, titled *Just Like This*. Later in 1999, a two CD set, *Showtime*, featured seven songs recorded at the Century Theatre, Buffalo, NY during the aforementioned December, 1976 tour.

Just Like This features blistering guitar work from Ronson and in the process spotlights an incredible band. Songs like 'I'd Give Anything to See You', 'Hard Life', and 'Crazy Love' are favoured tracks among the fans. Overall, these are wonderful additions to the collection and hint of the influence provided by Ronson's touring with Dylan. The songs feature lengthened guitar solos and have a jamming quality that, now and again, tips a hat to the blues. Having said that, it should be noted that Mick's sense of melody remained and a strengthened confidence in his vocal is evident.

John Holbrook says, "I think he had a very personal touch with the guitar in the way he bent strings and stuff. I remember him showing me how he grew a couple of nails on his left hand. Normally, guitar players grow nails on their right hand to do picking with, but he actually left at least one or two on his left hand long. I said, 'Why do you do that, isn't it hard?' He said, 'No, it's great because when I bend strings, I bend them so far, so much that, with these nails, well, I can sort of get under the other strings.' He had a certain way of bending strings and a certain attack. I thought that the sound he had, especially on the first demos that we did, was pretty distinctive. I don't think he sounded like anybody else."

Recording this complex talent was pretty straightforward, as John admits: "The sound was there. All we had to do was stick a mike in front of it. This was very much *his* baby, *his* project. He had a very musical approach, definitely on top of it. He knew what he wanted. Even then, I remember the music feeling quite intense at the time we were recording it."

Karen shares one amusing incident sparked by Ronson's Hull accent: "The band was in the studio and I was just always there. Some people showed up and everybody wanted to come into the control room, which already had too many people in there, not least because it wasn't that big. Ronson is drinking rum and coke. Somebody knocks on the door wanting to come in and he goes, 'Oh, come on in, we've got plenty of rum,' and everybody thought he meant 'room'. Before long, the control room is rammed full of people and all Ronson was talking about was that there was rum for everybody."

Mick continued to use Woodstock as a home base while travelling to and from London, depending on the work. While still in New York, Mick teamed up again with the band Topaz; this time joining Rolling Thunder's bassist/vocalist, Rob Stoner, guitarist Billy Cross and vocalist Jasper Hutchinson in the studio. Mick played guitar and piano and helped with arrangements on their self-titled album, featuring 'A Modern Love Song', 'Slice Of Night' and 'Some American Obsession'.

Meanwhile, as Britain was exploding with punk rock, Mick accepted the invite to work with The Who's lead vocalist, Roger Daltrey. The unforgiving punk culture forced Roger to pursue a renewed strategy and approach to recording. With this in mind, he employed a stellar group of musicians to appear on his third solo album titled *One Of the Boys*. Once again, Mick found himself in good company as John Entwistle, Eric Clapton and Andy Fairweather-Low also appeared on the record. Recorded at The Who's own Ramport Studios in London as well as at the Pathe Marconi Studios in Paris, Roger and friends created a commendable album, which peaked that summer at UK #45.

By the spring of 1977, Mick was back in the States, as Suzi was carrying their child. "I was expecting my daughter and Mick and I both wanted to stay in America. Mick said, 'Well, I suppose we'd better get married then', so it wasn't really a romantic big deal or anything! It was just one of those things that we always thought we were going to do and this was just a good reason to do it. We got married up in Woodstock, on the first day of spring, March 23, in a gorgeous Chinese restaurant owned by Albert Grossman. Barry Imhoff hired a couple of private rooms upstairs and we had a few great guests and that was that. No honeymoon. Mick went back to the studio. He was working with Benny Mardones at the time."

Mick met Benny through a referral from the owner of a local club called The Joyous Lake. He agreed to play all the guitars on his upcoming 1978 album *Thank God For Girls*. Benny's drummer, Jerry Shirley, remembers, "We did the first five tracks as a demo. Andrew Loog Oldham produced it. He took it to a record company and they said, 'Yes, go ahead and complete the record'. We went back (to Bearsville) and did five more tracks (only eight made the album) and that was the completion of the record."

Jerry adds that he found Mick very down-to-earth, seemingly concerned about "getting the job done quickly, efficiently and earning his money and looking after his wife and kid." Jerry got the impression that, at the time, he was struggling a little bit. "I don't think he was in the gutter or anything, but it just seemed to me like he was doing all he could to get by at the time. He didn't make a big fuss about what he did; he just got on and did the job. I seem to remember he and I talking about taking it a little easier with the drinking. It was a very uneventful session, very business-like. We got on very well, he was just a nice guy," adds Jerry.

In June 1977, Mick teamed up with Van Morrison, along with Peter Van Hooke (drums), Mo Foster (bass), and Dr. John (keyboards). This line-up played at a press launch for Van's new album *A Period of Transition* at Maunkberry's in London on June 15, 1977. This gig was filmed for the *So It Goes* TV show on Granada Television, airing on October 9, 1977. The group then traveled to Holland to appear on the *Wonderland* TV program, filmed at Vara Studios in Hilversum, Holland on June 22, 1977. The *Wonderland* show was also broadcast on FM radio in slightly altered form. For many years only bootleg tapes of the Holland broadcasts were available (featuring amazing versions of standard blues numbers like 'Fever', 'Baby Please Don't Go', and a sizzling version of a song Mick knew well, 'Shakin' All Over'), but recently bootleg DVDs in pristine quality from the *Wonderland* show have turned up as well.

Back in Woodstock, Mick looked forward to the birth of their daughter and hoped to provide a secure and loving home for her. Lisa Ronson was born on August 10, 1977 and became the apple of her father's eye. "He loved little Lisa, that was his girl,' states Suzi. "She is very much like her dad, two peas in a pod. They're very, very similar in looks, as well as personality. She is a darling girl and he adored her." These were happy days for the Ronson family.

Bob Harris remembers, "The Woodstock time was absolutely great. I was really pleasantly surprised to see Mick there. I remember having a long, long chat with him about how things were and he was very happy and comfortable and content."

The Old Grey Whistle Test did a programme that covered what was called 'the Bearsville Picnic', which was near Woodstock. "A lot of the members of that musical community were part of this special programme that we did. A lot of the artists that were on the Bearsville record label appeared on the show. Todd Rundgren and others all gathered around the studio. The Band were there and Dr. John too. John Sebastian and Mick Ronson were there as well. We recorded quite a conversation with Mick and he took part in a late night jam session, involving Dr. John, Levon Helm, even Leon Russell might have been there. That was the last time during my spell on that programme that we met up with Mick and featured him in any length."

Back in London, the jamming continued (in a warehouse) with Philip Rambow who he originally met in 1974 through Guy Stevens who was producing the debut album for Rambow's band The Winkies. Maggi was friends with Dave Corchoran the drummer and he and Phil asked her to do some back-up vocals with the band. Rambow told *Sounds* magazine "Mick asked her what was happening and what she was doing and one day we were rehearsing and Dave was asked to go down to have a jam. Mick was there with Dr. John and a couple of other people and I went down too and we just had a play." These jam sessions led to Mick (and Maggi) backing Rambow on a British tour that autumn. In December, they went into the studio and Mick played guitar on some demos, including 'Young Lust' which he later recorded with Ellen Foley. Sadly, Chrysalis weren't too keen and Ronson's other commitments banged the relationship on the head. The Rambow/Ronson demos did help secure Rambow a new deal with EMI records though.

Through his relationship with Philip Rambow, he was introduced to many prominent punks. Mick was right in the thick of it, watching groups like The Rich Kids and Slaughter And The Dogs gaining speed. The Rich Kids were formed by ex-Sex Pistol's bassist Glen Matlock, shortly after his departure from the latter. He and guitarist Steve New, drummer Rusty

Egan and vocalist Midge Ure had signed a contract with EMI and built up a solid live following in anticipation of the release of their first single in January 1978. However, before they began the process of recording their *Ghosts of Princes in Towers* album, they received a very unexpected phone call.

Glen Matlock tells it like this: "One day, the phone rang and there was nobody in the office at the time so I answered it, and it was Mick Ronson introducing himself. The conversation went on:

'Ah, you're Glen, aren't you?' he says.

'Yeah.'

'I've heard about you.'

'Well, I've heard about you," I replied, 'and you know what? We're looking for a producer, do you want to come and produce us?'

'Hmm, well, I'd like to see the band.'

'We're rehearsing tomorrow down in Putney. Why don't you come down and bring your guitar?'

'Alright.'

And he did! We were rehearsing in this place on Disraeli Road, so he joined us there. Then we went straight down to the pub."

Steve New remembers the anxiety attached to their first meeting: "I was really, really, really, *really* nervous that I was going to meet this guy, Mick Ronson. I had all of these projections about him because all I could relate to was 'Moonage Daydream' and that guitar playing. I'm thinking I'm going to meet this guy and he's going to be this bad mother and be like, 'Yeah, I did that solo, I'm Aladdin Sane, I'm the Cracked Actor,' but when I met him, he seemed to be just as nervous as I was. I think one of the first things he said to us was 'Give me a fag.'

Mick mastered some nifty tricks for The Rich Kids' tracks

he worked on in the studio: "Mick had some really good ideas. Like on 'Marching Men', the beat for the 'don't turn your back' part, that was Mick's idea. I don't think he liked the song actually, I think he thought it was a bit boring. That section of 'Sunshine Of Your Love', where the drums are the wrong way around, well, we did the same thing. The snare is where the bass beat should be and the bass drum is where the snare should be," says Glen. 'Marching Men' was the second single released.

Undoubtedly, Mick knew exactly what he wanted and how to get it. "One time he wanted to slow something down for whatever reason," recalls Glen, "but I said, 'Well, hang on a minute, if you slow it down it's going to be all out of tune'. 'No, no, no,' he says, 'slow it down from thirty ips to fifteen and it's exactly an octave lower. We're in A flat so, if you play the chord in F and play it at the third of the speed, it will be in G.' I went, 'Oh, wow.'"

Importantly, Mick also knew his limitations. Glen gives this example: "When we were doing the track 'Cheap Emotions' we asked Mick for a little piano and he obliged, but it didn't quite sound right. He said, 'Well, what do you want it like?' I said 'You know, like rock 'n' roll kind of piano, like sort of Ian McLagan,' and he said, 'Well, I can't play like that'. Instead, somebody in the studio suggested we call him up. We made Mick call him up and, sure enough, McLagan came down."

For Steve, the joyful experience of working with Ronson was mixed with the peculiar environment around The Rich Kids. "That record was a farce. Mick really contributed to the album in as much as he was there everyday, but the band itself wasn't really ever together. It was one of the weirdest bands ever; the band should have never existed, really. From a selfish point of view, however, it did contribute to my playing, via the comments that Mick offered me. Plus he was willing to let me do what I really wanted to do, guitar wise, even though Midge and Glen were like, 'Oh no, Steve, oh no!' I really believe to this day that Mick could understand my musical vision, which was a lot heavier than the Rich Kids.

He just heard things, he could hear the root. He could hear where the noise was coming from, which is a real gift. If all records were made like, 'Hey Ma, Get Papa', there would be some really good music out there. Mick was really tasteful with what did and didn't go on a record, he just *knew*. The Rich Kids never gave him that much space, but then again I'm not sure how much he would have wanted to be involved, because of our situation."

Mick is quoted in Campbell Devine's *All the Young Dudes* biography as saying, "It was great to watch Steve, seventeen years old. He didn't care if the guitar was in tune or not. He'd just plug in, turn it up and crank it out. I'd kind of forgotten how to live with music that way. I'd tended to get very serious about music."

The Rich Kids were burning out, but Glen fondly remembers Ronson's dry sense of humour. One particular session was dragging on slowly: "We were sitting in the studio and Mick turned to me and said, 'I wonder where it's going?' I said 'Oh well, Steve's just done that bit, you know, and I think Midge is going to do the bit next,' and he goes 'Oh, not there, I've got a horse in the 3:30, I'm wondering where it's going?'

Mick enjoyed the races and the thrill of a good gamble, "I can remember going to Walthamstow Dogs with him. The dogs were running but Mick suddenly starts walking away. I asked him, 'Where you going?' He said, 'Number Six is coming up quick on the outside, I'm going to try and get a bet on him before it's too late.' You know, for everything he'd done, he was so unaffected," says Glen.

Mick didn't go on the road with The Rich Kids, but he did appear at two of their gigs. "I always remember Mick being just as nervous as anybody else about going on stage," recalls Steve, "and that, to me, was another revealing thing. It wasn't just me that was shittin' myself, even guys like Mick Ronson got nervous before they went on. Just before we'd go on he'd be like, 'You all right then, you all right?' Then he'd kind of shut down a little bit and get into this semi-serious state. Sort of a little bit distracted, like he had other things on his mind. I was always hoping he'd say 'It's all right, you don't get nervous before you go on stage,' but now I understand, of course you do. Everyone gets nervous before they go on stage."

The Ronson-produced *Ghosts of Princes in Towers* was released several months later, in October of 1978. It reached #51 on the charts and was accompanied by three singles, but by the time of the last seven inch vinyl, the band had officially broken up. A memorable record and a few token memories were all that remained. "Mick was one of the most generous, funny, kind-hearted people I've ever met in the music business. But, what was also good about him was that he wouldn't stand for no shit. He wasn't a soft touch, you could only push him so far," says Glen.

Obviously still hungry to associate himself with the punk scene, Mick engaged himself with another British four-piece, led by one of his biggest fans, Mick Rossi. Slaughter And The Dogs were Mick Rossi (guitar) and Wayne Barrett (vocals) with recruited schoolmates Howard 'Zip' Bates (bass) and Brian 'Mad Muffet' Grantham (drums). Their gigs at The Roxy and Swindon's The Affair, combined with the buzz of an independent single had helped to establish their name and led to a deal with Decca. Having taken their group name from Mick's *Slaughter On 10th Avenue* and David Bowie's *Diamond Dogs*, the band naturally agreed with Rossi's idea of inviting Mick to the studio.

Rossi recalls, "I'd rung up Mick when I got my first Les

Paul. I told him we were doing an album and I was just messing about and said, 'You've got to come down and play on it.' When he said, 'Okay', I nearly fainted."

Mick's imminent arrival coincided with their third single for Decca, the 1960s classic, 'Quick Joey Small', in February 1978. "We were in Decca's studios and I was just so excited that we were in London doing the record," recounts Rossi. "Mick just turned up with his Boogie amp and his Les Paul and he played on two tracks, the forthcoming single and 'Who Are The Mystery Girls?' Right about then our friendship was kind of locked."

When asked about Mick's playing, Rossi notes, "It was his whole execution. It's all down to vibrato and the way Mick would play a note, it just seemed to sing. Having said that, he could do all the other stuff as well, but he just did it so tastefully. I think it was a combination of what was in his soul and what was going through his fingers that made him such a great player. He just had a great understanding of what was needed."

Do It Dog Style features the band's singles and various other punk-rock wonders. It hit the streets on June 13, 1978. Rossi still gives Mick the credit for influencing his direction and keeping him motivated: "When I would tell him that I wanted to be a guitar player, he would sit down and encourage me. Little things he would say would just give me so much drive." Remember, long before Slaughter And The Dogs were even a thought, Ronson had been befriending Rossi, the fan. "I remember once at his house in London, he gave me a distortion box. I thanked him and took it home but I couldn't get it to work, I was only sixteen. I rang him up, really embarrassed, and said 'Well, what do I do with it Mick?' and he said 'Well, you have to put a battery in it first.'

By summer of 1978, Mick had collaborated with two more

British-based artists. To this day, his involvement with the new wave band Careless Talk remains unclear, as they were relatively unknown. Another punk new wave production he did was with Dead Fingers Talk, assisting them on their *Storm The Reality Studios* record. According to Sven Gusevik, "The album caused some controversy when it was released because of the lyric contents; dealing mainly with gay topics." Mick, no stranger to controversy, must have felt delighted to leave his imprint on this new British sound.

Having tackled that, he next dived head first into a project with one of his mentors, Annette Peacock. Annette's decision to sign with MainMan in 1972 was during the peak of their relationship with Bowie. Annette was left biding her time in New York, studying musical theory after her *I'm The One* release. Eager for something to happen, she had moved to Surrey in England and spent the next four years recording her follow up, *X-Dreams*. "I just recorded in studios whenever I had the opportunity, with musicians that I wanted to work with. It developed over a period of time," she told Linnet Evans from *Sounds*.

A total of six guitarists were involved, including Mick and one of Britain's most versatile session guitarists, Chris Spedding. "There was an understanding between Mick and I, a mutual respect and admiration," says Annette. Songs like 'My Mama Never Taught Me How to Cook' and 'Questions' (both of which feature Mick) leave the listener with a stirring notion that this piece of wax is loaded with some sort of she-wisdom. Her lyrically sound explorations of men and relationships are complemented and perfectly balanced by the musicians she hand-picked, most notably, Mick.

'Too Much in the Skies' and (another) Elvis cover, the Otis Blackwell composed 'Don't Be Cruel', are the other two tracks that Mick plays on. "He showed up with absolutely no ego. He *had* no ego. He was very eager to determine what was needed and provide whatever that was," says Annette. *X-Dreams* was released and later reviewed in September 1978 by Ian Penman, writer for *NME*. "A hypnotic, taut-stomach, near-hysterical carnal escalation of sexual tension – so seldom caught, especially by rock music," he raved. Again, Mick had involved himself in projects that challenged him as a musician. Annette remains grateful, "He was a pleasure to work with and very, very professional."

Incidentally, the track 'My Mama Never Taught Me How To Cook' is featured in the 1997 film *Chasing Amy*. "When I heard that come on at the movies, Mick's playing on that was really an important part. At various times in your life, he reaches out and touches you. Not that many people can hold on to you that long and still touch you that intensely," says Annette.

A mooted collaboration including King Crimson drummer Bill Bruford and Japan's Mick Karn unfortunately foundered because of conflicting schedules. "I just abandoned the idea. The combination of those people would've been amazing," ruminates Annette.

Having spent so many months working with young, contemporary and cutting-edge artists, Ronson longed for the simple sounds of three-chord rock 'n' roll. He packed his bag and returned to New York, where a man in dark sunglasses anxiously awaited his arrival.

CHAPTER 10

JUST ANOTHER NIGHT ON THE OTHER SIDE OF LIFE

Even though Mick hadn't been working with Ian Hunter, they'd remained close friends. "He'd come to barbecues and parties, which was going on a lot at the time," recounts Ian. "He was always the guy that cooked. He'd be in the kitchen which Trudi loved because it took the heat off her! We'd have a lot of people around, which Mick loved, he marinated and all that kind of stuff."

Soon, the Ronsons became more than just visitors. "Mick, Suzi and Lisa lived with us for about a year. They came for a weekend and stayed for a year. We had a wonderful time. Suzi and Trudi were friends and I love Lisa like she was me own, so did Trudi. We seemed to be much more together when we didn't play then when we did. People loved it when Mick stayed with them because it was always a lot of fun. He was one of those guys who wouldn't make any mess or anything, but he would break things. You'd hear all these smashes because he'd be out of his brain from 8pm every night, but he would never apologise when he broke things!

I'd made this table tennis table. One night I heard this enormous smash. Apparently, he'd stumbled about and fallen on it. He never used to say, like any other human being would, 'Look what happened.' He'd just leave it until he was going and only then would he say, 'You know your tennis table? I broke it'. Not like, 'I'll pay for it', you know, like normal people, none of that.

He did the same thing with our letter box. He backed the car up the driveway and knocked the box over. I said, 'What did you do that for?' and he said, 'Well, it's not straight, that driveway isn't straight! How the fuck could I drive up the driveway backwards, if it's not straight?' Like it's *my* fault, you know? Unbelievable!"

Glen Matlock remembers an interesting incident that occurred around this time. "Bowie knew that I was in touch with Ronson and said that he'd been trying to get in touch with Mick. Bowie was asking me, 'What did he say?' I'd had a few drinks, so I said, 'I can't remember'. Bowie was like, 'No, c'mon, what did he say?' I told him that he said, 'You only ever call up when you want something.' I believe that Bowie was thinking of getting The Spiders back together at that time." Needless to say, it didn't happen.

In 1978, Corky Lang, drummer for heavy rock icons Mountain, was set to record his second solo album. The president of his record label decided Corky should assemble a superstar band, and the first person mentioned was Ian Hunter. Once Ian was on board, he recommended Mick as the guitarist for the project. Mountain bassist Felix Pappalardi then completed the line-up. The initial recording sessions were held at the Power Station in New York.

Several months later, they regrouped in Bearsville in the fall of 1978. This time, Todd Rundgren and Mountain guitarist Leslie West also joined them. The band completed basic tracks for eight songs before a shake-up at the record company put the brakes on the project. The recordings languished in the vaults until they were finally issued in 1999 as *The Secret Sessions*. The enhanced CD features an interesting (but poor quality) video, capturing Ronson, Hunter, Lang and Pappalardi performing 'The Outsider' in the studio.

In October, 1978, Ian began work on demos for a new solo album (*You're Never Alone with a Schizophrenic*) at Wessex Studios in London, with Mick on guitar and Glen Matlock on bass. While in England, Ian and Mick received an invitation from former CBS record executive Steve Popovich to join him for dinner. Steve had formed his own label (Cleveland International), and was coming off the huge success of Meat Loaf's *Bat Out Of Hell* album. Steve says, "I had known Ian from working with Mott the Hoople and while in England he was also producing Generation X. We had dinner with Mick and Billy Idol in London, because I wanted Ian to hear a demo of Ellen Foley doing 'All The Way From Memphis'. Then we got to talking and it transpired that Ian was on the verge of signing with Chrysalis. Ian and Mick were putting together the *You're Never Alone with a Schizophrenic* record. He played me some cuts and I really liked it, so Sam Lederman (Steve Popovich's partner in Cleveland International who mananged Mick's career for a short time and stayed close with him throughout his life) and I, along with Stan Snyder, who was our third partner in Cleveland International, took them on as the first act on our management company. Once we got the deal with Chrysalis, we managed Ian and Mick - not officially with Mick though, he was always kind of separate - for the next two or three years."

The Rats' first press shot with their new line-up, mid-1966.
Photo courtesy of David Wells

Left: With Geoff Appleby in Scarborough, 1967.
Right: With Geoff in Grantham, 1968.
Photos courtesy of Geoff and Moi Appleby

Mick plays the guitar with his teeth at a free festival in Hull, 1969.
Photo courtesy of David Wells

With Ziggy on stage, 1972.
Photo courtesy of Leee Black Childers

Left: A Ziggy-era Mick signing records backstage.
Right: The Spider from Mars, Cleveland, Ohio, 1972.
Photo courtesy of Leee Black Childers (l.) and John Kirk (r.)

On stage with Ziggy, a classic duo, Cleveland 1972.
Photo courtesy of Anastasia Pantsios

Top: Recording at the Chateau d'Herouville, France, 1974.

Photo courtesy of Leee Black Childers

Left: The Spider with the platinum hair, mid-1970s.

Photo courtesy of Anastasia Pantsios

Performing 'I Wish I Was Your Mother'.
Photo courtesy of Anastasia Pantsios

The Hunter Ronson Band, Cleveland, Ohio, 1988.
Photo by the authors

Live at The Newport, Columbus, Ohio, 1988.
Photo by the authors

Offering food backstage.
Photo courtesy of Steve Williams

With Ian Hunter.
Photo courtesy of Anastasia Pantsios

Signing autographs.
Photo by the authors

With Ian Hunter.
Photo by the authors

Joe Elliot, Steve Jones, Ronson and Hunter, November 1989.
Photo courtesy of Anastasia Pantsios

Sam Lederman remembers the evolution of the project: "Ian had originally decided that he was going to do the album in England with a whole different cast of characters. About two weeks into the project he called me up and said, 'Sam, this is not working out.' So I said, 'Shut it down and come home, don't worry about what it costs.' Steve and I were friendly with (Bruce Springsteen's) E-Street band and we decided to see if we could get them to work on this project. I called up Roy Bittan (E-Street keyboardist) and said, 'How much would it take for the E-Streeters to be Ian's rhythm section, work with him musically and cut the tracks on this record?' He gave me a figure and I said, 'Done'. They went up to Ian's house, rehearsed and then went into the studio."

Once back in the States, Ian and Mick began three months of pre-production for *You're Never Alone with a Schizophrenic*. During this period, Ian and Mick also joined with John Cale and Corky Lang to record another album which has yet to see the light of day. There was talk of putting this record out in 1989, but it remains unreleased.

With Mick and Ian co-producing, *You're Never Alone with a Schizophrenic* only took one week to record and three weeks to mix. Along with Roy Bittan, Max Weinberg and Gary Tallent from the E-Street Band, a couple of other special guests joined the sessions. John Cale added piano and ARP synth to the biting 'Bastard'. In addition, Ellen Foley, Rory Dodd and Eric Bloom of Blue Öyster Cult contributed harmony vocals to a couple of tracks. Eric says, "A few times, when I ran into trouble trying to write a new song, I would get in touch with Ian, who lived quite near me. One time I called Ian about a certain tune and Mick was visiting, so we tackled the song together. One of my favorite quotes came from this session and it was from Mick, a quote I use all the time. As we were writing the song, it came to a place where the lead would/

should be. Mick said, in his inimitable accent, 'You don't need a lead there – it's been done.' He was a great guy, self-effacing in his musicianship and talent."

Ian recalls how Mick earned a co-writing credit on 'Just Another Night', the powerful opening rocker on the album. "I wrote it in Wessex in London, but I was out of me brain at the time." The song was attempted with the E-Street Band, but Ian was not happy with the arrangement. "It was so Bruce Springsteen, because of Roy Bittan the keyboard player. It wasn't his fault, it just sort of came out that way. We were all playing it for maybe a day. It sounded quite good that way, but Mick said, 'Why don't you do it the way you started out doing it?' I said, 'What way was that?' I had no idea. Then he played it the way it ended up on the record. If it hadn't been for Mick, I wouldn't have remembered the original arrangement of the song.

He had the 'Schizophrenic' title as well, which he found on a toilet wall. I said, 'I've got to have that for this record,' but he said, 'No, you're not havin' it, it's for mine!' I kept badgering him, badgering and badgering. In the end I said, 'Look, you helped me out with 'Just Another Night', it would never have seen the tape had it not been for you remembering. Why not just give me that album title and I'll give you half of 'Just Another Night?' So he said, 'Alright.'"

The album was brimming with amazing playing from Mick and classic songwriting from Ian. Two cuts were retrieved from the past. The first, 'Cleveland Rocks', had been written back in 1977. Ian believed he had a sure-fire hit with the song if he changed the title to 'England Rocks.' When it was subsequently issued as a single in England, however, it bombed. He revived the song at these sessions with its original title, and prefaced it with a clip of Alan Freed's Moondog Show. Freed was the man who coined the term 'rock 'n' roll' and was Cleveland's most influential DJ. In March of 1952, he hosted the Moondog Coronation Ball at the 10,000-capacity Cleveland Arena. Upwards of 20,000 fans showed up and crashed the gates, causing this, the first rock concert, to come to an early end. In 2002, his remains were moved to the Rock and Roll Hall Of Fame. Ever since the days of Bowie and Mott, Cleveland had always been firmly under the spell of Hunter and Ronson, so now Ian repaid the compliment with this enduring anthem. To this day, the song is regularly played at Cleveland sporting events and on the radio, and heard on television as the theme song for *The Drew Carey Show*. Sam describes the atmosphere in the studio when Mick prepared to play his solo on 'The Outsider', a song originally attempted during the Corky Lang sessions. "Everybody would leave the studio," recounts Sam, "and Mick would go in with all the lights off and not do anything except listen to the track over and over and over again. I was at the board with Ian just hanging out and I said, 'Ian, when does he start playing?' Ian just said, 'This is Mick.'

After two hours of sitting there, they ran the tape and he started playing these licks that were just *fantastic*. He hit these really lovely notes. With him, less was more. It was one of the least commercial songs on the record but I loved it." Steve Popovich was also stunned: "What was always amazing about Ronson was that he never played the same solo twice. He was such a purist, more like a jazz musician than a rock 'n' roller. He always added something different to every solo." When the record was complete, Ian and Mick were pleased by the results but felt that one key element was missing. "We knew that we didn't have a single," says Ian. "We hung around for a while, trying to find one. We had people sending us songs, but we just couldn't find a single. That was the bummer; apart from that it was great. We went and toured and stuff, but a single would've took us over the million mark and we could've gotten quite big, probably." The album was a firm favourite with fans, and earned heavy FM radio play and a US chart position of #35.

Ian and Mick were scheduled next to co-produce the debut album by fellow Cleveland International act, Ellen Foley. Ellen had been the highly effective female voice on Meat Loaf's *Bat out of Hell* and her management were keen for her to release a full-length album. They went to the Full Tilt rehearsal hall (where Ellen had been practising) and were impressed by some of the musicians there that day. They chose Tommy Mandel on keyboards, Martin Briley on bass, Tommy Morrongiello on guitar and Hilly Michaels on drums to back Ellen on the upcoming recording sessions.

Ellen remembers, "I was a pretty young and impressionable girl when I met Mick. I developed an instant crush on him! It was totally innocent, because I love his wife Suzi, and we were all very close. I went up to Woodstock to work with them on pre-production and do some demos. Ronson was walking around with this torn T-shirt on. Two days later, I show up with a torn T-shirt and Ian was like 'Oh my God! What have I gotten myself into!' It was really embarrassing! We spent a lot of time up in Woodstock, me trying to keep up with them drinking. I remember having several wicked hang-overs. It was a little ambitious on my part."

Ellen's album (like Ian's) was recorded at The Power Station. It was daunting for the young singer, as she recalls: "It was my first record and here I was working with someone who was pretty much an icon." Ellen was pleased with the results, especially the string arrangements provided by Mick. "On *Hunky Dory*, Mick was really responsible for that sound that was so far away from the crunchy rock 'n' roll that you associate with him. They were simple, beautiful lines that he arranged. I wasn't a flat out rock 'n' roller. I tried to do some very theatrical and sensitive stuff and he really provided that for me."

Mick also introduced Ellen to two songs by Philip Rambow, the title cut 'Night Out' and 'Young Lust'. "The most fun track to cut was 'Young Lust', because Ian, Ronson and I did the vocal live in a darkened studio atmosphere, very clubby and smoky. We played it like a real performance. Ronson was just there churning out the guitar, and we were all dancing around, goofing off and having a great time. It really was a lot of fun. People didn't usually make records like that; it was a lot more sterile and a lot more contrived."

Ian wrote the album's beautiful closing number, 'Don't Let Go', while Mick came up with the idea of how to record it. Ellen says, "It was a live vocal track with just a piano. It was very emotional." Her impression of the duo was that, "Ian and Mick were like Yin and Yang in a lot of ways, they really pushed each other's buttons. Mick was 'Alright mates, let's just play' which sort of drove Ian crazy, but it also loosened him up and really got him to have fun and just rock out. That's why their collaboration seemed to work so well."

Ronson appeared not to take it that seriously. He was able to really enjoy it for the love of playing the guitar and producing the music, rather than churning out commercial sounds just for the sake of it. I think he really loved what he did. Without that, what you produce isn't necessarily honest. Ronson was nothing if not honest. In his playing, in the way he dealt with people. Sometimes he would say things that people didn't want to hear, I witnessed that on a couple of occasions. It got him into trouble a few times!"

While recording with Ellen, Mick ran into Genya Ravan who was also in the studio working on an album (Polish born Genya Ravan had been performing and recording since 1962, most notably with the blues based Ten Wheel Drive. She left that band in 1972 to go solo and had been putting out a string of impressive but non-commercial recordings ever since). Bobby Chen (from the 1976 Mick Ronson Band) was the drummer on the session. It quickly turned into another collaboration, resulting in the song 'Junkman.' "We were downstairs doing Foley," says Ian, "and she was upstairs and due to work with Van Morrison, but that didn't happen. So she was going like, 'I can't think of anybody to do it with.' Mick said, 'Well, why don't you try it with Ian'. So, I just went upstairs and we did it. It is good, she liked it a lot. I was scared because she's a real soul singer and I can't sing that stuff, but it worked out fine." Manager Steve Popovich was happy with the results of the work with Ellen. "They did a great job on Ellen Foley's album which ended up being real successful, in Holland especially." Ian has fond memories of the period too: "We were feeling really good then. I remember with Foley we could feel that we were coming into this kind of period, it's like bio-rhythms. We both felt great, we both felt creative and that was to continue for a while. In fact, that was the only time we ever really made money! Foley did about 650,000 copies worldwide, and then we got paid really well for *You're Never Alone with a Schizophrenic* as well. Mick managed to buy a house and get a car and stuff like that, which he never had before."

Next on the agenda for Mick was the production of *In Style*, the second solo album from former New York Dolls vocalist David Johansen. They had met during the Bowie days, when they both hung out at Max's Kansas City. The drummer for the project was Frankie LaRocka, who remembers his first meeting with Mick. "We met at David Johansen's apartment on 17th Street. I was a huge fan, so I was a little nervous before going into David's place. Mick was just hanging about, sitting on the floor playing guitar in his blue jeans and a button-down shirt and sneakers. I'd been used to seeing Ronson as this rock

God on stage, and here he was just laying around while David packed his bag. It was like a dream come true for us to work with him."

The three of them headed to Steve Paul's house, who was David's manager. Frankie says: "His house was in this real exclusive area of Connecticut. It was an estate tucked way back in the woods, it was monstrous, with cottages on the grounds and a built-in pool. First we had this huge dinner, then we got the fire going and Mick, David and I were just siting around talking about records, what we dug and so on. We spoke of songs that I had really wanted my drums to sound like, and we were talking about pre-production. In the meantime, we're drinking and drinking and drinking. All of a sudden, Mick spotted this bottle on the top shelf of this wall. It was on the biggest wall of the place, like at a library, where you need a lift to get up, except it was shelf upon shelf of liquor. There was this one bottle of Cognac up there and Mick spotted it. He didn't even bother getting a ladder, he just climbed up from shelf to shelf, knocking over all these bottles on his way, like something out of a movie. He finally got to the bottle and instead of coming down to drink it, he opened it up fifteen feet in the air and started drinking. It was unbelievable!"

By the end of the night, Mick had passed out. "We left Ronson in the huge living room because we couldn't carry him. We put him on the couch and tucked him in. The next day when we got up, we were still completely out of it." As they stumbled down the stairs, David and Frankie could hear a commotion in the kitchen. Mick was cooking a huge English breakfast, making eggs and beans. "He looked like nothing had happened to him (the night before), no hang-over, nothing!" Mick continued on with this ritual right through the sessions. "We had this really cool Jamaican cook that would come in and cook for us daily. Every morning Mick would make some concoction for breakfast.

He was a great cook. He'd have his little apron on and make something really edible out of just left-overs."

The record took two months to make and every day the band would have a surprise waiting for Mick at the console. "Every time Mick would come in to the studio, we would put different pictures up of him and Bowie, like the one where Bowie's getting down on him," laughs Frankie. He'd look at it, rip it up and say, 'C'mon guys, give me a break!' If you didn't know Mick to talk to, but you saw pictures of him, it was like two different people. Mick the Rock God and Mick the regular Joe."

In Frankie's eyes, Mick was the perfect producer: "Besides making you feel comfortable and getting the right performance out of you, he was such a groove master. We'd be playing in the studio and suddenly he'd do one of those little turn-around-and-bend-down-things that he did on stage, crouching down then just give you that look, that little face of his, doing that Ronson groove thing. Sometimes, we really had to twist his arm and practically beg him to do whatever he did. Then he'd play this ridiculous lead. Then we'd be arguing with him to save it, saying, 'We've got to keep this, you can't erase it!' He would erase it and say 'Rubbish!'"

Mick even brought his daughter to the sessions. Frankie and the other musicians fussed over her: "Lisa was only one-year-old and was the cutest little thing. She looked exactly like Mick, in fact, she'd got the best of both of them. We would all pal around, her and a bunch of our kids. I really dug it, she was really sweet."

Before the final mixing sessions, Mick asked Ian Hunter if he would like to contribute some piano to the album's final cut, 'Flamingo Road.' "We did it in Manhattan. That was a real thrill for me, being a huge Mott fan," enthuses Frankie. "When we found out that Ian was going to come to the studio, everybody came, the whole band. He came down and gave us an "'ello". There were just one or two takes, Ian was the perfect guy for that feel."

Ronson's intense workload continued to pile up. Joined by the band they had assembled for Ellen Foley's record, Ian and Mick hit the road in support of the *You're Never Alone with a Schizophrenic* album. Billed as 'The Ian Hunter Band Featuring Mick Ronson', the long tour started in June and culminated in a week of November shows at The Roxy in Los Angeles. These LA shows formed the bulk of the double live album, *Welcome to the Club*, co-produced by Ian and Mick and issued on April 4, 1980.

Ian explains his thinking behind this swift release of the live album: "The idea was to get another album out quickly after *You're Never Alone with a Schizophrenic*. We sat in San Diego for ten days while I tried to write and it cost us $30,000 just sitting there. I was desperately trying to write these songs and I just couldn't do it, principally because I *had* to. Mick wasn't writing hardly anything and if he did it was at two miles an hour and very scenic. I found out then that Mick just didn't write rock 'n' roll. He would write some good songs, but then he would piddle about with them. He had this one song called 'Time Bomb' for years, but he kept on changing it. You know how you have a joke a year, which you have to tell everybody, right? Well, with Ronson it was the same with a song, one a year maybe.

So this wasn't helping. You really needed a Mick Ralphs to come in with four rockers, then you'd come in with four rockers yourself and you'd write two in there, you know? But by that time, I was so smitten with Mick's playing that, as long as he was around and wanted me to use him, I was going to use him. I just couldn't hear anybody better."

Welcome to the Club is prime Hunter/Ronson, filled with energy and excitement. Mick takes the spotlight right from the beginning with his arrangement of The Shadows standard 'F.B.I.', which shows his skills in adapting material and turning it into a piece all his own. Elsewhere, the live versions often eclipsed the studio takes. Mick's playing kicked everything up a notch. As a bonus, the fourth side of the double album featured three new songs, recorded at Media Sound in New York. Mick received a co-writing credit for his down-and-dirty riffs on the raunchy 'Man O War', a long-time favourite of Hunter/ Ronson fans. The album closed with a beautiful live version of 'Sons And Daughters' from the Roxy shows. Mick's country-styled picking adding to the feeling of regret and loss expressed in Ian's number about a failed relationship. Even though *Welcome to the Club* wasn't a blockbuster seller, it was the perfect souvenir of a great tour. The band travelled to London for one final show at the Hammersmith Odeon on November 22, before taking a break from the road until April.

In February of 1980, Mick continued his frenetic pace of studio work with production on *Have A Good Time But... Get Out Alive,* the second album by Pittsburgh band (and fellow Cleveland International act) The Iron City Houserockers. Mick helped Steve Popovich organise the musicians for the project, which was recorded at Media Sound Studios in New York. Steve says: "We had a great time with that. We also brought in Ian Hunter and Steve Van Zant. All three of those guys were major contributors to it. Mick was always fun to hang out with and in the studio he was so spontaneous. He'd always come up with a great idea. Even if I came up with an idea, he was one of the few that wouldn't laugh at it! He kind of liked what I liked, mandolin and accordion, not hip kind of stuff. I even played him folk music that I'd brought back from Yugoslavia, and he went nuts over a couple of them. He was into every kind of music. Mick played mandolin on the ballad from that album. One of the songs had this big Russian-sounding chorus that was me and Mick and Ian."

Steve was more than impressed with Mick's skills, both behind the board and on guitar. "We had a problem coming up with a guitar line, a key hook. The band was trying to work it out and Mick was just sitting there. All the sudden, he picks up his guitar and out comes the line. He just went in and laid it down. First take, brilliant. A spontaneous, creative genius."

Ronson's influence seemed to infect all genres of music. In March 1980, The Human League released their album *Travelogue*. It included a cover of the Ronson/Richardson composition 'Only After Dark' from *Slaughter On 10th Avenue*, updated and dressed up in their harsh, electronic Bowie/Kraftwerk-influenced style. It was strangely effective and proved what a great song it was in the first place.

On April 20, 1980, Mick joined Ian and the band for a television appearance on Germany's *Rockpalast*, a programme that broadcast live rock concerts from the Grugahalle in Essen. The live show featured the two Ronson showcases, opening ('F.B.I.') and closing ('Slaughter On 10th Avenue') the concert as they had during the previous tour. In the next two days, the band performed in Paris, before heading back to the United States for yet more concerts.

Mick surprised everyone when he announced his intention to leave the group just before they were due to play the Dr. Pepper Music Festival in New York on July 11, 1980. He told Kirk Blows in a 1989 interview that, "I didn't want to play the guitar that badly. I didn't want to go out there and play 'All the Young Dudes' again."

Back home in Woodstock, Mick began to hang out with the Johnny Average Band (aka The Falcons). Mick played lead guitar on 'Gotta Go Home' from the *Some People* album, released on Bearsville Records. Suzi Ronson received a credit on the album as 'hairstylist.' Fellow Bearsville resident Eric Parker (who had taken over Hilly Michaels position as drummer in Ian's band) played on 'Gotta Go Home' as well. Mick 'Johnny Average' Hodgkinson recalls those glory days in Woodstock: "There were just so many clubs and there were so many musicians that just got together and played. Bearsville studio was the main place. The first week I came to Bearsville, I met Mick along with Levon Helm, Dr. John, Steve Cropper and everybody. Butterfield lived here, Bobby Charles, it was just happening. There were so many things happening. Obviously, that was one of the things that Mick loved about it."

Sven Gusevik best explains the core group that made up The Falcons. "The band had an ever-changing line-up, depending upon who was available – and most members used pseudonyms. Regular members included Mick Hodgkinson (aka Johnny Average) and his then-wife Nicole Wills, Ian Kimmet, Frank Campbell (aka Brian Briggs), Bill Mundi, John Holbrook, Mick Barakan (aka Shayne Fontayne) and Wells Kelly. John Sebastian and Randy Vanwarmer also did stints with the Falcons." Mick Ronson's pseudonym was Ricky Monsoon!

Mick Hodgkinson remembers that 'Ricky Monsoon' not only had his own unique playing style, but his own tuning method for guitars. "Mick had the hardest fingernails that you've ever known on a guy. He had long nails, not super-long, but nails that were longer than most guys who played guitar. When you picked up one of Mick's guitars, it was always far out of tune. He could never tune his guitar with a tuner. He had to tune it out of tune. So when he played it, he compensated for how he bent, because of his long nails."

After this short break, Mick once again hooked up with Ian Hunter at the end of 1980. Ian had joined forces with Todd Rundgren for a series of shows benefiting John Anderson's presidential campaign. During the October 20 show at the

Akron Agora, Mick appeared as the duo's special guest. Shortly after this, Mick agreed to co-produce Ian's *Short Back n' Sides* album with Mick Jones of The Clash. Jones recalls that, "I first came to meet him through Glen Matlock, who I'd been pals with since the Sex Pistols days, when Mick was producing The Rich Kids. Then we sort of got to know each other a bit." On a visit to the studio, Mick Jones' ideas impressed Ian. "They were working on a track and I just started sitting in with them and they liked what I did. Ian asked me if I wanted to get involved. In retrospect, I think I was way out of my depth. I mean, I was sitting in the studio with those guys and I was totally in awe of them. I did me best, but I realise now that I should of just stayed away. I was so young then, I was thrilled to be asked and thought that I could handle it. I couldn't."

Mick Jones enjoyed spending time with Mick: "I even had the good fortune to go out and stay with Mick out in Bearsville. He had a serenity. Mick was always so calm, I've only learnt to be calm like that just now, I've just realized that's a very important thing in life. He was a lovely man."

Short Back n' Sides featured Mick on lead guitar, keyboards and vocals. Along with Ian's touring band, there were guest appearances from Ellen Foley, Todd Rundgren, Roger Powell and Miller Anderson. Mick Jones also brought in Topper Headon on drums and Tymon Dogg on violin, (who had recently worked with The Clash on their triple album *Sandinista!*) to give a couple of the tracks a dub/reggae feel.

'Lisa Likes rock 'n' roll' (Ian's ode to Mick's daughter Lisa) was one of the album's best tracks. Suzi says, "Lisa was too little. She had been in there to sing 'here's my daddy' and she was like three. She was very, very small. When we first came back from England and we lived with Ian and Trudi, Ian fell in love with Lisa, she is a difficult child not to fall in love with. They would go to the studio all night and in the morning when they came back, Lisa was just getting up so Ian used to go out and walk with her. Then they would play the mixes and she would just dance around."

Short Back n' Sides was re-issued in 1994 and included a bonus disc called *Long Odds And Outtakes* featuring many interesting songs left off the original album. One of them features an inspired lead vocal from Mick. Mick Jones says "Mick's beautiful song 'China' was just Cockney rhyming slang, china plate, mate. It's a song for your mate."

After Ian's album was completed, Mick decided along with the members of The Falcons to form a group called The New York Yanquis. The short-lived band consisted of Mick on guitar and vocals, Mick Barakan (Shayne Fontayne) on guitar, Frank Campbell (Brian Briggs) on bass and Wells Kelly (drums). Dee Dee Washburn and Ann Lang were on occasional lead and background vocals. Karen Baraken remembers that "Shayne was a huge New York Yankees fan and I think it was him that came up with the name."

The New York Yanquis recorded some demos and went out on a short tour in August of 1981. Their set list included 'Hard Life', 'Crazy Love' and 'Just Like This' from the 1976 Mick Ronson Band days, along with other material that has still not seen an official release, such as Mick's 'Time Bomb.' Karen Barakan says, "I was the sound mixer and road manager for the New York Yanquis, from Boston down to New York. "There was this one night in the Red Creek area, Rochester it was. Mick Ronson got on stage and they booed him. It was heartbreaking. They booed him because he started up with some slow love song when they were looking for the Spider From Mars. I don't think it even affected Mick, but I think the rest of the band was quite catatonic by the second song. Then they got into a groove and the audience joined in. After two or three tunes, he'd won them over, such that they were jumping in their seats by the end of it. It turned out to be a wonderful, wonderful night."

The New York Yanquis only played about twenty live shows, with the last one held at The Savoy in New York. Karen says, "It was a great club and a good place to mix the live sound too. I'm a female doing the sound which is always a wrestling match. The band always walks in with their amps and say, 'where's the sound guy?' Afterwards, I was upstairs in the dressing room, frazzled, sitting on the floor. Mick was taking all of this adulation from these people who thought it was a wonderful gig and wanted to meet the sound guy. Mick just pointed down to the floor and said, 'There she is.' He told me that night, 'You did a great job and if I ever go out again I wouldn't hesitate to use you.'"

At one New York Yanquis gig in Connecticut, the opening act was a Canadian band called Lennex. Rick Rose (lead singer for Lennex) says, "Mick was looking for new up-coming bands to produce, because he wanted to get back into production. I was introduced to him at the gig. I told him that I had been a big fan of a lot of his work. We talked and I sent him a tape a week or two later and he liked it. The next thing you know, he was willing to come up to Canada to work on demos and secure a deal. We just hit it off." Mick produced an album for Lennex called *Midnight In Niagra*, which was never released. Rick says, "We did one whole record that we scrapped because the musicianship was pretty bad." Only two Lennex songs were issued. The first was called 'Struggle' and was issued on a flexi-disc included inside *Music Express* magazine. The other was 'She's Got It' which did well on a Q-107 radio contest and wound up on a various artists compilation album of the winners, released in Canada.

Back in Woodstock, a ceaseless work ethic saw Mick contributing guitar to Meat Loaf's second album *Dead Ringer*, adding guitar to a track called 'More Than You Deserve'. Steve Popovich recalls that, "Mick wasn't a big lover of the *Bat Out Of Hell* album. Especially when he had a few drinks and would say what was on his mind!" The album eventually reached #1 in England.

Another project was started in 1981 for a film soundtrack called *Indian Summer.* Mick played all the instruments and with the help of a drum machine, created some very interesting pieces. Suzi remembers that, "Mick usually composed everything in his head, but he could write music as fast as you and I can write letters. He was very good at just writing music. He had his own studio and he would go in there and crank it up." Many songs for the project were revived from previous sessions at Bearsville including, 'I'd Give Anything to See You', 'Jack Daniels' and 'Midnight Love.' 'Blue Velvet Skirt' was co-written with Suzi. Karen Barakan still has a version of 'Blue Velvet Skirt' that Mick played on The New York Yanquis tour, the only time he ever did it live.

Sadly, the script for *Indian Summer* was bland and predictable and both the movie and soundtrack were never completed. When the tapes and notes for the project were discovered in 2000, NMC issued a double CD of the material. The second CD contained some screen-test dialogue that gives a good indication of why the movie wasn't completed. However, the instrumental work is impressive and proves that Mick could have enjoyed a strong career in movie scores.

In October, Ian Hunter was in the middle of a tour in support of *Short Back n' Sides* when tragedy struck. "Tommy Mandell went down with an aneurysm of the brain while we were on the road," explains Ian. "We're thinking, 'Who knows the songs, who can do them?' We decided to try Mick on keyboards." Manager Sam Lederman remembers the incident: "They were on their way to Texas when I got a call from Ian saying, 'Get Mick a ticket for Texas, he's going to join the tour.' I said 'What are you going to do about replacing Tommy?' Ian said, 'I just did.'" Sam was confused, "'You're replacing a keyboard with a guitar?' Ian said, 'No, Mick's going to play keyboards, he can handle it.'"

Ian laughs as he remembers Mick's first day as keyboardist. "He came down and we spent a nightmare first day with him. He got on the bus and consumed everything he could find, no matter what it was. Then he started saying he wanted to shoot this owner of a pawn shop in Texas. Unlike Mick, this bloke actually had a gun, under his counter with his hand on it, staring at Mick. I'm thinkin', 'Jesus, I can't deal with this.' So, we left Mick there.

Two hours later, Mick's sitting in the gutter. We took him to the gig but he started making these bloody awful noises, because now he was comin' down after getting completely out of it at 6:00am. I remember sitting on the bus with John the tour manager and saying, 'He's going to have to go, we're going to have to put him on a plane, I can't take this.' Then all of sudden we start hearing 'Standing In My Light' sounding *really* good. By the time we'd done three or four gigs he was great, the same as always. And he was happy because he wasn't playing guitar."

When Sam and Steve Popovich joined the tour in California, they were impressed. Sam says, "The show used to open with the band coming on without Ian. Mick would lead them in an instrumental ('F.B.I.'). So when these latest shows opened and Mick wasn't on guitar but on keyboards, the place would go berserk! I was astounded. Then he did the last two numbers of the encores on guitar and the place went wild... I went wild! After that, he went through this period of time where he no longer had an interest in guitar."

Ian says that Mick lost interest in the guitar because, "He got so disenchanted because of all the famous guitar players, he hated fast guitar players. It didn't make any sense to him.

He used to say, 'They may as well be draftsmen or something, because they're not saying anything. They're just going up and down the fretboard.' He just felt, if that's the way it was going to be, then he would rather not play. So, he didn't."

Towards the end of 1981, Cleveland International split up as a company. Sam Lederman and Stan Snyder became Ian's manager and, unofficially, Mick's as well. Mick began 1982 working on some demos with Ellen Foley for her third album. Her second record had been produced by Mick Jones, who she was dating at the time. Ronson was only aboard to give Ellen a hand and the project was eventually produced by Vini Poncia.

After so much relentless session and live work, it was time for a change. The bulk of the next two years were spent working in Canada. Mick became involved with A&M Records, consulting and producing many of their up-and-coming artists. For example, Mick brought along Mick Barakan from The New York Yanquis to help him on a album by Australian singer Lisa Bade. Mick wound up playing on five songs from her 1982 *Suspicion* album. He was also set to work with Canadian artist Stanley Frank (also signed to A&M) but it's not known if they ever committed anything to tape.

Ian Hunter was in the studio again during the winter of 1982/1983, working on his latest album, *All of the Good Ones Are Taken*. Recording sessions were held at Wizard Sound in New York. Ian says, "That was a bad time in my life. I said to Mick, 'You gotta come play on this,' but he was always like really disinterested if you'd done something already and you just wanted him to play on it. He was much happier if he was totally involved." Mick wound up playing lead guitar on the song, 'Death 'n' Glory Boys.'

Mick's biggest success with A&M was the first album by The Payolas, *No Stranger To Danger*. Manager Sam Lederman says, "He produced their first record and it was a phenomenal success up there. It won all kinds of Juno awards and was a multi-platinum record." Their single, 'Eyes Of A Stranger', was even a Canadian #1. Mick joined the group for their 1982/1983 winter tour, playing keyboards. Split Enz were the opening band on the tour, and at one show Mick came out and jammed with them. The guitarist in The Payolas was Bob Rock, who has since become a famous record producer himself, most notably for his work with Metallica. A second successful Payolas album (*Hammer on a Drum*) followed in 1983 with similar results to the first. However, excellent sales and acclaim in Canada (and another #1 single, 'Never Said I Loved You') were never replicated south of the border in America.

Seemingly without pausing for breath, Mick flew to Miami to check in with old pal John Cougar Mellencamp. Mick played on four tracks featured on Mellencamp's *American Fool* album. One song that was almost dropped from the project was rescued by them and went on to become an international hit, namely 'Jack And Diane'. After coming up with a new arrangement and adding some acoustic guitar riffs, everyone involved knew it was a hit. The song was John's first #1 record.

After the sessions, Mick immediately returned to Toronto again to work with Rick Rose of Lennex. Rick says, "When Mick came to Toronto, we heard 'Jack And Diane' on the radio. He said, 'I just did that one, Johnny's an old friend of mine from the MainMan days.' I'm thinking, does this guy have any kind of ego in that brain of his?"

When the record company insisted Lennex change their name, Mick stepped in and became more involved with their sound and approach, working under the revised name of Perfect Affair. "There was never that intimidation, often found with producers in the music industry," recalls Rick. "Some producers can make you feel like you're at a lower level than they are. Mick never did that, no matter who you were. He was a hands-on guy too. If a guy was having trouble with the bass part, he would play it.

He always looked at songs like pieces of art, almost like little movie soundtracks. He would even get involved with the lyrics sometimes. He would say 'What does this mean Rick? What was going through your mind when you wrote this?' It wasn't for compensation or money, he was more concerned whether it was going to leave an impression musically. He would never let a record that did not sell bother his ego or his pride. He knew when it left the studio with his name tag on it, it had to feel good." Perfect Affair's self-titled debut (released in 1983) was a success in Canada, spawning two Top Thirty singles.

Another Canadian artist Mick produced at this time was Ian Thomas. His *Riders On Dark Horses* album was recorded in 1983, but not released until 1984. It seems Thomas wasn't sure about the production Mick had done and brought in Max Norman (who had produced Ian Hunter's *All of the Good Ones Are Taken* album) to re-mix it. The album was issued in Canada and the US, but was not a success. Mick's original mix remains unreleased.

His next project for A&M was the Los Illegals, a band of Mexican immigrants who could barely speak any English. This didn't stop Mick, who wound up contributing guitar and keyboards to the project. He later said how much he enjoyed the experience. The resulting album, *Internal Exile*, enjoyed critical acclaim but only modest sales.

Mick then decided to work with Seattle band Visible Targets. They recorded their mini-album with him in Vancouver. The album was only available locally in Seattle through mail order. The band managed to secure an opening slot on a Simple Minds tour, but broke up soon after.

After such a string of varied successes and occasional failures, Bob Seger offered Mick a high-paying gig in his touring band.

Instead, Mick hooked up with his friend from the Rolling Thunder Tour days, T-Bone Burnett. T-Bone had secured the opening slot for a few dates on The Who's Farewell Tour of 1982. Mick was not impressed with The Who. He told Jimmy McInerney in the *Lounge Lizard* fanzine that, "they looked bored out of their brains. For the most part it was bloody miserable. They must have gone out and done it for the money." He then joined T-Bone in the studio for three songs on his *Proof Through the Night* album, released in 1983.

In the midst of all this production and live work, Mick heard the news that his old friend Geoff Appleby was sick. He immediately wanted to visit. Geoff's wife Moi says, "Geoff was severely ill in the hospital after a brain hemorrhage. He was still semi-comatose and unable to speak. At the time, I was unsure if he knew who his visitors were, as he showed very little sign of recognition or emotion. One day Mick phoned to ask if he could visit Geoff. I had to warn him not to get upset if Geoff didn't recognise him, but, undeterred, Mick made the journey to the hospital not knowing what to expect. However, within a few yards of Geoff's bed, Geoff burst into tears of recognition, closely followed by Mick and then myself, until all three of us were hugging and sobbing with emotion. I shall never forget that special moment. I knew then that Geoff's memory was still there somewhere and that he was capable of showing emotion, something the doctors were hoping for.

I shall always be grateful to Mick for being there for Geoff when it mattered and helping to bring those feelings out of himself. Mick continued to keep in touch with Geoff throughout the following years whether it be a phone call, a visit or an invitation to a gig. He never forgot about the people he cared for and despite how busy he was, he always found time for them. That's the way Mick was."

CHAPTER 11

THE HUGHMANN
TECHNIQUE

Back in Canada, Mick became involved in a project that immersed him once again in someone else's music, another opportunity for him to lose the 'guitar-hero' tag and to carry another artist to a new peak of creativity.

Lisa Dalbello had enjoyed a run of funk/pop hits in her home country, but had withdrawn from that scene to work on new, more experimental music. Unaware of Ronson's stature in the music industry, even oblivious to his best-known work with David Bowie, she failed to recognise him when he called her out of the blue after catching some of her work on a retrospective TV show, asking if he could work with her. They met for "a cup of tea and a talk," as Dalbello describes their first meeting. "We got together and he was so quiet and shy. He was really timid and very difficult to get to. Yet one thing led to another and we just kept having tea. He met my mom, who's also English, and then I never saw them again for two hours!"

The fact that Lisa did not know Mick's previous work was a key to his enthusiasm for the project. "I don't want you to judge me by anything I've done," he told her. "I just want you to accept me for who I am now. I'm not here to bring my agenda to the table. I'm here to hold up the mirror in front of you."

Between sessions in Vancouver, producing *Hammer on a Drum* for The Payolas, Lisa and Mick met and corresponded over a period of more than a month, talking about music and their shared attitudes, learning the stories of themselves. Often they would send one another pictures that illustrated the music non-verbally (Mick's were "usually pictures of rain and weather"), building a gradual image of the work that they would produce. Lisa's album was titled *Whomanfoursays,* a pun on the phrase 'human forces'. A series of home demos grew into a song-by-song set recorded in the studio, working on each track as it grew into the next so that each had an individual, unique flavour within a homogenous whole.

Mick was able to take Lisa's ideas and turn them upside down, retaining their individuality but injecting something new all the time. This was particularly evident on 'Gonna Get Close to You', the first single from the project. Lisa remembers Mick sitting at a synth in the studio and finding a new tempo and groove for the track, giving it the sinister mystery that it had otherwise lacked. Lisa was then herself inspired by Mick's involvement to invert the drum beat, swapping the snare and kick beats to insert a new level of discomfort.

"We only had a four-track machine at the house," remembers Lisa. "We started to over-dub and build the song from there. With that kind of pre-production and walking through the song at home, by the time we got into the room with the Fairlight we were basically just hunting down the sounds we had already imagined in our heads. It was so much fun!"

Mick was still reluctant to play guitar. He told Lisa that he "hated guitar solos," but she did coerce him into sharing a lead vocal on 'Guilty By Association,' a song about being judged by whom one is associated with – an ironic touch for this reluctant hero of so many other people's albums.

On 'Cardinal Sin', Mick and Lisa's own conversations are mixed into the middle section of the song. Lisa wanted a serious, muted section of dialogue to be miked up and included in the track, but Mick insisted on fooling around and making her laugh instead. Against her own instinct, and with the support of Lenny DeRose (a recording engineer who worked on several albums by well-known Canadian artists, such as Saga), the conversation was included as recorded. "It's little moments like that," recalls Lisa. "that show Mick's whole way of performing and expressing himself was based on instinct."

On 'Target', Mick brought in Lisa's own "shitty little Yamaha guitar amp" through which to put her vocal performance. The track became a kind of 'sound performance', with emotion rather than content being handled by Mick and Lenny DeRose's direct manipulation of microphone and amplifier. "Mick would turn up the volume of the guitar amp when I wasn't singing, to pull in that performance," says Lisa. "We were like mad scientists in a lab." She wishes they had been able to tape more: "From that point on, I've taped every record I've ever made in a sort of tribute to Mick, because I kept thinking that all I have are these amazing snapshot memories of the greatest ideas. He just went against the norm."

Playing back the album for mastering, the pair was overwhelmed by their creation, actually weeping at the realisation that what they had done revealed so much about who they were. Ronson's involvement, usually over once his production or playing time was finished, extended way beyond the norm on *Whomanfoursays*, and, besides his inspiration for the title of the album, he became instrumental in the cover art as well.

"We wanted something where (the cover artwork) didn't box me in," says Lisa. "So we removed my first name. My face is on the cover, but it's painted in this Aboriginal New Guinea paint. That was a way of saying 'the paint may be a mask, but it is also the individual, unique colours of who I am and what the music is.'"

Everything had an agenda and Mick was involved along the whole way, even working with Lisa and Mary Margaret O'Hara (who did the lettering of the lyrics on the inner sleeve) to explain the paths of each individual lyric, as each was scrawled according to this journey. "The final touch was that we put on the inside credits that this album was recorded with the 'Hughmann technique'" laughs Lisa. "People kept asking us where they could get the machine. 'Hughmann' was just this word that we had made up, an obvious play on the word 'human'."

Early reviews of the album were encouraging. The press were intrigued by the duo, and Lisa feels that "Mick's involvement created a whole career for me in Europe and back in Canada. It would never have happened without him." Although the only radio play they enjoyed initially was from stations that failed to realise that the album was by Lisa Dalbello (some thought that 'Dalbello' was the name of a band!), the critical response was excellent. Rick Rose considered it "one of the best albums in Canadian history. They made great music together. Alanis Morrisette is doing what Lisa Dalbello was doing years ago, and Mick created that - it's a classic record." High praise, in a culture that has given the world some of the most highly-rated performers and songwriters, including Leonard Cohen, Joni Mitchell and Neil Young.

THE SPIDER WITH THE PLATINUM HAIR

While Mick and Lisa were in the studio, David Bowie - riding high on his album *Let's Dance* and the 'Serious Moonlight' tour - was in Toronto for two nights (at Toronto's CNE on September 3 and 4, 1983). Mick decided to pay his old sparring partner a visit and to catch the shows and took Lisa along as his guest. Lisa laughs as she remembers her introduction to Bowie: "We went down to the hotel and Mick says to Bowie, 'Oh David, I'd like you to meet Lisa, she's really, really smart...' And David goes, 'Oh yeah? Well, what's the meaning of life?' I just wanted to clobber Mick on the head!"

Bowie invited Mick to come to the following night's performance. "Maybe you can play something," he suggested. Lisa recalls how, "Mick was, like, 'Yeah, maybe, whatever!' We go down the next day and Earl Slick (Bowie's tour guitarist) comes up to Mick and says, 'Check this guitar out, man.'" He had a cool little prototype that someone had made for him in New York, so Mick was tempted by the offer of playing the thing on stage with his mate."

After so many years, the reunion that so many music fans around the world had longed for was about to take place at last. The premiere Spider agreed to join the former Mr Stardust on stage once again!

The show rocked like Toronto had been hit by a major earthquake. Before 'Jean Genie', Bowie halted the 60,000-strong audience and introduced Mick to a reception like no other. Earl Slick handed the guitar over and before long Mick was camping it up with David. Lisa remembers Mick getting so involved that he nearly fell off the stage: "He was doing his whole spiel and Bowie is acting like there is no problem, 'if he falls, it's all part of the show.' Mick's doing all these major pyrotechnics. Remember, I'd never seen Mick perform before, so I was in shock!"

So involved was the erstwhile quiet, shy Yorkshireman,

that "all of a sudden he goes to do this major stroke on the guitar, and the strap comes undone and the base of the guitar (hits) the ground. He's almost on his knees, and this guitar goes 'BBBPPPPPPPRRRRRAAANNNNGGG!!!!'"

In shock, Slick's hand left his own guitar as he put it to his face in horror. As quick as a flash, the newly liberated 'guitar-hero' Ronson realised that here was a chance for a bit of showmanship, and seamlessly incorporated the whole accident into a Hendrix-like pantomime, hitting the guitar on the floor again and again, spinning it with his left hand as it wailed. Bowie joined in, going over to Mick's spot on the stage and making sure the audience clocked the whole performance. Lisa thought that Slick would never forgive him for abusing his little wonder-guitar: "He just sort of took the guitar back, nodded at him and smiled!"

After the show Rick Rose ran into Mick in the parking lot. "We told him that he sounded great up there and he said, 'Really, I did? It sounded okay?' Remember, there were 60,000 people going nuts." The reunion of the Spider and the Spaceman was, of course, a blistering success. Another nine years would pass before David and Mick would work together again.

Capitol Records had been impressed with Mick's work on the Dalbello album and were interested in having him work with another of their recently signed artists, the legend Tina Turner, who was on the comeback trail after leaving husband Ike. Mick's manager Sam Lederman says, "They wanted Mick to do at least a few of the cuts, if not the whole album. Tina had just taken on a new manager named Roger Davies who'd had tremendous success with Olivia Newton-John. At that time, Tina was being rediscovered through a fiery version of the Temptations' 'Ball Of Confusion'. The song was included on *Music Of Quality And Distinction* a project credited to B.E.F. who in reality were Craig Marsh and Martyn Ware of Heaven 17. When Mick first found out that they were interested in him, he said, 'Sam, can you believe it? Me producing Tina Turner! I would do that for nothing.' I said, 'Number one, you're not doing it for nothing. Number two, just make sure you don't fuck up the interview.' He was never really good one-on-one with business executives and A&R. So we flew out there and Mick totally fucked up. We meet with Tina and Roger all day but Mick got tongue-tied, he just couldn't explain what it was he wanted to do. The next morning I get a call from Roger and in a nice, indirect way he basically told me they were not interested in having Mick on the project.

Later that day, we were in the bar and Mick knew that I was not happy with him. He says, 'Well, Sam, maybe this is all for the best.' I looked at him, started laughing and said, 'Ronson, there ain't any fuckin' way that this is for the best!'" (the album Turner made was the multi-platinum selling *Private Dancer*)

Three other projects Mick was involved with in 1984 failed to see the light of day. The first was some demos with Girls Next Door, a band that featured actress Daryl Hannah, but the project never got off the ground. The second was with Charlie Sexton who was known for his guitar skills, but after the pair worked on some demos, record company politics intervened. Mick received a nod in the 'thanks to' column on Charlie's debut album *Pictures For Pleasure*, released in 1985. The third was with Norway rockers Can Can. Vocalist Anne Grete Preuss told Sven Gusevik: "My band Can Can played a gig at the Sardines club in Oslo in November and Mick came backstage after the concert. He was in town doing promotion with Dalbello and had really enjoyed our set. I was invited to join them for a late breakfast the next day but for some strange reason I chose not to go. To this day, I still regret that decision." Shortly thereafter, Can Can's label made contact with Ronson but due to time restrictions, a recording failed to prosper.

Sadly, in 1984 Mick's father George passed away. Ex-girlfriend Sandra Goodare recalls that, "Actually, Mick and I had lost touch. We went our separate ways and both got married. When my mother-in-law died, I was at the hospital and I came out of the ward waiting to get into the lift, when I bumped into Minnie and Maggi. I'd kept in touch with them although not all the time, we'd maybe write or contact each other a couple of times a year. It was then that I learned Michael's dad George was dying of cancer." When Sandra found out Mick would be coming over, she was surprised. "I hadn't seen him for about ten years and it was a bit of shock to the system actually. A great jolt to be honest, I think, for both of us. I spent the week with his family and it was really lovely."

After this series of disappointments and difficulties, Mick was more than happy to help out Ian Hunter on a song for the Nick Nolte movie, *Teachers*. '(I'm The) Teacher' was recorded at The Power Station in New York and produced by Mick. He also shared the writing credit with Ian, who was just beginning to get involved with songs for various soundtracks. Subsequently, Mick helped out Ian again when he co-produced and played guitar on 'Good Man In A Bad Time', featured on the *Fright Night* soundtrack of 1985.

Mick's last co-production with Ian was on a 1985 album by Urgent, a band from New Jersey. Ian remembers, "Mick was usually skint. We got together and produced this album in LA. He was looking for money and that project, if we both did it, was $30,000. I did it because he wanted to do it. So I just sat there and let him do it. I'd watch the telly! That way he was happy and I'd make a few bob as well. It was always a bit unfair because I'd written songs and got paid very well for them, but you don't get paid well for playing guitar, other than gigging. So I always had made more money than Mick had. It's not really that fair, but that's the way it goes." In addition to contributing guitar and keyboards, Mick shared co-writing credit with Ian on a number of tracks featured on the 1985 album *Cast The First Stone*.

Back in New York Mick worked with a super group fronted by Psychedelic Furs saxophonist Mars Williams. Mars told *Goldmine* magazine (#469) about his all-star line-up featuring musicians from Billy Idol's band, Duran Duran, Psychedelic Furs, and anyone else who wandered in: "Ian Hunter came and rehearsed and did a show. This band would never fly because there were too many egos involved. It was wild, we were in the studio fooling around, writing some things. There were three guitarists, Ronson, Duran Duran's Andy Taylor and Steve Stevens, with John Taylor and Tommy Price providing bass and drums." It was a short-lived project for Mick, who was feeling ready to return to London after many years away.

Upon his arrival in England, Mick came upon the demo tape for a band named One The Juggler. He decided to work with them on their second RCA/Regard album, *Some Strange Fashion*. They first cut a single together called 'Hours And Hours', but by the time they entered Marcus Studios in London to record the album, only two members remained. Rokko Lee was the lead singer and Lushi was the bassist while Mick provided guitar, keyboards and production. Mick and Rokko stayed in touch throughout 1985, writing some songs together and doing a few gigs together in London accompanied by a drum machine.

Mick then got back in touch with Tony Defries who was nurturing a new singer/songwriter from New York named Sandy Dillon. Mick had met Sandy back in New York earlier in the year and was eager to team up with her for an album. Glen Matlock helped the pair out during the early stages of their collaboration. "We just sort of kept in touch over the years," says Glen. "When he worked with Sandy Dillon, I went down there and rehearsed with them for a while. It was always sort of nice to be asked by Mick to do things, you know?" Recordings began for the album and one single ('Flowers/ Heavy Boys') was released in the UK on MainMan Records. It wasn't a smash hit, but did attract loads of favourable press. In August of 1985, Mick and Sandy did a session for BBC Radio 1. They were both interviewed and performed 'We Can't Go Back' and 'Heavy Boys.' A string of successful gigs followed. In November, they performed a gig at The Fridge, Brixton billed with Angie Bowie's band, just days before the riots there claimed two lives. Unfortunately, Sandy's album *Dancing On The Freeway* was never released. In 1996, it was scheduled to finally be released in the US and UK, but plans for the project were cancelled and it remains in the vaults to this day.

Mick never seemed to take much time away from working. While in London, Mick hooked up with Cockney Rebel's Steve Harley. Steve had known Mick since the glam days, having been introduced by photographer Mick Rock. Steve was in the midst of recording a new album for RAK Records that was being produced by Mickie Most: "Mick plays guitar on a track called 'Lucky Man', which has never been released. It's a white-reggae rhythm. This session was responsible for bringing Midge Ure and Mick Ronson back together. Mick was as easy as could be, musically very quick and adaptable. I experimented with several guitar approaches. Naturally, they were all well within Mick's scope." Steve also recalls some people in the studio indulging in various things. "Cognac, too much of it. Cocaine, same goes. Music too, but never too much!" Unfortunately Steve Harley's *El Gran Senor* album was never released, although 'Lucky Man' did surface as a UK single.

Mick's reunion with former Rich Kid Midge Ure lasted all of two weeks. Mick began tour rehearsals with Midge, but at the last minute it was decided that Mick's style didn't ideally fit the band. A version of the old Visage number 'Fade To Grey', recorded on September 29 which featured Mick, was issued as a 12" single in 1985. Another song from the rehearsals (including a memorable solo by Mick) was dubbed 'Wastelands' and broadcast by BBC television.

The frustration continued with another failed project in 1985, with Belgium singer Axelle Red. Mick was impressed with a demo he'd heard and met up with her in Belgium to discuss working together, but arguments with potential record companies and other businessmen ended the project before it even began.

Mick next travelled to Italy to begin working with Andi Sexgang on an album. Mick contributed guitar and keyboards to the project and co-wrote the song, 'Belgique Blue.' The album was released in Italy in 1986 on IRA Records, credited to Arco Valley and titled *Love And Danger*. Years later it was issued in the US and UK, but this time credited to Andi Sexgang and called *Arco Valley*. Other out-takes from these sessions surfaced on the US compilation *Western Songs For Children*. Mick's time in Italy was enjoyable and he returned later in the year to work with another band on IRA Records called Moda. He co-wrote the song 'Malato' and produced their album *Canto Pagano*.

Back in England, Mick worked with Lisa Dominique and her brother Marino on some demos. Eventually Scorpio Records released a three-song tape from these sessions. Lisa and Marino were Mick's neighbours in Hull when they were growing up. The three eventually did a gig at London's Marquee Club where it's said they were joined by Jeff Beck and Bobo Phoenix from Dead Fingers Talk. Mick co-wrote a song called 'Gypsy Lover' with Marino, that was recorded and eventually released in 1998. Another British project involved the group Kiss That. Mick played keyboards on and produced their *Kiss And Tell* album and 'March Out' single. Both were released in 1986 on Chrysalis in the UK and gained favourable reviews but disappointing sales.

By spring, Mick was back in America and teamed up with XDavis a three-piece power band from Brooklyn. Vocalist and guitarist Michael Jeremiah shares this memory: "Mick comes to Brooklyn to our studio and gets lost. He's two blocks away, not bad, except it's Bath Avenue. Bath Avenue is a Mafia breeding ground. Anyway, he calls and tells me he's in a pub. First of all, there are no pubs in Brooklyn. They're bars. Second of all, [this place] is a private social club or as we know them, Mafia bars. Oh boy – I fly down the street to see him, in all his glory sipping a white wine at the bar. Guys with bloodshot eyes are trying to figure him out. I smile and get him out of there quick. He never knew the potential of that one. We rehearsed for a week, and then recorded for another week or two in a studio on 48th Street in NYC. We started five songs, but only completed four. These were hot sessions and a real lesson from a pro. I knew I would always treasure my time with him and I still do."

In June, Mick began working with Cody Melville. They recorded four tracks in Detroit that again never got released. Mick handled the production along with playing most of the instruments. He also did cello arrangements and co-wrote one track called 'Voices.' A decade later, Cody finally released an album, but none of the tracks recorded with Mick were featured.

Also in 1986, Mick played with Woodstock band The Phantoms on a track called 'I Forgot', that was released locally on a cassette compilation with various Woodstock bands called *A Woodstock Sampler Vol. 2*. The Phantoms eventually released their own album that included a version of the song, but Mick wasn't involved in those recordings. He was also again approached by Urgent to work on their next album 'Thinking Out Loud.' This time Ian and Mick passed on the production and just contributed songs to the project.

Mick received a call from Rick Rose asking him to give him a hand on some new material. Rick told Sven Gusevik, "At the time we had our own studio in Niagra Falls. My brother Fred ran the studio. I was in a rut and I called Mick to see if he could help out. We wrote about five songs together. We had a great time and no pressure from record labels. One of the songs 'Gypsy Jewelry' won a radio station contest and 1000 singles were pressed up and distributed through CBS Records." Mick not only co-wrote the song, but also produced it and sang backing vocals.

Again feeling perennially restless (Hunter called him a "wilful little gypsy" in an interview with *Goldmine*), Mick travelled to Switzerland to produce four songs for Maire-Laure et Lui, a duo featuring Marie-Laure Baeraud and her partner Phillippe Bourogne. Mick took on keyboard, bass and drum duties on the recordings. Only one single was released in France ('C'est pas le Pérou/Sam Me Glace') before they split up. The rest of the recordings remain unreleased. On Mick's many unreleased sessions Ian commented that "He did some great production work in Europe and up in Canada. Most upsetting was the way that time after time it would be with some screwed up little record company that sometimes wouldn't even put it out. And when they did, they didn't have two pennies to spend on marketing or anything like that, so it never saw the light of day."

Back in the United States, Mick hooked up with the group Funhouse to produce an album for them. He spent seven weeks at Prince's newly-opened Paisley Park Studios in Minneapolis working on the album, but it was never released. One track ('Twisted Heart') was featured on a 1991 cassette-only release. He told Holland's *Music Maker* magazine "I was at the new Prince studio and it was nothing special, really. There's a nice control room and a custom-built mixing desk, but it's nothing extraordinary. In fact, many people would say some of the things he has there are junk. But if you listen to his records…"

The next stop for Mick was Nashville. Steve Popovich tells how Mick wound up producing his first country album. "There was this singer/songwriter called David Lynn Jones. I had this idea to bring Mick down to co-produce with David and his manager Richie Albright. I sent Mick a tape and he loved his songs. He came down and stayed at my house for a month or two and made this wonderful record. 'Bonnie Jean' was the first single we had and at the time it was kind of against the tide of what was happening in country music. They really didn't want to hear about rock and rollers. That year David was named the 'Best New Country Artist' in *Billboard*. We also did a video for 'Bonnie Jean', which Mick is in, and it's a great video."

The corresponding album, *Hard Times On Easy Street*, also featured a guest appearance by country legend Waylon Jennings. Everyone in Nashville was quickly impressed by the former Spider From Mars, so other offers began coming his way. Sam Lederman says that, "the album showed the versatility Mick really had. Imagine working on the early Bowie stuff, the straight ahead rock 'n' roll, to basically the southern country thing. Mick loved Nashville and country music." Maggi Ronson agrees: "He enjoyed the Nashville experience, for sure. I know he liked the country music scene very much and he really enjoyed doing that album with David Lynn Jones." Mick helped David on a follow-up album, but the tracks were eventually re-recorded with a different producer after Mick left the project.

Heading back to Woodstock, Mick hooked up with Rokko

Lee from One the Juggler who had recently relocated to Woodstock and changed his name to Sham Morris. Mick and Sham immediately began working on writing songs together and recording demos in Mick's in-house studio. Sham told Justin Purington, "I've got one really good one called 'Satisfy Your Pain' that's really good quality and should be out there. Mick plays guitar and harmonica on it."

Keen to find a new direction and at the same time concentrate on what he knew best, Mick decided to form a new Mick Ronson Band with Sham. They even played a handful of gigs in February of 1988. The first gig featured Jerry Morotta and Tony Levin from Peter Gabriel's band, but after that other musicians were brought into the picture. A bootleg tape of a Poughkeepsie show features 'Get a Grip on the Arm of Love' and 'Open Your Eyes'.

By the end of February, Mick was preparing to work with a group out of Holland known as The Fatal Flowers. Mick had initially been set to produce their debut album back in 1986, but his busy production schedule had ruled out that possibility. By chance, Mick had seen a poster for the band in their record company offices in New York, and after talking with the record executives got back in touch with the band's management. They were still keen to work with him, so he flew to Holland to sit in on some rehearsals. The band had a festival gig while Mick was in Holland, and he wound up coming out on stage to jam with them. Initially they were going to play 'Suffragette City', but Mick decided to teach them one of his original numbers backstage before the gig. After these rehearsals, Mick and the band flew back to the States to begin work on the album at Nevessa Studio in Woodstock.

Richard Janssen, lead vocalist/guitarist with The Fatal Flowers, remembered that little Lisa Ronson was "lots of fun. We had her up when Mick was playing a guitar solo. He had certain phrases he would say to you, like 'just play', for example. Lisa was behind the desk one day when he was playing and in the middle of a solo, Lisa pushed the button and said, 'Just play Dad, just play.'" The resulting album, *Johnny D. Is Back!* was released in the US and Europe and earned good reviews and decent sales. Later, when asked by Sven Gusevik about his favourite productions, The Fatal Flowers was the first name mentioned. He was also regularly seen sporting one of their T-shirts throughout 1988/1989.

The Toll (a band from Columbus, Ohio) were in Bearsville Studios working on their album *The Price Of Progression* at the same time The Fatal Flowers sessions at Nevessa were coming to a close. Mick stopped in to check them out and wound up contributing characteristic lead guitar to the closing track on the album 'Stand In Winter'. In the 'special thanks' section, Mick is credited as Mick 'ya know wot I mean?' Ronson!

In spite of the massive work-load and occasional deflating commercial success of this multitude of session projects, this latest guitar-based rock 'n' roll had inspired Mick. He was beginning to become interested in playing guitar again. He told Kirk Blows in a 1989 interview for *Raw Magazine* that "being in the studio all the time, it was like I was doing a regular nine-to-five job, but (avoiding) that was precisely why I wanted to get in the music business in the first place, because I wanted my freedom."

For a time, the former Spider from Mars seriously considered going to college to develop his knowledge of cooking and become a chef. Mick admitted that "there was a while there when I kind of lost myself." Now though, he was sure of one thing.

He picked up the phone, called Ian Hunter and said, "I wanna go play guitar."

CHAPTER 12

SWEET DREAMER

During 1986 and 1987, Ian Hunter had done several short tours with Roy Young in Canada and discovered audiences were still excited to hear his brand of rock 'n' roll. So when Mick telephoned to let him know he was anxious to play guitar again, Hunter proposed some low-key Canadian dates together. "I'd been up there and knew the money was good and that it was no problem. I also knew eventually I'd be doing a record. I knew it would be good for me and Mick to be playing together again, because we hadn't played in a long time. It worked like a dream."

The early Canadian shows started in June, 1988. After only a couple of gigs, it was clear that the magic was back. Joe Elliott says, "That was the first time I joined Ian and Mick on stage, in Toronto. The Hunter/Ronson Band was playing this place called Rock & Roll Heaven downtown. We'd (Def Leppard) had a night off the day before and they were playing about an hour away from where we were. So me and our sound engineer rented a car and took a trip there to watch them in this scuzzy little place. The next night, both bands were playing Toronto, we were due to finish at eleven, but Ian and Mick didn't go on stage until midnight. So for that next show, I didn't even want to do the encore! Talk about taking your own gig for granted! I ran offstage, got changed, didn't even have a shower. I was just sweating horribly! I jumped in the car and said 'Take me to Rock & Roll Heaven – now!

Ian dragged me up to do the encores. We did 'Cleveland Rocks' and 'All the Young Dudes'. Then they got me to stay up and do 'While You Were Looking At Me'. I'd never heard the song. Ian said 'Just keep singing 'while you were looking at me' and try to sound like Jagger', so I did! It was in a little club which was a really strange shape, so some of the people in the club couldn't see the stage and they had all these monitors up. So I've actually got it all on video."

The Canadian shows were great. Ian remembers that, "We went up there to do maybe twenty gigs and then this guy rang up from LA and said, 'Would you do a couple of weeks down here?' Mick organized the whole thing and would keep coming back and asking, 'Do you wanna do three weeks instead of two', then, 'Do you wanna do four weeks instead of three?' In the end, it was nine weeks!" Ian and Mick then chose Bob Ringe (who had arranged these LA gigs) and his partner Greg Lewerke of Vault Management to be in charge of their affairs.

Joe Elliott wasn't the only visitor at the Rock & Roll Heaven gig. Canadian band The Fentons were also there to meet with Mick, who had heard their demo and was interested in working with the band. Mick suggested they join him in Woodstock at Nevessa Studios in September, before the Hunter/Ronson tour was set to begin. Paul Fenton told Justin Purington that, "During the next month or so, I received a few phone calls from Mick on my answering machine. He was always up and easy-going and kept saying what nice barbecues we would have. It seemed like he was more excited about that than the producing end, but as it turned out, he was a hard worker and fast too." Paul was surprised when he returned one of the calls and found himself talking to Mick's mum who was visiting from England. "I got quite a kick out of that. She was very sweet and said she'd pass on the message to 'Michael.'"

Like The Fatal Flowers before them, the band was to stay at Nevessa (conveniently located only ten minutes from Mick's house), which included a room above the studio with three beds and a bathroom. They worked with Mick for ten days, and in that time completed five songs. The band convinced Mick to play on the recordings, and he pulled out his old Ziggy-era Les Paul one last time for the occasion. He would soon donate the guitar to the Hard Rock Cafe in Australia.

Paul told Justin Purington that, "On 'Radio Wasteland' Mick broke the sixth string and I was amazed when he proceeded to record the whole song with just five strings. 'I don't need that string', he said when I suggested we stop the tape to replace it." Mick played acoustic guitar on a song called 'Houseboy' and all the rhythm guitars on 'Shadow Play', a cover of an old Rory Gallagher song. The Fentons last night in Woodstock was spent drinking beer and pulling rock 'n' roll stories out of Mick, who was in the midst of reading *Full Moon*, the Keith Moon biography. Unfortunately, record company politics led to The Fentons tapes being shelved. The only evidence of Mick's work with the band came on a promotional compilation that featured 'Radio Wasteland' re-titled 'Radio Has No Sound.' These recordings remain in the vaults.

The new Hunter/Ronson touring band featured Pat Kilbride on bass, Howard Helm on keyboards, and Shawn Isenber on drums. At one point, Mike Garson was thought of for the tour, but schedules didn't permit what would have been an exciting partnership.

The band began their tour on September 27, in Ontario. Several dates in California and the southern states followed, before hitting their traditional stronghold on the east coast. They were beginning to fill the clubs, and the November 25 show in Cleveland quickly sold out. Fans were responding enthusiastically to the remarkably well-paced set, which was book-ended by Ian's taped readings of D.H. Lawrence's *A Sane Revolution* and his own 'Shades Off'. Sandwiched in between were old favourites and a heavy helping of amazingly strong new material from Ian, most of it highly personal in nature.

Mick took the spotlight during a re-worked arrangement of Patsy Cline's 'Sweet Dreams' and 'Slaughter On 10th Avenue' which closed the show. The crowd, completely rowdy for the rest of the set, would stand in stunned silence at Mick's mastery of the guitar. You could hear a pin drop during the songs, and then a huge explosion of applause would follow. The same reaction came in 'Just Another Night' when Ian shouted "Take it Ronno!", signalling a squealing lead to come forth from Mick's blue Telecaster. Mick Ronson, 'Guitar Hero', was back.

While the tour was in full swing, Great White were enjoying a Top Ten US hit with 'Once Bitten, Twice Shy.' This lucky coincidence raised interest in the original version and the tour. With the response the new material was getting at the concerts (and the renewed interest in Ian as a songwriter) it was only a matter of time before the record companies came calling. RCA and Epic were interested, but the nod went to Mercury/Polygram.

The US leg of the tour ended in Kentucky, and they took a break for the Christmas holiday before making the journey to Europe. Drummer Steve Holly would join them for these dates. The band visited Norway, Sweden, Finland, and Germany with multiple shows at some of the venues. Ian said, "When we got over there, we were doing real well. Instead of having days off, we would have to go back and do another date at the same place."

The tour ended with two sold-out shows at The Dominion Theatre in London on February 15 and 16. The British press complained about the lack of old Mott the Hoople material, but the fans didn't mind. The first Dominion show was broadcast on the BBC, and eventually the opening half of the concert was officially released in 1995. A film of the event remains un-issued. Ian says, "That was a great tour, I really enjoyed it and Mick did too."

Meanwhile, the strain of Mick's constant globetrotting was finally beginning to take its toll on his marriage. Suzi recalls that 'Mick and I did break up for a period of time. Our relationship deteriorated mostly because of not being together. Mick was always away and it is hard to maintain a relationship when we were apart for so long. I was used to being part of the action and was not happy being left alone for such long periods of time. After Lisa was born we still travelled together but when she reached school age it was impossible."

While in Stockholm Mick met Carola Westerlund and Estelle Millburne, two local girls who had their own band named EC2. Mick liked their demo tape and decided to fly back to Sweden to produce them. They worked on writing some songs together and landed a deal with Polygram. He soon began a relationship with Carola Westerlund, one that led to the birth of his third child, a son named Joakim.

It was time to get all of the new Hunter/Ronson material down on tape. As Mick had said he just wanted to show up and play guitar, they chose Bernard Edwards (of Chic fame) to be producer for the project. The month-long recordings were held at The Power Station in New York and started on

Ian's birthday, June 3. By the time sessions were completed, they had finished thirteen tracks. The vinyl had ten tracks, while the CD format (with its longer playing time) included all thirteen. Three of the songs were jointly credited to Ian and Mick, but Ian says, "I hate to say this, but usually it was some kind of deal between us. I really resented the fact that, as good as he was, he never got any extra money, whereas a guy who wrote the songs did. That would very often be the case. To be honest with you, those three songs ('Cool', 'Following In Your Footsteps' and 'Women's Intuition') I think I wrote. Maybe 'Women's Intuition' we might have done between us."

Whatever his actual involvement in the writing process, Mick's musical stamp was all over these recordings. From the Stones-like rockers ('The Loner', 'Women's Intuition') to the exquisite ballads ('Livin' in a Heart', 'Sweet Dreamer') the recordings were fuelled by one hundred per cent classic Ronson guitar. 'Sweet Dreams' was re-titled 'Sweet Dreamer' to reflect Mick's new arrangement of the Don Gibson-penned tune. Mick's mother says that "his soul is poured out in that tune," and she's right. When fans complimented Mick about the song on tour, he said he still wasn't satisfied with it and spent hours 'laying in the bath, thinking of ways to make it more bluesy.' Mick Rossi says Mick was "a man who had understanding beyond understanding. The most tasteful guitar player I've ever heard. When you listen to 'Sweet Dreamer' that speaks for itself, really. A real genius in my eyes."

Bassist Pat Kilbride realised that Mick possessed the talent of "where to leave space. It's that kind of musicality that shows he's a monster musician, with great ears. He was just one of those guys that knew what was musically right."

The album was called *Y-U-I Orta* (after the Three Stooges catch-phrase) and was the first time the duo had released an album credited to Ian Hunter/Mick Ronson. The album was released in the first week of October 1989. The record company made promotional posters and ads were placed in a few key magazines. The rock press were generally in favour of the album, with most of the reviews being positive. Unfortunately, the album didn't stand much of a chance. Just at the point when Ronson's public profile was really beginning to shine again, one of the Polygram executives that had been instrumental in signing Ian and Mick left the company. The promotional rug was pulled out from under the project and went out of print shortly thereafter.

Shortly after the release of *Y-U-I Orta*, Hunter and Ronson were back on the road for over seventy more concerts, this time with Moe Potts on drums. The tour began on the east coast with former Sex Pistol Steve Jones as the opening act. Of course, Cleveland was waiting with open arms for their appearance at the Cleveland Music Hall on November 4, 1989. This time the concert was a benefit for The Rock and Roll Hall Of Fame, and it too sold out. Mayor George Voinovich was waiting to present Ian and Mick with the keys to the city. Ian says "I've got a couple of keys to that city, all because of 'Cleveland Rocks'. It used to be comedians' joke point, Cleveland. I still lived in England then and I used to think 'Why do these people on the coasts joke about Cleveland?' Cleveland's hipper than the places on the coast. When you played that circuit that you do before you make it, most of them are empty. Not Cleveland, it was always full. They just go and see if they like 'em or not. The people's attitude towards rock 'n' roll music was amazing. Better than anywhere else in America."

Joe Elliott was set to be the not-so-secret 'special guest' performer at the concert. "It was such a trip for me to do that. I flew straight in the night before, kind of jet-lagged, straight on to the stage to play with my heroes. Doing fifteen minutes, you don't quite get the orgasm, so it was very frustrating but still good. Steve Jones was there as well. He was going to sing 'Suffragette City', but at the last minute he said, 'I don't want to sing it man, I just want to play guitar.' So I said, 'Oh bollocks, I'll sing it!' I'd already been up and we'd did 'Cleveland Rocks' and 'All the Young Dudes' and then we did 'Suffragette City.' After the gig, me and Mick got completely arse-holed and told stupid English jokes to each other for ages!"

Due to popular demand, the set list for the tour now included two cover songs sung by Mick, Johnny Moped's 'Darlin' Let's Have Another Baby' (surely inspired by the upcoming birth of Joakim) and Lou Reed's 'White Light/White Heat.' Ian says "People used to think I was this horrible svengali and Mick was this like sweet innocent little choirboy! When we'd go in the dressing rooms, there'd be these girls, 'Poor little Mick, and here's that rotten bastard that won't let him sing.' Especially when we were doing two hour shows, I'd say, 'Mick, for fuck's sake, sing a song will ya? I could do with a break, apart from which people like it.' It would always be his amp. He had to be near it. If he wasn't near it, he was constantly worried. But to get over to the mike, he had to leave it. I nagged him into it. To be honest, I'm not crazy about singing on stage. I think writing is my strong point. I don't mind doing it, but I don't mind someone else doing it. Especially if people like it. He held a tune really well."

Throughout the tour, Mick joined fans to pose for photos, sign autographs and talk to everyone. Pat Kilbride said, 'he was one of thee sweetest guys I ever met. I could try and come up with a more masculine word, but really that's what you think of when you see him. One thing I noticed, was that in almost every town there seemed to be people with this strange chemistry, friends that were around him, women and men who cared really deeply about him."

When the tour hit Toronto, Mick paid Lisa Dalbello an unannounced visit, as she recalls: "I was doing a performance in

Toronto. It was a live telecast of a gig that we were doing at a club that was going live at the same time across Canada. I was in the middle of 'Gonna Get Close to You' and I decided to do this performance by starting in the audience. While walking through the audience, I looked up and there was Mick. Of course, my energy just shot up, it was just the most amazing kind of support."

Pat has more practical highlights of his touring days with Mick: "I just have pictures of him getting excited over food. When ordering in restaurants, he would ask about everything on the menu. Also betting. He would bet on lotteries that he had no chance of checking up on later. One time we were in Vegas and Mick had been on this slot machine all day, he ended up losing $200. Then Ian, who had been saving his voice all day, walked in, dropped a couple of coins in the slot machine and won a couple of hundred bucks. Mick just sat there with this long face. He and Ian should've had their own TV show, they were like two old women."

The North American leg of the tour ended in December in Canada. After a short break for the holiday season, the band flew off to Europe. Sweden, Norway, Finland, Germany, Denmark and the UK were all on the schedule. The shows were great, with most of them selling out in advance. By this time, however, Mick was getting a bit restless again. One night, he complained to Ian about playing the same tunes every night and they had an argument. Ian threw a vase at Mick but missed. The vase was worth £100, so Ian paid the hotel girl and went back to the tour bus where Mick was waiting. "What are you getting so upset for?" Mick asked, to which Ian replied, "You owe me fifty quid!"

After the completion of the tour, Mick travelled to Switzerland to work on a second project for The Fatal Flowers, their album *Pleasure Ground*. He brought along Lenny DeRose, the engineer from the Dalbello album. Once again, Mick added some guitar and keyboards to the songs. Richard Janssen told Sven Gusevik how he had some lunch with Mick one day and Ronson began recounting some of his experiences: "Mick just loved to tell stories. He was angry about how a lot of people had ripped him off. He said people would call him and say, like, 'Oh, Mick, we're having a nice little jam in the studio, would you come along and play a little guitar?' or 'We are working on a song and we are not quite sure.' Then he would come along and do his thing. A few months later it would be in the charts and Mick would hear his riff, and nobody ever said thank you or anything. He said that happened to him a lot. He was always very cheerful, but that was the only time I ever saw him, well, grim."

Mick returned to Sweden to live with his new girlfriend Carola and began production of an album for EC2. Three singles were issued (all with songs co-written by Mick) and he appeared on Swedish television with the duo to promote them. On the show they performed 'Passion', 'Once Bitten, Twice Shy' and 'F.B.I' but the singles were not well received and the album was not released.

In the autumn of 1990, Mick went to Bergen, Norway to work with Secret Mission on their album *Strange Afternoon* producing and adding guitar, keyboards and backing vocals. Mick co-wrote one song titled 'Call Out Her Name' and the CD single for it includes a version with an extended guitar solo from Mick.

Mick also worked with American musician Dave Nerge, who was residing in Sweden. Nerge explains: "It was decided that I would meet Mick at the Hard Rock Café, 2pm. I sat at the bar and had a beer, sure that nobody even close to Mick Ronson would arrive, but lo and behold I saw a small figure in big shades, a great coat and 80s hairstyle walk through the door. We sat at that bar for seven hours and drank way too much beer, chatted about music and life, and agreed to work together. I had a band then called Nerge Wind and Fire, a have-a-good-time, extra money-making band, all covers. Mick joined us as a special guest. We rehearsed and went on tour in Sweden for many, many months. Mick and I became good friends, hung out and spent birthdays and Christmases with our families together. We also recorded three original songs that we co-wrote, pretty good tunes. I have the only copy. He was a great guy."

Mick's love life began to fall into disrepair. His relationship to Carola came to an end soon after the EC2 sessions and he found himself living with Johan Wahlstrom (a Swedish concert promoter). Johan had an idea for a tour called *Klubb-Rock*, where he would bring together some of Sweden's most popular artists for mostly cover songs. The twelve date tour started on March 6, 1991. Mick received a solo spot during the show and played a new song co-written with Sham Morris called 'Trouble with Me.' His cover of 1970s Australian band The Angels 'Take a Long Line' was also a highlight.

In May, Johan organized the month-long *Park Rock* tour. This time Ian Hunter came along and the two of them had a featured set in the show that included '(I'm The) Teacher', 'F.B.I.', 'Sweet Dreamer' and others. The shows were successful with the fans and the press.

While on the tour, Mick met many Swedish musicians and wound up contributing to a number of projects, including work on a successful album for The Leather Nun called *Nun Permanent*, guitar for three tracks on Dag Finn's *The Wonderful World Of D. Finn*, and was scheduled to produce Sonic Walthers *Medication* album. He also recorded an album with Casino Steel, which featured Mick and Casino on the cover and was billed as *Casino Steel & The Bandits Featuring Mick Ronson*. In addition to the commitment to do the Sonic Walthers album, Mick had a September 1991 Swedish tour booked with Casino Steel and another solo tour booked as well. His work ethic never seemed to waver, no matter how exhausting the schedule.

He returned to Woodstock to work on an album by Randy Vanwarmer called *The Vital Spark*. Old buddy Shayne Fontayne was also on hand to help Randy out on this album. Unfortunately, this was yet another album that was initially shelved and didn't see release until 1994.

While back in Woodstock, Mick was starting to believe there was something seriously wrong with his health. In Sweden, he had experienced shooting back pains and was feeling weak and run down. Lisa Dalbello remembers Mick calling her from Sweden. "At the time, he didn't know what was wrong. He just kept saying 'I've been going for my walks and I just keep getting this back ache and I don't know what it is, I don't understand." He decided to wait to see a doctor until he went back to London in April.

Kevin Cann remembers that, "I picked Mick up at Heathrow on April 30, 1991 and drove him to Chorleywood, where I had arranged for him to stay while we recorded a lengthy video interview. He told me that weekend that he knew something was wrong with him. The day after the interview, I drove him to Maggi's and she immediately got him into a hospital. I think all of this happened within a week. We all knew the worst straight away after the exploratory operation." Mick was diagnosed with liver cancer and was informed he did not have long to live.

Maggi says that, "When he first got the news he was very shocked. He was only forty-five when he was diagnosed. It's very young to be told that you're going to die. He felt that his life was just really kind of coming together and he was about to do things that he wanted to do. He felt that it was all a bit unfair. He worked hard trying to stay positive. He tried everything he could to get rid of this cancer. He didn't want to accept the fact that he was going to die." David Ronson says that his brother "put a brave face on in typical Michael fashion. He was thinking more for the people around him, than for himself. It couldn't have been easy."

Friends and family were astounded at Mick's bravery, he just refused to believe the worst. Steve Popovich says, "when he found out he had cancer, he had the most positive attitude. He was seeing different doctors, trying different diets. 'Some days are better than others,' he'd say. His whole attitude was just really inspiring."

Ian recalls that, "when he rang me, someone else had told me so we already knew. I was dreading his call. He rings up and he goes, 'I got cancer and it's inoperable.' What can you say? Those bastards at the hospital. I was there in November and he comes back white as a sheet one day and says, 'They told me I won't make Christmas.' How can people do that? I mean he was fine; they just did him in by saying it. These assholes just get so immune to it, they think they can talk to people like that."

The Casino Steel and Sonic Walthers projects were cancelled while Mick underwent treatment. Incredibly, his illness didn't stop him from going ahead with the proposed Swedish tour with Graham Parker even if it meant major inconveniences for him. Graham couldn't believe it. "He was flying back to London from Sweden for chemo-therapy every Tuesday. The promoter made sure that this day was free. Mick would fly back, have chemotherapy then come back out on the road with us. One day he had a conversation with the drummer who said something like, 'How ya feeling, are you all right?' and Mick just said, 'It's nothing ya know. It's just, my body is outta whack but I'm going to beat it.' He was suffering from terminal liver cancer but he didn't want to believe it for a minute."

Mick's illness brought about one obvious and major change in his life: his diet. On the Swedish tour, Graham says, "He had just got into vegetarian food. Before, he was this quintessential Englishman living in Woodstock and probably still eating egg and chips. Somebody said to him, 'Look, if you've got something seriously wrong you've got to get into vegetarian food, you've got to clear your system out.' So, he did."

The accomodation on the tour was quite spartan but Mick didn't mind. "We would check in to our hotel and then meet up for the sound-check and I'd be like, 'I can't even swing a cat in my room,' and Mick would say, 'What's the matter? It's got a bed, it's all right.' He was obviously uncomfortable all the time, his back was bad, and he's in a room that the lowest of road crew wouldn't want, yet no complaints, ever. And every night his playing was incredible."

The concerts were divided into sections, with Mick playing guitar throughout the one hundred-minute sets. Johan would open the show with his spot, then Mick would do a set and Graham would do the final slot. Mick was doing 'Take A Long Line' and 'Marseilles' by The Angels, and sticking in his recent collaborations with Sham Morris such as 'Trouble With Me.' Mick got to show off his guitar chops with 'F.B.I.' and 'Sweet Dreamer' which impressed Graham: "Obviously, great rock guitar players have a style and it's identifiable, immediately. I'd never saw anybody actually bend the B string of the guitar up. Right across the fret, so that it was touching the bottom E string. I mean he just bends the hell out of those strings. He made the most un-earthly sound, the most funky sound."

In spite of his illness, Mick still put his fans first, refusing to turn anyone away for a quick chat, an autograph or a photo. Graham says that, "after a gig I would go backstage and be in my underwear changing. People would walk in and I'd go, 'Get these fucking people outta here!' Mick would say, 'Oh, what's the matter? They're all right.' He had more humility than anyone I've met."

CHAPTER 13

HEAVEN
AND HULL

In the early part of 1992, Mick made one of the best decisions of his career. He accepted an invitation to produce *Your Arsenal*, an album by thirty-three-year-old Stephen Patrick Morrissey, a record which is widely acknowledged as a high point in Moz's post-Smiths career. His fourth album since the demise of The Smiths, Morrissey set out to create a record which had a real sense of physicality to it: "I chose Mick because he's a very strong musician," Mozza told Lorraine Ali in *Alternative Press*. Both he and Ronson were credited with a fine album that was loved by both fans and critics alike.

Your Arsenal is brimming with the cunning songwriting and acerbic lyrics that one might come to expect from Morrissey. The difference is that this time he rocks. Boz Boorer (guitars), Alain Whyte (guitars), Gary Day (bass guitars) and Spencer Cobrin (drums), along with Mick and Moz, created ten songs that would forever change Mick Ronson's status as a producer. It was nothing short of a razor sharp masterpiece.

Mick's contributions and influence are threaded throughout the album and it seems that he must have picked up the guitar on occasion during the sessions, although the album notes do not suggest this.

Morrissey defended one of the favoured tracks, 'I Know It's Gonna Happen Someday', during the *Alternative Press* interview: "The 'Rock 'n' Roll Suicide' riff was an absolute accident. David Bowie mentioned to Mick that he thought the end of the song was from 'Rock 'n' Roll Suicide' and it's true. Now that I listen, I can hear it, but at the time it was completely accidental. It wasn't something that Mick threw on or instigated."

Accident or not, there is no denying that the guitar parts are, big, heavy and Ziggy-ish. Mick shared his feelings on *Your Arsenal* and his work with Morrissey during a KROQ Radio interview with Rodney Bingenheimer and Chris Carter: "It's great, I mean, that was real easy. I think maybe it was because he was from Manchester and I'm from Hull. I think we have a bit of an easier time together from that end, because he's very Northern and I'm pretty Northern too. That way, it was real good. Also musically it was real good."

Released in July 1992, *Your Arsenal* had a big build up in the press and rekindled genuine interest in Morrissey's previously varied solo career. The album sold on the strength of a number of factors: Morrissey fans naturally bought it (indeed, in Grand Rapids, Michigan, over 3,000 fans turned out for a personal appearance by Moz, and the store's entire stock of over 500 copies was sold in a little over an hour); those drawn to re-investigate Morrissey were brought back to the fold on the back of the album's ace reviews; finally, Bowie and Ronson fans bought the album, recognising the neat link between these three unique British talents, made obvious by Morrissey's choice of producer.

Within three weeks, *Your Arsenal* had sold over a quarter of a million copies, and the single 'Tomorrow' was a #1 hit single on many US modern rock radio stations. Ronson's reputation as a producer had never been higher, and at last it seemed as though he had made the grade in the eyes of the critics for this side of his talent. The album made many 'best of...' lists in the music press and Mick won a number of 'Producer of the Year' plaudits for his contribution. Morrissey himself joined the praise in a *Modern Rock Live* radio interview:

"It was one of the greatest experiences I've ever had. He's really a wonderful person. I was obviously a fan twenty years ago when he worked with David Bowie, and I actually saw Mick in 1972... so for me, it was just an enormous compliment that he actually agreed to produce the record... I think it's worked very, very well, and for me to work with him was an inexplicable thrill."

Ronson was, as usual, modest when asked of his own contribution. On being congratulated for the 'rock-iness' of the album, Mick humbly declared that, "Well, he wanted to. That makes it easy... if someone wants to!" He also declared that he would like to work on Morrissey's next album and that the ex-Smith sounded good as a rocker. Unfortunately, the pair never worked together again.

On Monday, April 20, 1992, Mick Ronson joined some of the world's most renowned musicians to play his biggest ever gig at Wembley Stadium, in tribute to Queen's lead vocalist Freddie Mercury, who had sadly died of AIDS on November 24, 1991. The aim of this show was to celebrate Freddie's life and his music while increasing the public awareness of the disease. The concert also raised funds to help AIDS sufferers across the world.

Live television and radio broadcasts would burn the circuits of seventy six countries worldwide, from the USA to Russia. At 6:00pm, the remaining three members of Queen, John Deacon (bass), Brian May (guitar) and Roger Taylor (drums) took the stage.

"I always knew I was a star - and now the rest of the world seems to agree with me," Freddie Mercury once said. Undoubtedly, everyone on the planet knew he was a star, a fact reflected in the intense coverage of this event. It was a mammoth production and for those working behind the scenes, a huge undertaking to successfully pull off a show as huge and monumental as this.

The star-studded line-up provided their time and talent for one full week of rehearsals prior to the show. Two known rehearsals took place with Ronson, one with Ian Hunter on Thursday, April 16, and one on Friday 17, with Ian and David Bowie; both at exactly 6:00pm and both with the remaining members of Queen.

Joe Elliott remembers the Freddie Mercury Tribute as unbelievable: "Mick was working on the Morrissey album up in Wales. About 5:00am, he got up and drove down. Considering he was on chemo at the time, it was a very tiring thing to do. We got to the gig and went into our little dressing room, then wandered around and went and got a coffee from the machine. I was just looking around and opened this curtain and there was Mick asleep on a couch. I thought I'd better leave him there as he must be tired. Yet he was kind of up and around about two minutes after that and we were chatting. He was saying how well the Morrissey album was going and how he was glad to be there and looking forward to the show."

Queen's special guests for the celebrations included Bowie, Ian Hunter, Mick Ronson, Def Leppard, Roger Daltrey, Annie Lennox, U2, Elton John, Guns N' Roses and more. Artists mixed their own material with classic Queen covers, and whether you were one of the 72,000 lucky ones in the stadium, or one of the audience of millions in homes, bars and pubs around the world, it was pure sensory overload, a night to remember.

Mick had written in the concert programme that the gig was "a great thing to do," and he was clearly looking forward to his part in the event. Few in the audience, though, seemed to have put two-and-two together, for the response to Bowie, Hunter and Ronson walking out together to perform 'All the Young Dudes' was ecstatic, loaded with surprise and delight. Add to this the fact that their backing band was Queen, and for those present a 'once in a lifetime moment' was imminent. It remains one of the most memorable Mick Ronson events ever caught on film.

Inevitably, emotions were high. Fans, family and friends worried about Mick's ability to carry this appearance off. His illness was known to many of his fans and sister Maggi remembers that, "I've always been concerned with how he's feeling about everything... always. Even at the Freddie Mercury thing. It was great because he's playing... but is he all right?"

They needn't have worried. Exhausted after the show (Hunter recalls that the appearance "got to him a bit. He went home not long after the gig"), Mick nevertheless pulled it off, once again proving himself more than capable of 'the big event' and not afraid to trade riffs with Bowie again after all these years. He strutted out, after David's introduction, his trademark platinum hair blowing in the wind... a sight to behold. Queen hit the first notes and rocked like crazy, Ian took the lead vocal and Bowie played sax to Joe Elliott and Phil Collen's (of Def Leppard) backing vocals.

Joe Elliott: "I stood at the side of the stage with Phil Collen. I turned around to Phil and said, 'Come on out,' and he went, 'Nah!' I said, 'Phil - think about this for a minute. If you don't, you'll regret it for the rest of your life.' So we both went out and did the backing vocals... we even did the 'oh, oh, oh-ooohs.' We were just grinning from ear to ear for weeks afterwards. It was like 'Wow! – we've just been on stage with Bowie, Hunter, Ronson and Queen, playing the best song ever written!"

Phil Collen remembers it with equal affection: "(It) was a wonderful night. There were no egos around, well, there were egos, but no one was expressing them. We hadn't played a show in three years. We had a great time there... we were like kids in a toy store!"

Hunter left the stage grinning like a Cheshire cat, leaving David and Mick to run through a storming version of 'Heroes.' The camera caught Mick looking a trifle unprepared for the song (he told KROQ that the night was "pretty hectic. There were so many people, you know... wondering which amp you were going to plug into..."). He needn't have worried. Over 72,000 voices cheered the duo on as Queen set up the song and Mick pulled off another incredible performance. As ever, Bowie's vocals led the way and Mick worked through them, into them and around them, complementing the singer's performance while cementing his own.

"We loved it," says Hunter. "The week before... they'd taken over a film studio just outside London, and everybody was there. (Mick) was fine – he was really okay at the time. We really enjoyed it. We had a ball that whole week and we got to show off properly, like we used to. I was laughing out there... there was a lot of very nervous people, but I thought, 'This is great. This is the way it *should* be!'"

Mick described the event to *Rolling Stone* as a "magical" sort of day. "Everybody was smiling, and that made me really happy. I didn't know Freddie Mercury, but I know he brought a lot of happiness into people's lives." Few realised – though the implication was obvious – that Mick's opportunity to bring that same happiness into people's lives was running out. It was fitting that Ronson shared the biggest stage of the year with Bowie and Hunter, and that so many millions of people were reminded of his true context: among the greats. It was to be his last ever live show.

In the spring of 1992, David Bowie began work on *Black Tie White Noise,* a new album bringing several of Bowie's former collaborators back into the studio. Chic's Nile Rogers (*Let's Dance*), Mike Garson (from the Ziggy tours through to 2002 and albums from *Aladdin Sane* onwards), Frank and George Simms (backing vocals on the 'Serious Moonlight' tour) and many others contributed to a strong album. Bowie's recent career had been blighted by double-edged reviews, 'difficult' albums such as the three cathartic Tin Machine releases, and the little-loved *Never Let Me Down* of some five years earlier. David was keen to re-establish himself as a major contributor, as relevant in the days of Suede as he had been in those of the Sex Pistols and before. When he and Ronson were both in New York, Bowie called up his former side-kick for their first studio work together since *Pin Ups.*

Bowie singled out 'I Know It's Going to Happen Someday' from Morrissey's *Your Arsenal,* as he told an interviewer for the *Black Tie White Noise* world premier weekend: "It occurred to me… that he's possibly spoofing one of my earliest songs. I thought, 'Well, I'm not going to let him get away with that.' I think he's one of our better lyricists in England. I think he's a fabulous songwriter. And I thought it was an affectionate spoof because he was working… with Mick Ronson. So I thought, 'Well, I'll take that song that he's done and I'll do it my way, so we'll have David Bowie doing Morrissey doing David Bowie." Ronson, of course, had defined the original 'Rock 'n'

Roll Suicide' track to which 'I Know It's Going To Happen Someday' owed so much.

The track on Bowie's album that Mick worked on was a cover of Cream's 'I Feel Free,' a shared favourite from their earlier days. Bowie (again from the above interview): "He said he'd be delighted to do that, and he came along and played his usual breathtaking solo on the song. (An) extraordinary man, extraordinary guitar player."

A version of Dylan's 'Like a Rolling Stone,' cut with most of Bryan Adams' backing band that Mick was particularly keen on, was also recorded. Sam Lederman remembers that, "David had given him the right to go ahead and see if he could make a singles deal with it. They had hired a lawyer who was trying to get a deal going, and nothing was happening. I said 'Mick, let's do a whole album with people that you've been involved with. Do an album of songs that *you* want to do, the type of album you've always wanted to do for yourself." Thus began a project that was to become Mick Ronson's musical last will and testament, the well-received and well-loved album, *Heaven and Hull*.

Lederman and Steve Popovich took it upon themselves to lobby the record companies on Mick's behalf. Popovich: "It was just amazing: some of them said, 'Uh – it'll sell three copies,' and were really cold about it." The one executive who recognised not only something commercial but something innately worthy in the project was Tony Martell. His own son had succumbed to cancer and Tony had dedicated himself to funding research into leukaemia cures, running benefit concerts that had raised millions of dollars and helping fund real advances in finding a cure. Martell understood the project immediately and set to work turning wheels within CBS/Sony in order for it to come to fruition. Popovich calls it a "real labour of love" for Martell, and remembers that it really added an incentive to Mick's remaining time. Many times during the album's germination, Sam Lederman told Martell that "if this record never sells a unit, I will consider it a tremendous success, because this project prolonged Mick's life by about a year."

Mick set to work making lists of tracks he wanted to record and who he wanted on the album. "He was just totally full of it," remembers Ian Hunter. "Instead of sitting around thinking about the illness, he was running around like a maniac." Knowing that his friends – Sam, Steve and Tony in particular – had brokered a deal that he could bank on with confidence, Ronson really became passionate about *Heaven and Hull*, knowing that the album was for once guaranteed a release. Reviews for Morrissey's album *Your Arsenal* were coming through with nothing but glowing praise for Mick, he was confident of his recent collaboration with Bowie and, for the first time in a long time, his career, enthusiasm, passion and vision were simultaneously on the crest of a wave.

In many respects, this period became a golden time for Mick, despite the illness that was slowly eating away at him. Tony Visconti remembers meeting Mick a number of times in 1992, discussing the new album and laughing over good times in the past. Ian Hunter remembers a painful few weeks when Mick and many of his family and friends thought that his cancer had been beaten: "He was on this stuff. He said, '(It's) supposed to work after six weeks and the six weeks are up and it's not hurting.' So he stopped taking the pills, he started driving around London and we started having a laugh and it seemed to have gone. But it just went for ten days and then came back. That's the cruel thing..."

Sham Morris, now back in England too, joined the project and four of the songs he co-wrote with Mick made it to the final cut. "It was a bitter-sweet thing, doing the album. It was great to be back in the studio with him, but he was really hurting for most of it," remembers Morris. His four songs are highlights of the album in themselves; 'Trouble With Me', 'When the World Falls Down,' 'Colour Me,' and 'Life's a River,' demonstrate both Sham's own musical diversity and the strength of his professional and personal relationship with Ronson. A late-comer into Mick's life, he inspired him and they spent a lot of time together in the studio in Mick's last year and a half, trying to get as much of Ronson onto tape before the inevitable end came.

With Sham's material recorded, along with the Bowie collaboration 'Like a Rolling Stone,' Mick sent rough mixes of the first few songs to Sam Lederman: "We were really excited, because it proved that we had all underestimated how good this guy could be, had he been given the (space to work). We were all at fault - including myself - for not being able to give him that arena before. He desperately wanted this record to show who he was, musically."

Suzi Ronson remembers how Mick thought it was going to be a big hit. It was his saving grace. Maggi agrees that though it was hard work for him, he was determined to work the project through to the end: "I had to drag him out of the studio to go to the doctor. I'd say, 'You've *got* to go,' when he was noticeably unwell and in pain. (The album) was therapeutic for him, it kept him extremely busy."

Ian Hunter remembers the activity around Mick during these crazy days, how family and friends - Maggi and Suzi in particular - buzzed around Mick, caring for him, helping him through. "You can lose friends when the chips are down," notes Ian. "If anything, he doubled them!" Hunter remembers that Mick never talked about the illness until he had run out of all other things to say about the album, about life: "Then it would be, like, 'How're you feeling?' and he would say, 'Great!'"

Suzi and Mick had now reconciled. "I never stopped loving him and do to this day. When he was diagnosed with cancer we got back together. We were very happy being together again during those last three years. I was living in the US, working for Defries, but I really wanted to be with Mick all the time then but Lisa was at school. Mick had nowhere to live, he stayed with his sister for a while but Mick wanted his own place, I was lucky enough to be able to help him get it. Tony Defries supplied him with a house in London and his assistant Maxine Marshall carpeted it for him so he was comfortable. I came and went. His mum and Maggi were with him a lot and he had a record to do."

The imminent release of *Black Tie White Noise* meant that early in 1993 Mick was sought after by journalists keen to cover the new Bowie album. In a notable interview (for KROQ), Mick inadvertently broke the embargo on information regarding the collaboration. Bowie's camp had asked that no information on which songs Mick had played on be released until the album was out. Not realising this, Mick told the interviewers that, 'I Feel Free' was one of them. When learning that it was supposed to be a secret, he quipped back in his rich Hull voice, "Well, don't tell them I told you!" Broadcast on January 10, 1993, this would be another final chapter for Mick, his last interview on public radio. However productive and rewarding the sessions for *Heaven and Hull* were, time was running out.

As work on *Heaven and Hull* continued, other names came on board. Peter Noone (bass) and Martin Chambers (drums) of The Pretenders were already on board. Chrissie Hynde met Mick in South Kensington: "We went and had lunch. He was still looking beautiful, but he really didn't look well." Hynde recorded vocals on one of the stand-out tracks, 'Trouble With Me,' her trademark street-smart growl complementing

Ronson's soft, semi-spoken vocals on the guitar-driven number. "He was very up and very cheerful," remembers Hynde. "I could tell he was very weak... I never really asked him about it or anything. I was aware of the fact that he was going down, so it was a very sad event."

Long-time friend Cherry Vanilla recommended a variety of 'cures' and alternative, holistic treatments for Mick, which he adopted with great gusto. As well as adapting his diet he adopted a course of colour therapy, reflected in the opening lyrics of 'Colour Me'. The repeated refrain, 'You make it better when you colour me,' closed the song with a convincing optimism. "There was no doom or gloom in his mind at all," remembers Cherry. "He was full of vim and vigour and was determined that he was going to live and live and live. No doubt about it - I believed he would, no matter what the doctors said he had. I had never seen him as a strong guy before, but I guess when things like this happen everybody gets strong. Maybe he always was."

Mick threw one last session in, other than those for *Heaven and Hull,* when he agreed to play on an album for The Wildhearts. "We had this one song called 'My Baby is a Headfuck,'" remembers Ginger, the band's vocalist. "We were thinking of dropping it, but we got in contact with Mick Ronson and said, 'We'd really like you to come down and do some guitar,' thinking he would say he was too busy. But he just said 'I'd be honoured.'" The band remember Mick playing their own old Les Paul - a standard edition of the instrument out of which Mick wrought the most beautiful, unexpected sounds that the band themselves had never imagined. "He was playing this great bottleneck," Ginger told *Making Music.* "I've never met another musician like him." (Authors' Note: The Wildhearts album *Earth Vs. The Wildhearts* was released in 1993 and dedicated to Mick Ronson. This would be one of many dedications and tributes that would occur over the next several years).

"He was amazing," confirms Ian Hunter. "That's what made it unbearable for everyone else, the way he handled it... He was also keeping everybody else happy, because he knew everybody was worried." Ian remembers that even if Mick only felt good for half an hour a day, he would use that time to make telephone calls in which he would reassure everyone that he was fine.

It was at one such juncture that Mick decided he fancied a trip to Dublin, perhaps sensing himself that he didn't have much time left. Joe Elliott picks up the story: "Mick was staying at Tony Defries' place in Hasker Street. I went round there one night and he was playing with his demos. We had tea and he was in great shape at the time... he'd been having his treatments and looked really healthy. He was being very positive about the whole thing. I said, 'Great – whenever you want to do it and I've got a break in the tour, I'll be there (to lay down vocals)'." In March, Elliott got a call from Hunter, to tell him that Mick had recently had a major relapse and was not at all well. "If you're gonna sing on his album," Hunter told Elliot, "I would suggest you do it sooner rather than later."

Conveniently, about ten days later, Elliott got a two-week tour break. He called Mick to arrange the session: "Of course the big liar (was pretending) to be fine," recalls Elliot. He was very up and positive on the phone. Joe invited him over to Dublin and Mick flew over on the Saturday morning with Suzi, staying until the Monday. Joe's wife Carla cooked him a roast dinner with Yorkshire pudding – food he hadn't eaten for years. In the studio on Saturday and Sunday, they worked on at least three tracks: 'Don't Look Down,' 'Take a Long Line' (on which Joe did vocals) and 'Life's a River', on which Elliott added vocals to those already on tape. Joe Elliott remembers a bright side to these few hours in the studio with Mick: "I've heard Ian tell stories about him and Mick having some serious scraps, but that only happens when you're with people for a long time. He was never gonna be feisty with me after two days in the studio... I (saw) Mick Ronson through rose-coloured glasses."

While in Ireland, Mick's condition worsened and Elliott warned Hunter that he may not have long left. Hunter called Ronson and arranged to come over for a session. It was due to take place on Wednesday April 28, but events intervened to prevent it ever coming to pass. Sam Lederman recalls that Mick so wanted the project to be a 'Mick Ronson' album that he consciously kept Ian away, which hurt his friend. At the same time, Ronson was planning a Spiders reunion. Woody Woodmansey remembers his sadness that it never happened: "After so many years, the three of us were just about to get together. Mick was doing his album and he wanted us to actually play something on it - it would have been the first time we'd actually played together since the early days. We were so close to meeting up. His spirits were good right up to the end... he was very much, like 'I'm going to beat it,' and he didn't have anything negative to say about it."

Annette Peacock also paid Mick a visit at this time, and, having heard that Morrissey too was a fan of her music, they planned for the three to work together. Annette was moved deeply by her last visit to see Mick. "I was just overcome with the whole experience. I surrendered to it," she says of her visit to the studio. "I remember hugging him - there was no substance to his body and that sort of really took me back. Yet he seemed to have this incredible spirit... indestructible. The whole experience of knowing Mick was delicate and here this might be his last record... He had incredible enthusiasm and his life force was overpowering. Everyone was affected by that – you could hear it in his playing, and when you were in his presence."

Mick was calling around other friends, including Geoff and Moi Appleby. "We didn't realise at the time (that) he was so close to death. We know now (that) he wanted to say his final goodbyes to his friends," says Moi.

Ian Hunter got to Mick just in time. "I couldn't believe it," he says. "He didn't look like Mick. Nor did he until after he died…(when) he looked like Mick again." Hunter – a virtual life-long friend – had promised Mick that if things got bad, he would be there for him. "Nothing drastic happened," he recounts. "His heart didn't give out or anything like that. He just dropped off. He was on his feet until Monday… largely because of his attitude towards it, he just refused to acknowledge it, let alone give in to it. I dread to think how I would be. I caught him on his own a couple of times when he was having a little cry, but I just barged in because I knew he would stop the moment I came in. He's an old Northern boy – you don't do that!"

Mick Ronson, the 'old Northern boy', the Spider from Mars, the ace producer and electrifying guitarist passed away of liver cancer at his home in Hasker Street, on the border of Knightsbridge and South Kensington. Suzi, Margaret and Ian were with him. He was forty-six years old.

Although they had expected the inevitable, Mick's friends and family were obviously devastated by his death. So many of them had shared Mick's own defiance and enthusiasm for life that when his ultimate end came, it was a dreadful shock.

Minnie Ronson feels that Ian Hunter in particular took the death very badly. Ian himself remembers "a big relief. Privately I just felt, 'Thank God', it was so big and heavy. His mum told me I was his best mate – something we never spoke about. I was proud of that."

Joe Elliott was about to walk into a sound-check in Sweden when he heard the news: "It was Carla, my wife. She said Suzi Ronson had just rung and that Mick had passed away that night. It bummed the entire band out. I just said to everybody, 'I want to do 'Ziggy Stardust', so we did this acoustic section in the middle of the set. I told the audience that 'a very close friend of ours died today and I'd like to do this song in memory of him.' The entire audience were holding lighters up. But they weren't doing it and swaying like they do with ballads in arenas. They were holding them dead still, kind of a candle-lit mass. Mick had lived in Stockholm, and they were very familiar with him there."

Sam Lederman got the call from Ian himself. He walked out to his car and drove around the neighbourhood deep in thought, until he wound up in a Barnes & Noble bookstore. Drawn to the music book section, he picked up Angie Bowie's autobiography, and read page after page about Mick, reminded of his own first meeting with the man who became his close friend: "My original impression when I first met Mick was that he must have been a mould for the Greek gods. I told him that: 'You're the best-looking man I've ever met.' He had that sculptured face and hair that a lot of women would have died for."

Back in Woodstock other friends paid their own respects. Mick 'Johnny Average' Hodgkinson: "There's a park here called Wilson's State Park, which is a kind of camp-ground where we planted a tree for him. We had our own ceremony. George Cowan and a lot of Mick's friends from town were there." John Sebastian cooked a vegetarian kebab barbecue and photographs of the event show a group of deeply moved friends paying their own respects in their own way to a man who had influenced all their lives.

Countless obituaries were written about Mick, but this

concise paragraph extracted from David Sinclair's tribute in *Rolling Stone* says so much: "Mick Ronson was one of rock's great unsung talents. His death from cancer, on 29 April at the age of forty-six, deprived the world of a musician who not only shone in his own right but had a rare gift for making the talents of others shine more brightly." Bowie himself was quoted in the same magazine as saying, "Mick was the perfect foil for the Ziggy character. He was very much a salt-of-the-earth type, the blunt Northerner with a defiantly masculine personality, so that what you got was the old-fashioned yin and yang thing. As a rock duo, I thought we were every bit as good as Mick and Keith or Axl and Slash. Ziggy and Mick were the personification of that rock 'n' roll dualism."

Family and friends gathered for a Memorial Service for Mick at the Church of Jesus Christ of the Latterday Saints in London on May 6. The service started at around 2.30pm, and included prelude music, hymns, a choir, readings and a closing prayer. The closing music was 'Sweet Dreamer.' The following day, Mick was buried in his home town of Hull. A blessing was said – a prayer to dedicate the grave – and as it was in progress a gust of wind blew hundreds of fresh pink petals off a nearby cherry tree. Those in attendance noticed how blossoms, falling like pink snow, blew directly into Mick's grave and landed nowhere else.

"Michael was an angel," says his mother Minnie. "When (he) died I built a wall around myself. I couldn't talk about him or mention him. I couldn't bear to even play his music or to hear it. I thought I would die. It made me ill. I had cancer too and I believe that was the cause of it." Thankfully, Minnie was successfully operated upon for her cancer: "The day I went into hospital, Sandra came to visit me. She went down (to the grave) to change the flowers, and when she was going there the tears came and I thought 'Michael's going down there with her.' When she came back she said to me 'Michael's come!' It was real."

Suzi Ronson remembers with mixed feelings the thoughts of getting the *Heaven and Hull* project finished. It wasn't easy: "I was with him a lot of the time while he was cutting it and then, after he died, I picked it up with Joe Elliott, finished it off and put it out. I had a hard time with that. I really didn't care about it after he died, I didn't give a damn if it ever came out. It had done what it was meant to do, to get Mick to where he was going. I didn't want it to be a hit... I couldn't imagine having a big hit and having all that money and him not having it. It would have been awful. I wanted him to be remembered, of course, but it seemed a bit pointless."

Hunter, who'd been denied his last session with Mick as his friend slowly passed away, feels that the album was "aborted." "It just seemed to come to a halt with his death," he says, reflecting that the album is perhaps ultimately too short to give credit to its originator's intentions. Sam Lederman, aware of the sad irony of Ian being unable to contribute while Mick was away, dubbed vocals from the former Mott frontman onto a few tracks. Joe Elliott took over and finished it off, overseeing the mixing. Lederman recalls the things that Mick had still wanted to do, including a Michael Kamen-arranged version of 'Slaughter on 10th Avenue', with a full orchestra. There was to have been a session including Bryan Adams and Mick was due to fly to the USA to finish off the recording there, including sessions with John Mellencamp. Mick and Suzi's tickets were booked for the day of Mick's funeral.

Frankie LaRocka remembers thinking about the tape left by Mick that he and Joe Elliott finished. How would Mick have wanted each song finished off? Who would be best to do the work: "Sham Morris would come up occasionally, or whoever knew the song best. My thing was just to get it done for no money. We all just wanted to do it because we wanted to do it. Joe knew where everything was and with Pete (Denenberg) and

I, at least we had a couple of sets of ears there." They edited here, made cuts there, and embellished the project as they felt that Mick might have done himself. Joe Elliott felt it lacked a little something: "It needed a bit of gloss put on it: it needed spin-offs on things, and it needed a bit more size to it. I remember Mick saying to me, 'I want 'Don't Look Down' to sound like Def Leppard, I want it to have that big sound.' When I heard the first mix it didn't have that. So I rang Frankie. Two days later he phoned me up and said 'I've booked your plane, get over here!'"

Elliott, according to LaRocka, was on a mission. "I'm telling you man," he put everything he could into it… the bulk of it was complete. Mick left a blueprint of what he wanted. We just tried to elaborate and get as close as possible to that, because he left rough mixes for everything." He was impressed, on studying the tapes, to find the level of care and complexity that Ronson had put into everything. As a drum fanatic, it struck him that even this area of the recording had been dealt with using the utmost care, dubbing bits here, changing mikes a little there. "That was a valuable lesson," he laughs. "You can't find that stuff out yourself. I just had to sit back… I thought 'the little shit! That's how he did it all of these years!'"

Joe reworked the Bowie track 'Like a Rolling Stone', using an alternative mix that Mick had made. John Mellencamp and Mick's vocals on 'Life's a River' were mixed together as a duet, as both had given supreme vocal performances. He also added cymbals to 'Colour Me', playing a set of cymbals set up around an imaginary kit with no extra drums: "I was actually playing air-drums, just hitting the cymbals where they needed to be hit. It made the song come to life so much more."

Bowie gave permission for the version of 'All the Young Dudes' from the Freddie Mercury gig, playing his sax part again for the final cut, as the live version had recorded badly. "Everyone was there, and periodically people would come up to hear what was going on," says Frankie. "We would all have dinner together and everybody just connected, Suzi, Ian, Lisa and Trudi, Peter, Joe and everybody. We would reminisce about Mick while we were eating our dinner, a lot of funny little things (that) pulled everybody through. It got a little tough at times though, you know?"

The album suffered from a bit of 'music business' intervention. Ian Hunter explains that while he was up at Bearsville working on a Def Leppard track he realised that there was a lot more material that was of high quality and should be included on the album, but certain parties wanted more money. So *Heaven and Hull* was released as is, and Joe's selection of ten tracks was a successful album without the 'lost' pieces that eventually came out on *Just Like This*. Frankie feels that if they had been allowed to use the full range of tracks it might yet have been better. Joe Elliott was especially disappointed: "Everybody loved it. They went, 'Wow – this is cool.' I always heard the album with those four songs, as soon as they went off it sounded twenty minutes too short."

The cover artwork comprised a back cover shot of the stunning Humber Bridge, one of Hull's most notable landmarks and the largest single-span suspension bridge in the world. Mick chose the image as the most characteristic image of his home town and it became a symbol for all the artists and musicians involved with the album. Beneath the shot on the cover, Sham Morris referred to this, adding "Mick has crossed the bridge now and left us this swan song."

Photographer Karen Barakan remembers the front cover artwork too: "They were doing a playback at the end of the night. Mick was just listening and it was a serious day. I was just sitting at the producer's desk while he was sitting, listening on the board. It was like he was meditating on the music, and I took the shot." To get the most out of the black and white image, Barakan overlaid three different colours – pink, blue and yellow. It was Suzi that chose the final blue colour.

A montage of video clips and special footage - Spiders, the Mercury tribute, film of Mick himself and with Ian, plus footage of Joe too - was used to compile a video for 'Don't Look Down,' a commercial rock song that, according to Elliot, had potential as a single. Filming was done in a little theatre in Pennsylvania, because of existing footage of Ronson playing guitar in a similar venue. Spliced together, it looks as though Elliott and Ronson are performing in the same theatre, but this footage was held back for a documentary. Of the recording of this music itself, "Mick was very focused," says Elliott. "He knew what he wanted, but at the same time was willing to let me have a little bit of freedom on how I did it… I insisted heavily that I double-track myself rather than do it in a single voice, because it adds just that little bit more of a commercial touch to it. Mick did all the low ones and I did the high one and the blend was brilliant."

The single made #45 in the UK singles chart, a respectable position for the man from Hull who had not been seen in such a forum for many years. *Heaven and Hull* was released with two extra instrumental tracks: the acoustic 'You and Me,' credited to Suzi, and 'Midnight Love,' a rendition of Giorgio Moroder's theme from the 1978 movie *Midnight Express*, which Mick had been playing and refining for years. Further additions were additional Elliott/Hunter vocals on Mick's version of 'Take A Long Line,' and similarly added Elliott/Bowie vocals on 'Colour Me.'

Family and friends all have their own feelings about the final released version of the album. Maggi was glad that it was finished, released and successful but prefers the demos. She feels that a bit of the rawness and 'British-ness' was smoothed off in America. Suzi loves the record, but cannot listen to it. She says that, "it served its purpose… it helped him through. While he was in the studio playing, he didn't think about what was wrong with him or what might be happening to him. And for that it was a gift." Brother David Ronson feels that not only was it a shame that Mick himself didn't get to finish the project, but also that it hinted at a rebirth for him musically for the future: "He was hitting such a rich stream," he says. "I think he really got himself set on what he really wanted to do musically for himself for a change. He was actually getting down to putting some very good stuff together." Tony Visconti remembers, as have so many, Mick's animation during the process of recording the album. "His eyes would sparkle and light up, and he would get very excited in his speech when he was talking about it. That's all we have left of him, so we have to love it and have it in our lives."

Press acclaim for the record was strong – take this quote from Keith Chagnon in *Hits* magazine: "Never before has a mere mortal squeezed notes from a Gibson or a Fender with such animal grace and sexual prowess. Whether slamming through the middle of 'Like a Rolling Stone,' the most rollicking cover of a Dylan tune to shoot from the heavens in many a moon, or roaring through the pensive 'Life's a River,' one thought remains: Ronno, we'll miss you."

Rolling Stone's Alec Foege was equally impressed: *"Heaven and Hull* brims with the kind of muscular but melodic guitar leads that earned Ronson a cult following among musicians. Ronson himself warbles in a pitch-perfect tenor on the midtempo stomper 'When The World Falls Down'. But it's the voices of friends that bring the other tracks to life."

Part of the proceeds of the record went to the TJ Martell Foundation to help in its future cancer research projects. Mick's labour of love would go on to help others suffering from the same illness that brought his work to an end, a gesture of which the generous Ronson would no doubt have approved.

CHAPTER 14

MICHAEL PICASSO

Soon after Mick's passing, the wheels for a tribute concert were put into motion. Maggi remembers how it began: "I went to see Ian Hunter perform at The Forum in London. It was just three months or so after we'd lost Michael. I met Kevin Cann after the show, he and Michael had been involved in a couple of things as a result of which he'd been to my house. After Ian's show, Kevin suggested us doing this concert together and I thought it was a great idea.

It was quite a feat. I'd never done anything like that before in my life. My children were still quite small and I was still working. Kevin was busy too but in six months we put that concert on, which was totally an act of love. It made me realise that with love anything is possible. It was just incredible the way it all came together, the spirit was very, very strong. I was so motivated by my love for Michael and also for all the fans that obviously hadn't been able to take part in his death in some way. He'd died and some people didn't even know that he was ill. I just thought this would give everybody an opportunity to share in something for him. I don't believe in 'when you're dead, you're dead, that's that,' anyway. I believed very much that Michael would receive it all, from everybody. That's really what motivated me to do it. It was really hard work, but it was a great experience and I felt it was very successful."

The warmth of affection for Mick was reflected in the huge number of people who wanted to help out in advance. Kevin Cann reveals this about Defries: "When we put on the Memorial concert, Tony Defries and MainMan were extremely helpful, which also reflected the way they treated Mick after it became known that he was unwell. Tony immediately arranged for the loan of a beautiful house near Knightsbridge. Basically they made sure Mick was comfortable during those difficult years. Mick told me that he enjoyed long walks around Hyde Park. Tony gets a lot of difficult press and he was a tough businessman, but it might surprise people to know there is a kind and generous side to his nature. He came up trumps."

The concert was held at The Hammersmith Odeon on April 29, 1994, exactly one year to the day after Mick's death. Inside the venue were two different posters and a programme to commemorate the event and raise money for several different charities. Ian Hunter feels that, "Mick's Memorial Concert was like the Freddie Mercury one. Such a great atmosphere, because everybody was there for the right reasons. They just bring the best attitude. I was fuckin' terrified! With Freddie, it was like I knew him, but we weren't that close. This was *for Mick*. Then Kevin Cann showed me the programme, which I thought was amazing and that made it even worse. The better the night looked the worse I was feeling!" Mick Jones felt that Mick, in addition to his musical contributions, "had some angelic quality as well. In the programme for the Memorial Concert that really came across."

The week before the event was spent rehearsing and

reminiscing about Mick. The warm feelings carried over on the night, as Joe Elliott recalls "It was great backstage. We were just all hanging out around the dressing room, signing all the posters and having pictures taken. We were hearing little stories about this, that and the other. Then we'd nip downstairs and see Roger Taylor, Roger Daltrey, Steve Harley and Ian. Amazing."

The evening began with a 1975 video of Mick from *The Old Grey Whistle Test*, followed by a snatch of 'Moonage Daydream' from the Ziggy retirement show, held at this very same venue some twenty years earlier. The video segments throughout the evening successfully brought Mick into the show, with rarely seen footage that was highly effective.

Bob Harris compered the evening: "A lot of the people that had worked with Mick and/or had been influenced by him appeared on stage that night. Mick was such a nice guy and that was the common bond between everybody there that night. When you are putting together a tribute to someone that you all liked so much, you want that atmosphere to prevail. We all felt touched by him in some way. So, his spirit was very much the atmosphere of the night. If Mick had been there, he would have just loved it. It exactly represented him in the best possible way."

The first band to perform was appropriately The Rats. Benny Marshall, John Cambridge, Keith 'Ched' Cheesman, and John Bentley were joined at the last minute by Tony Visconti. They performed 'It Ain't Easy' and 'I Feel Free' along with a solo guitar medley that contained bits of Mick's most memorable melodies. Tony says, "The concert was so well organized. They just wanted me to give a speech, but then Kevin remembered that I also played and they offered me the chance to play with The Rats. I thought it was very ironic that I would play with The Rats. We rehearsed for two days. It was like role reversal; I came in really scared and nervous and didn't even know the songs. John Cambridge almost missed the show completely.

He went back to the hotel to pick up his wife and some other people. The stage manager just said, 'if that drummer isn't here in one minute, you're not going on,' so, that was really funny. I think John being late was a little indicative of how nervous he was. Then by the time we got to the stage, the whole band was a bunch of nerves and I was cool! I was having a ball and they were dying, they were shaking like leaves! Seriously though, it was a great time and all worked out."

Next came two blues numbers from Dana Gillespie, who was remarkably joined by Rolf Harris for a bit of wobble board. Bob Harris and Gus Dudgeon shared some memories before Glen Matlock and The Mavericks took the stage for a well-received trilogy of energetic rock 'n' roll numbers. Glenn says, "We played 'My Man' which was written for my son but I thought it was kind of cool thing to do because it all wasn't that far removed from the sentiment of the song."

The next segment was the screening of the original *Slaughter On 10th Avenue* promo film, which was an amazing moment for fans who for all these years had wanted a glimpse of this long-sought-after relic. Chris Carter, covering the show for *Creem* felt, "There was nothing boring during the whole show at all. It just kept moving along, like an old 1950s show. In between the songs they had all these different clips." More stories came from Johnny Walker (who spoke about the BBC sessions with Mick) and Tony Visconti, who told the story of how Mick became involved with David Bowie.

As Big Audio Dynamite began their turbo-charged two song segment, Maggi (who was in the wings) began to enjoy the show. "When they went on, we kind of got to a point in the evening where it seemed to be going to time and everything seemed to be working. It was great to see Mick Jones up there enjoying himself and that really made me relax and enjoy myself." Mick Jones says that, "It was a very emotional day. It really excited us.

It was the only thing we did until the very end of the year, for the rest of the time we were recording and stuff. So we kind of came out especially to do it. We did the concert and it was great because the money went towards the stage up in Hull. We got to know Maggi quite well, she's lovely. Then we also recorded 'Suffragette City', that was more of a permanent tribute."

Maggi followed Big Audio Dynamite's performance with a short speech (reproduced here word-for-word):

I just wanted to say a big, big thank you to everybody that's here tonight, that's taking part in this concert and the artists that are taking part. I can't thank them enough. I mean they've been absolutely brilliant. They've really worked hard, they've given all they've got to take part in this evening. I also want to thank all the production team, everybody, everybody else on those fringes that have made this show work tonight. Most of all I want to thank all of you because if I didn't thank all of you, well this show just wouldn't be here if it wasn't for all of you. I'm very, very grateful that we're all able to take part in this together. It's a real together thing for me to do this show and I want you all to know that. Michael's great love, as we all know, is music and it's very symbolic the way that things have kind of linked in to this concert, what with his album and with the proceeds of this concert. I want to talk just for a second about the proceeds of this concert. It's because of you that these things are really going to happen. There's a stage that is going to be built in Hull and that's going to be The Mick Ronson Memorial Stage and it will have the names of the bands who are taking part this evening in that piece of concrete. It will be used freely and it'll be listened to freely. I just want you to know that you're putting a little brick into all that's happening there, in Hull. It's symbolic obviously because Michael's album is called Heaven and Hull *as well. It just had to be. Also, the children are going to benefit from all your proceeds tonight in a holiday home. Michael was always into everybody having a good time and sending everybody off on holiday. So, that's something I felt was really important. As well, the MacMillan Nurses, the great work that they do. In helping people like Michael in the latter stages of his life to be able to get on and do the things that they really want to do. Like trying to finish the album off. I'm thankful to them for helping my brother do that."*

This was followed by a moving solo piano version of 'Whiter Shade Of Pale' performed by Procol Harum's vocalist, Gary Brooker. He was then joined by Bill Wyman's Willie And The Poor Boys, who had everyone dancing with their brand of 1950s rock 'n' roll. Next was a segment of Kevin Cann's 1991 Hammersmith Odeon interview. It was chilling to see Mick sitting in the same theatre, talking and playing guitar. It truly felt as if he were actually among the crowd.

Everyone was quickly jolted from the mood by the antics of Captain Sensible, who was a last minute replacement for Johnny Moped. Maggi says that, "I wasn't expecting him to moon everybody! That's rock 'n' roll for ya, I mean, I was quite glad, you need a bit of craziness, so that was all right." Charles Shaar Murray was the next speaker and Morgan says, "he told a nice heart-warming anecdote at that gig, about Mick being on a tour and when the bus pulled up at a truck stop, he rushed out and bought ice creams for everyone. He was there to make things happen and make them work. This is northern soul!"

Beethoven's Ninth Symphony heralded the arrival of The Spiders From Mars. Joe Elliott did an admirable job of filling Ziggy's shoes for the evening and a wide range of guest guitarists ripped through some of Ronson's most classic solos. Woody remembers "The problem we had was that there were a few guitarists that obviously wanted to play Mick's stuff and the Bowie stuff with us. Different people had promised different guitarists that they could play certain solos. When we got into rehearsal and we were running through the numbers, every guitarist there was playing all the solos. That was the hardest bit, saying 'Well look, don't you play on that one?' and it would be like 'but I always wanted to play *that* solo!'"

Joe was anxious to join the Spiders from the beginning. "When Maggi rang me about the Memorial Concert I told her, 'Look I'll do anything you like, but I'd really like to play with Woody and Trevor!'" They came out fast and furious with 'Width of a Circle.' Joe remembers "that was a lot of fun. Just for hearing Trevor and Woody doing all that middle section again, twenty years on. They were giving it some serious gusto. Very, very cool. Then we brought Bill Nelson on and did 'Ziggy Stardust'. Then 'Angel #9', 'Don't Look Down', 'Moonage Daydream', 'White Light/White Heat' and we finished with 'Suffragette City.'" Unfortunately, the brilliant 'Billy Porter' was dropped after a few rehearsals. Joe learned why Mick never performed his solo hit. "I wanted to do 'Billy Porter'. They tried rehearsing it and said, 'You can't do 'Billy Porter'. That's when I realised that's why Mick never did it in 1975. Two guitarists and a keyboard player tried to do it and it just didn't sound right at all. It's obviously a complete studio creation. So we dropped 'Billy Porter' and we put in 'White Light/White Heat' instead."

It was obviously an emotional reunion for Trevor and Woody, who hadn't played the Bowie material in years. Trevor says, "I slept on the couch for about four days at Kevin Cann's. Woody stayed there as well. He talked to me all night long, I didn't get any sleep! We had about three hours sleep and then off we'd go to rehearsals again. I've done a couple of things with Woody over the years, but just studio sessions. To actually start playing that stuff again, especially at Hammersmith, it brought back so many memories when we were up there. It was hard to play actually. All the memories came flooding back of our last night, except Mick wasn't there. I kept looking around to see if he would walk on stage..."

'Moonage Daydream' brought down the house with Phil Collen's perfect guitar solo the highlight. Phil had grown up with Mick's playing: "I'd definitely taken parts of his playing and put that into my own. Definitely the vibrato was based on Mick. The real thing that makes any guitarist kind of unique is vibrato. Mick was very much out on his own when it comes to that, it was a very exaggerated vibrato. Even now, there's no one who plays quite like that."

After The Spiders left the stage to great applause, a video montage was shown accompanied by 'Sweet Dreamer' and another clip which showed Mick playing one of his mother's earliest favourites, 'Black Hawk Waltz', on the piano.

Steve Harley says that "I finished a song, 'The Last Time I Saw You (El Gran Senor)' only after being invited to play the Memorial Concert. I was proud to dedicate it to a dear friend and proud to be one of only two artists who performed a new song (Ian Hunter being the other). I'd read about the concert several months earlier and was bitterly disappointed not to be involved. My then-representative said, 'It isn't important.' I told him it was vital for me to be there." Steve led the crowd in a sing-a-long of his biggest hit, 'Come Up And See Me (Make Me Smile)' which featured Roger Taylor of Queen on drums. Steve notes that "As a thank you I gave him a forty-five year old bottle of port. I hope he decanted it twice!"

Roger Taylor returned the favour to Ian and Mick for appearing at the Queen benefit by showing up to drum with Ian and Steve Harley. He also performed a version of Queen's 'It's a Kind of Magic' to an appreciative audience.

Then, fittingly, it was finally Ian Hunter's moment. With one "'ello", he had the crowd in the palm of his hand as he roared through his traditional opener, 'Once Bitten, Twice

Shy'. He then slowed the pace for the beautiful 'Resurrection Mary'. At its conclusion, the opening notes of the Who classic 'Baba O'Riley' filled the air and Roger Daltrey made his entrance. Roger was in fine voice and, ever the entertainer, twirled that microphone for all it was worth. He stayed onstage for a spirited and spunky 'Summertime Blues', with Ian doing the low-voiced bits admirably.

It was then time for Ian Hunter to perform his very own special tribute to his friend and partner: "I wrote 'Michael Picasso' in or around Mick's death, maybe just before or just after, I don't know. I just wrote it. I knew I'd write one, I had to write one and it had to be simple." Simple and effective, just the way Mick liked 'em. Few made it through the heartfelt modern classic without shedding a tear.

There was only one thing left to do. An all-star jam brought the concert to an emotional climax as the stage filled with musicians, friends and family for an extended 'All the Young Dudes' that – of course - brought down the house.

The musicians and fans partied at the Embargo Club into the wee hours of the morning. Jean Genie, a Ziggy Stardust and the Spiders tribute band were the entertainment for the evening but, all of the sudden, Trevor and Woody got up to jam. It was surreal to see them play 'Suffragette City' and 'Width of a Circle' with 'Ziggy'! Woody says, "That was definitely spontaneous, it was fun. I had heard about them but I'd never seen them. I couldn't believe it when we walked in. It was so wild."

The evening was a success and Maggi was happy and relieved it all came off so well. "I remember there was a write up afterwards, and in their music paper terminology they kind of said there were a lot of 'old fart' musicians there. But then, at the end of the piece, they pointed out that the spirit was there, it had the feeling. For me, that was the whole purpose of it."

Sixteen days later on May 15, after the glitter started to fade in London, another Memorial Concert took place in Tokyo, Japan. This concert was organized by one of Japan's hottest acts, The Yellow Monkey. Kazuya Yoshii (vocals, guitar), Hideaki Kikuchi (guitar), Youichi Hirose (bass) and Eiji Kikuchi (drums) paid their respects by remembering Mick, the only way they knew how: with rock 'n' roll and with honour. Choosing to call their homage *Ronson Play Don't Worry In Heaven*, they successfully presented a total of three different Mick Ronson Memorial Concerts between 1994 and 1996. "For me, the core of ideal rock 'n' roll was Mick Ronson. Of course, I love The Beatles and The Stones, etc. etc., but Mick Ronson will always be *the* most important rock star," says Kazuya Yoshii.

One of the band's special guests was former Mott the Hoople member, Morgan Fisher. "I was touched by their decision to do the Memorial gigs and was, of course, willing to be involved. Especially as the profits went to the same charities as the London show and also to the Kobe Earthquake Fund, which affected me personally as I have friends who lost their homes, friends or family in that disaster."

The band distributed petitions at their concerts in an effort to put pressure on Mick's record company to reissue his first two solo albums in Japan – eventually they did reissue *Slaughter On 10th Avenue* and *Play Don't Worry*, giving them their first proper CD release in Japan. On a larger level, these copies were the first (in the world) to be issued as separate entities featuring the original album artwork.

Morgan actually had a printed letter to Mick in the *Ronson Play Don't Worry In Heaven* Concert Programme. It reads like this,

Dear Mick,

I wish I'd known you better. When you joined Mott the Hoople

the band was shaky and finally you helped to shake it into two halves. At least, I think so. You and Ian went to the States and never came back. If only we had taken the time to talk about it more, maybe Mott could have stayed together. When I played in your memory on April 29, with Ian and the two Rogers (Taylor and Daltrey) and everybody talked about you, I began to realise what a great guy you were. It was unfortunate that we spent such a short time together. It was infinitely more unfortunate that you spent such a short time with us all. Now when I listen to your music, your talent reaches me. Now, when I speak about you to people who knew you longer, your kindness touches me. 'I wish I'd known you better' - I always think that when someone dies. Good luck Mick, you made many, many people happy with your music and your being.

Morgan Fisher, Tokyo, 1994

Maggi Ronson and family were very grateful to The Yellow Monkey and their efforts in pulling off the first Japanese Memorial Concert. Here is the letter that she wrote Kazuya Yoshii shortly thereafter. This hand-written letter was reproduced in the second *Ronson Play Don't Worry In Heaven* concert programme.

Dear Yoshii,

Well at last I've finally put pen to paper, forgive me for taking so long. My family and I are very grateful to you and Yellow Monkey as well as everyone else who took part in the concert in Japan. It is a great feeling, knowing that yourselves in another part of the world have the same feeling of love towards Michael that we do. Your love and support have been gratefully received. I watched the video and I love it. I wish we could have been there. The money that you sent us contributed greatly towards the stage in Hull being built. We have been struggling a bit trying to get the money together so we really appreciated the Yen! We're hoping to go ahead with the stage in the New Year and by next spring, the second anniversary of Michael's passing, we hope to have a concert in Hull. We intend to have the names of the artists and bands imprinted on the stage and of course Yellow Monkey will be there with the rest. We hope you will be pleased about this. I can hardly believe that Michael left us a year and a half ago. We miss him so much. He was a very beautiful person inside and out and it has been very painful losing him. He has left me with many beautiful memories and I try to be like him because he was a great example to me. I could go on about how I feel towards my brother but it is hard to write about. It's good that we can carry on honouring his life and his music. I hope we can stay in touch and again, Thank You!!! From Kevin, my family and myself.

Lots of Love, Maggi.

Ian Hunter had this touching message printed in the programme for the April 29, 1995 show:

Two years ago tonight I sat with Suzi and Maggi Ronson at the house in Hasker Street where Mick spent his final months. Two years of extreme optimism, extreme pessimism, hopeful lies and brutal truths ended that night when Mick quietly "left the building". Mick loved people loving him. I know he would have gotten a kick out of you all being here to celebrate his work this evening. For those of you in the audience that never got the chance to hear Mick play, there will never be another "Ronno", but the artists playing his music tonight perpetuate the legend and isn't that what every artist ultimately wants? To be remembered? I thank you all for remembering him and honouring him.

Truly, Ian Hunter

At the third Japanese Memorial Concert, another message was printed in the programme, this time from the Ronson family.

To The Yellow Monkey and Fans,

On behalf of my family and myself I would like to thank you for your love and devotion towards Michael, his memory and the music he made. Michael was a very modest person and I'm sure would be very proud, if not to say surprised, of the love, honour and appreciation that you show him. We miss him greatly, he was the brightest light in our lives and although he has left us for now, hopefully as we believe, we can be together again one day. We feel his spirit around us and through your music and the things that you do, it helps to keep his spirit and memory alive and living on. We feel Michael knows what is going on through your music, love and the thoughts that you send out to him. We hope you have a wonderful time tonight at the concert. We wish we could be there with you in person but you are in our thoughts. We are really looking forward to seeing you when you come over to London. Until then, take care, have fun, enjoy the music.

With love from the Ronsons,

Maggi, Minnie and David Ronson

Maggi wouldn't have to wait very long for The Yellow Monkey's arrival in London, as they were one of the many-honoured guests who agreed to play *The Mick Ronson Memorial Concert II* in his hometown of Hull in the summer of 1997. As Naomi Fujiyama puts it, "Mick has become very popular in Japan now, and it would not have been possible without The Yellow Monkey's efforts." Having said that, it's incredible yet not surprising, that The Yellow Monkey brought 600 Japanese fans to Hull with them. Four years after Mick's passing, on the weekend of August 9 and 10, it was as if a piece of the Orient landed in Hull.

The Japanese fans weren't the only ones present, as family, friends and fans from all over the world planned their holidays in Hull that summer. Due to the combined efforts of Kevin Cann, the Ronson family, Pete Allen (a friend of Mick's), Hull City Council and many others behind the scene, an entire weekend was planned.

Hull's support of the Memorial weekend was commendable, as you couldn't walk two city blocks without seeing banners stretched across the streets stating, "Welcome to Kingston upon Hull – Mick Ronson's home town". Carefully planned, these banners were printed in both English and Japanese. Printed flyers and bulletins were posted throughout the city, detailing Mick's history and the planned events for the weekend. Guided "Ronno" tours of the city were offered and stores decorated their windows accordingly. A record fair was organised featuring dealers that specialised in Ronson, Bowie, Mott and related memorabilia.

Many of the artists were lodged at Hull's Forte Hotel on the Marina, located within walking distance of everything Ronson. Both Big Audio Dynamite and Glen Matlock were scheduled to play the *Memorial Concert II*, at Hull Arena, later that night. Mick Jones didn't think twice, deciding to spend his afternoon at the record fair, happily searching for a treasure amongst the tables that formed a maze around the room. Before performing the first turn, Jones was spotted scooping up a nice 1970s paper collectible. When asked about it, he happily revealed the Mott the Hoople *On Broadway* playbill. He had also picked up the *Slaughter On 10th Avenue* flexi and a David Bowie 'Sorrow' seven inch single. Jones was one of many fans who scored that day.

The Saturday night concert took place at the Hull Arena, known as the most versatile venue in the city. The queue was halfway around the building, as hundreds of fans (most of which were Japanese) waited for the doors to open. Both UK and Japanese television crews were on hand, capturing the excitement.

The show was scheduled to start at 7:00pm with appearances by Ian Hunter, Joe Elliott and Phil Collen, Mick Jones and BAD, Steve Harley, The Spiders From Mars, Glen Matlock & Steve New, The Yellow Monkey, Michael Chapman, The Rats, John Shuttleworth and Colin Lloyd Tucker. Throughout the evening Geoff Appleby, Maggi and other special guests appeared on stage, complementing the performers. In addition, The Wildhearts were scheduled to play but as it turned out, were unable to attend.

"It was different to the other one, I think," says Benny Marshall. "The first one was more special for us because it was in London at the Hammersmith. I did enjoy the second one too, I just think it was lower key."

It was well after midnight when the after-party started at the Forte Hotel. Fortunately the hotel had an accommodating bar as Ian, Trevor, Joe, Phil, the Ronsons (celebrating Lisa's twentieth birthday) and friends partied into the wee hours of the morning. Nonetheless, everyone arrived at Queens Gardens the following afternoon in fine form for the dedication ceremony. Finally, on August 10, the dream that was foretold by Maggi from the London stage in 1994, became a steadfast reality.

Queen's Gardens, in the heart of Hull's city centre couldn't have looked better on that sunny English day as the park was in full bloom and filled with people. The idea of building a permanent stage in memoriam to Mick came from Pete Allen, Assistant Director of Hull Leisure Services. Pete had known Mick when he had worked for the Council in the Parks Department all those years ago.

In April, work began on the stage and a low-key ceremony took place with Maggi cutting the turf. Four months later, it was officially opened, thanks to money raised from the 1994 Memorial Concert and generous donations by Yellow Monkey. Additional money was raised for the stage through the release of the 1994 double live CD of *The Mick Ronson Memorial Concert*, on Citadel. This recording was released and available for the first time at the Arena show. Notably, this recording has since been re-issued by NMC in superior quality and is now a three

CD set. Disc three is video enhanced, featuring 'It's a Kind Of Magic' and 'All the Young Dudes'.

Maggi explains that though it only took a few months for the actual construction of the stage, there were many other elements involved that continually delayed the project. "We had to establish more money, so that was a bit of a hold up, plus where the actual stage was actually going to be."

There was a musical line up planned for the day, but due to timing and unexpected guests (some of whom had played the night before) it turned out to be much more of an impromptu event. Many local bands played, paying their tribute to the man who once roamed these gardens. Later, a Bowie impersonator (dressed in *Earthling* attire) posed as David for a few numbers, which created a few whispers in the crowd.

By late afternoon, the stage crew were throwing water on the fans, in an attempt to cool them off. Temperatures increased as The Rats, The Yellow Monkey, Glen Matlock and Mick Jones and BAD kicked out a day's worth of blazing rock 'n' roll. By the time the Spiders hit the stage, the only heat that mattered was that of the moment. They played an astonishing set that compared to Saturday's performance, except Sunday, they didn't play 'Life on Mars?'. Next, Ian Hunter made his grand entrance, joining them for the closing number. Even on a hot day, the coolness exudes from him. Ian would truly christen Mick's stage that afternoon singing 'All the Young Dudes' with a band that was bang on.

In addition to the memorial concerts, a new road in a development at Greatfield Estate, Hull was called Ronson Close. The road (in the same estate where Mick grew up) was named in his honour shortly after his death. Mick's influence continues to thrive, in modern music, arts and performance.

CHAPTER 15

MOLTEN GYPSY SOUL

Since 1997, many people have come forward to nod their head to Mick Ronson and his legacy. One such testimony comes from one of modern rock's most intriguing singer-songwriters, Billy Corgan, who wrote the following words exclusively for this biography (reproduced here with original typographics intact):

when I was 9 in 1976, I had heard about this weird guy named david bowie. people were saying he was from outer space and gay, but I had never heard his music, but when I saw the album cover of the spiders from mars I knew that it looked like the kind of thing I would want to hear. so I saved my pennies, bought the album and immediately fell in love with it. every song sounded fresh, as if they had indeed come from outer space. and what intrigued me was although the music was really different, it rocked. mick ronson played the guitar with flash and style without resorting to heavy metal trickery. most lead guitar players played some form of the electric blues, but mick's playing had molten gypsy soul. he played like a lead singer, giving a sensuality and taste to guitar that was unheard of before him. what strikes me now, having heard his playing thousands of times over the years is the way he complemented a vocalist so well. his style and songwriting seemed to embrace the best the world had to offer.

Billy Corgan July 1999

Billy Corgan is one of many that were influenced by Ronson at a young age. Likewise, guitar collector-dealer, Rick Tedesco, was only thirteen when he discovered Bowie/Ronson. The image of Mick with his Les Paul as seen in *Ziggy Stardust: The Motion Picture* changed him forever. "That was the guitar that made me want to play guitar," says Rick. His story of dedication to Mick and his absolute love of Ronson's work is so typical of the thousands of people who have been deeply affected by Ronno. The final destination of Mick's Les Paul, and how it arrived there, remains the perfect analogy of, and epitaph to, this acutely unique man.

Rick Tedesco opened his own guitar shop when he grew up, selling some of the finest six strings around. He became a very close friend of the Hunters and supplied Ian with many guitars. One day he expressed an ambition to acquire Mick's sanded-down, natural top, Les Paul. "Well, good luck finding that!" said Ian. "Knowing Mick, he just gave it to some guy while he was crossing the street."

Tedesco made countless calls and sent several e-mails before he scored a contact at The Hard Rock Cafe in, of all places, Australia. "I called them and got in touch with their head guy. He said, 'Sure, it's been hanging here for twelve years, I'm looking at it right now.' After months of research, I was finally talking to a guy who was staring at it."

Mick had donated the guitar to The Hard Rock in the late 1980s. The headstock had been broken so many times that Mick had to get a new one custom-made. Rick believes that "when he got it back, it just wasn't the same guitar to him that he remembered. He really wasn't all that thrilled with it anymore, so he donated it and signed it, *To the Hard Rock Cafe, I'm still rockin', Mick Ronson.*

I really wanted to get that guitar and have it in the (Cleveland) Rock And Roll Hall Of Fame. I thought it *belonged* there, not in a bar. Suzi Ronson sent me a bunch of pictures of Mick with the guitar and close ups of the top. Thankfully, Mick sanded the top down because as a result there was clearly identifiable wood grain; it was like a fingerprint. It was *that* guitar.

I negotiated a bunch of memorabilia in exchange for that guitar. Ian gave me a guitar, I got a guitar from Joe Bouchard from Blue Öyster Cult, I swapped them stuff, I just pulled everybody together and gave them this big package of memorabilia."

Rick was beside himself, anticipating the arrival of Mick's Les Paul. "It was funny because I unpacked the guitar in the same room that I first discovered him, all those years ago as a kid (of course, UPS left it outside). The strings were still on it that Mick had used, twelve-year-old strings. It looked like there was buffalo wing sauce on it. My first thought was 'I don't know if I can donate this thing now.' It clearly had so much history, it just had this mojo to it. I'm sitting there, gazing at this old Les Paul, surrounded by guitars worth $50,000. Yet, this particular guitar, *the* Les Paul, sent shivers down my spine."

"I put new strings on it," explains Rick, "saving the original strings, of course, and set it all up. I adjusted the truss rod, plugged it in, then played 'Ziggy Stardust'. I mean, *what else could I do?*"

Mick's 1968 Gibson Les Paul arrived at the The Rock and Roll Hall Of Fame Museum on August 15, 2001. Thanks to Rick's generosity and the Museum's curators, the Les Paul cements

Mick Ronson's noble position in the iconic upper echelons of modern music history.

Friends, family and colleagues from around the world who were interviewed for this book still miss him greatly. So do millions of fans. The picture that they all build of Mick Ronson is of a lovely man: kind-hearted, generous, more interested in others than in himself, a true friend and a great father, husband, brother and son. And at the very end, a brave man.

Michael Picasso, The Spider with the Platinum Hair, touched our lives. In turn, there remains an on-going commitment to keep his memory alive. Through heart, soul and song - here, there and everywhere, he will be remembered.

"Mick's not going anywhere," says Ian Hunter. "I think Maggi sometimes panics and thinks it will all die away, but it won't. The best never does."

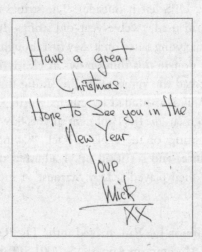

Have a great
Christmas.
Hope to See you in the
New Year
love
Mick
XX

CHAPTER 16

THIS IS FOR YOU

It's been seven years since Ian Hunter claimed, "Mick's not going anywhere" because "the best never does" and as expected, Ronson's best and perhaps wisest friend is right on target. As we take a closer look at Mick's life, his career and his record collection, let it be said that this new chapter is inspired as much by the present and future of Ronson's legacy as it is by his rich and ambitious past.

In March of 2003, a 30th anniversary, digitally remastered copy of *Ziggy Stardust And The Spiders From Mars – The Motion Picture* made its rounds to independent movie theatres across the USA. Fans were given the opportunity to watch the 1973 final performance of Ziggy and the Spiders on the big screen, for the first time since its initial run in 1983. The new stereo and 5.1 Surround Sound mixes by Tony Visconti intensified the experience and when the larger-than-life Ronson stomped across the screen with his famous Les Paul, a popcorn run was completely out of the question. The movie house promo was in support of the official DVD and CD release that followed on April 1, 2003. Both releases were available in a limited edition format that included a silk-screened printed clear slipcase, pull-out poster and mock ticket.

Britain's *UNCUT* magazine put David Bowie on the cover of their 70th issue with a blazing headline that read: 'Ziggy Played Guitar – BOWIE – The Rise And Fall Of Glam's Greatest Idol'. This 21-page spread was adorned with great photography and quotes from DA Pennebaker, Ken Scott and Mick Rock to name a few. One of the sidebars was titled 'Mick Ronson – Forgotten Icon' and quoted Marc Bolan admitting that when with Bowie, "No other combination, including Jagger-Richards, was as visually strong. They were riveting." The article coincided with the release of the *Ziggy Stardust Motion Picture* DVD UK release and the article also mentioned the forthcoming 30th Anniversary edition of *Aladdin Sane*, scheduled for a UK release in May.

Meanwhile, after a two year lodging at Cleveland's Rock and Roll Hall Of Fame And Museum, Mick's Les Paul guitar returned in 2003 to owner Rick Tedesco in Brookfield, CT. Rick's guitar shop The Guitar Hangar has been "serving the earth's guitarists since 1999" and in 2004 he offered the public the opportunity to buy a replica version of Ronson's legendary Les Paul. This guitar replica is a stunning piece and was limited to just 100 numbered units. The guitars are modified to the specs of the original Les Paul and since the original is in their Museum collection, they can pull it off with authenticity. The actual guitar has a decal of Mick's signature on the back of the headstock. The replica guitars still include the bonus memorabilia package including an 8x10 Mick Rock photo "Certificate of Authenticity" suitable for framing and signed by Suzi, Lisa and Rick, an autographed copy of this book, a Ronson guitar pick and one random record from Mick's personal record collection.

The August 27 edition of *Rolling Stone* magazine positioned Mick at #64 on their list of the '100 Greatest Guitarists Of

All Time'. A year later, in December 2004, the song 'All the Young Dudes' came in at #253 on the magazine's list of '500 Greatest Songs Of All Time' while the album itself that credits Ronson as the orchestral arranger and conductor ranks #491 on their list of the '500 Greatest Albums'. The Rock and Roll Hall Of Fame have also recognized 'All the Young Dudes', putting it on their list of the 500 songs that shaped rock 'n' roll. A closer look at the *Rolling Stone* article will reveal other winning titles that Ronson contributed to such as David Bowie's *Hunky Dory*, *Aladdin Sane* and Lou Reed's *Transformer*. Another credit worth noting is the fact that *Words & Music – John Mellencamp's Greatest Hits* (2004) gives Ronson a guitar and backing vocal credit on the song 'Jack & Diane'.

Ronson's enduring legacy has been fuelled still further by the dot.com age. When youtube.com launched in February 2005, the public suddenly had a convenient channel to share and view videos for free on the internet. The ease and confidence with which one can now search for entertainment has increased at such a rapid rate it's no wonder that formats such as VHS and PAL are extinct. Using hard digital discs for music and video is already a dated format for many users. The majority of fans agree that typing 'Mick Ronson' into a search engine and pulling up 500 plus videos, interviews and photomontages at any given moment is the superior option and a lot less spacious. Speed and space are just two of the advantages of living and collecting in the cyber age. Audio experts claim that the trade-off is in the sound and it's an immeasurable loss. Regardless, there's a brand new way to turn on Mick Ronson and it's called the world wide web.

One business that quickly gained speed online after launching in 2005 is Worn Free, a T-shirt company based in Los Angeles, California. Reproducing original tees famously worn by rock legends such as Mick Ronson, Ian Hunter, Debbie Harry and Iggy Pop is their niche. The shirts offered at Worn Free are custom-made vintage and fully licensed from the estates and the individuals concerned.

Back East, Rick Tedesco teamed up with Dennis Dunaway – the original bassist for the Alice Cooper Group – to record *Bones from the Yard*, officially released in September 2006. During the course of those recordings, Ronson's Les Paul was used on several of the tracks, "most notable was the solo for 'Man Is A Beast'," says Tedesco.

Recent audio discoveries include recordings by a short-lived band consisting of Ronson, Hilly Michaels (Ian Hunter Band) and Les Fradkin (Left Banke). The band recorded a song called 'Spare Change' and it remained unreleased until Les Fradkin put it on his 2006 album *Goin' Back*. Meanwhile, six EC2 tracks have finally made it up on the web and new information reveals that bands The Proof (1981) and The Mundanes (1982) both worked with Ronson but the songs remain unreleased.

Also of interest are the previously unreleased (1986) Cody Melville sessions. Cody explains that "Ronson played most of the instruments on the four tunes. I played some bass and the vocals. Johnny Melville (brother) did the live percussion and programming with Mick aside from the cello, Mick played everything else." Cody posted all four songs on the web.

Four classic titles definitely worth seeking out are the expanded versions (see discography) of Lou Reed's *Transformer*, Bob Dylan's *Live 1975,* Roger McGuinn's *Cardiff Rose* and Hunter/Ronson's *YUI Orta*.

While the digital download age dominates the music industry, good old-fashioned bootlegging and collecting continue to evolve. Take for instance the six-disc version of *The 1980 Floor Show (uncut)* that surfaced early in the year. Amanda Lear, the Astronettes, Carmen, The Troggs, Marianne Faithfull and what some declare to be the best visual footage of Bowie and Ronson ever. One fan points out that "'Space

Oddity' is especially cool since there is no spaceship footage obliterating Mick's lift-off sound effects. Plus, it's great to finally hear 'screw', 'whore', 'wanking', and 'god damn' again."

An unofficial eight-disc David Bowie (audio) set culled directly from the Ryko vaults surfaced shortly thereafter. The first two discs showcase Ronson by featuring alternate versions to the original tracks ranging from several versions of 'Memory of a Free Festival' to 'Hang On to Yourself' with different lyrics. The multiple versions of 'Life on Mars' are a treat with a favourite being the one you can hear Mick instructing Rick Wakeman on how to play the piano parts. There are alternate versions of 'The Supermen', 'Song for Bob Dylan' and 'The Bewlay Brothers' and tracking sessions (multiple takes) of 'Star', one including alternate lyrics. Though this set is still considered rare and difficult to find, it is certainly worth its weight in gold.

In May 2007, Gibson.com paid tribute to Ronson by pointing him out as an "understated guitar hero" and someone who could bring "subtle elegance and exquisite economy to his string work." Elsewhere, as Ian Hunter worked out an arrangement for the loan of the piano on which he composed 'Cleveland Rocks' to be donated to the Rock and Roll Hall Of Fame and Museum, Suzi Ronson was making some arrangements of her own. In June of 2007, Spontanuity a film company based in London run by Susan Ashworth and Marc Coker, approached Suzi about creating a documentary on Mick. Suzi wisely secured the domain name: mickronson. com, thanks to the cooperation of Ed Di Gangi and brought in Webmaster Justin Purington, assisted by Madeline Bocaro and other faithful supporters. Hundreds of photographs and news articles are up and available to view. It's tremendously satisfying to visit the new official website where news is current yet there remains an obvious commitment to archiving data. If you're on the web, it's the place to go for all things Mick Ronson.

Back in Connecticut, Rick Tedesco and Dennis Dunaway regrouped, this time paying tribute to Ronson by choosing to record 'Moonage Daydream' for the MainMan Records David Bowie Tribute CD called *Hero*. "Mick's guitar was the only guitar used on that song and the solo was done note for note in honor of Mick," says Tedesco. "Dunaway sounded very enthused about the project during the mixing of the track and told us 'Ian Hunter has already given it the thumbs up.'" The official release followed shortly thereafter and featured 35 tracks spanning across two discs.

In November, The *Classic Rock* Awards 2007 honored Mick by giving him the Tommy Vance Inspiration Award. Prior to the ceremony, many artists came forth (including Joan Jett and Duff McKagan) to be filmed for the Ronson documentary. Joe Elliott and Ian Hunter presented the award and Lisa and Suzi Ronson accepted, both honoring him with heartfelt speeches. Lisa admitted to being nervous but her message was lovely and read as such:

"I think about my dad everyday. A lot of people list him as an influence, but no one was more influenced by him than me. To this day when I meet people who have met him, they usually don't talk about his guitar solos or his production skills. They talk about what a decent, funny, down-to-earth person he was. If ever someone felt out of place, he had a way of making them feel liked or loved or accepted because to him, they were. He taught me to be strong and courageous but most of all he taught me to be kind. A rather small and gentle lesson to receive from someone who appeared so much larger than life, wearing more make-up than I ever have. He taught me it's nice to be important but it's more important to be nice." The January 2008 issue of *Classic Rock* covered the event in full and complemented it with a feature story by Campbell Devine. Tagged as the 'all star' salute to Ronson, the article doubled the value, making it a genuine keepsake.

THE SPIDER WITH THE PLATINUM HAIR

In April, the legendary Ziggy Stardust concert from Santa Monica was finally given an official release sanctioned by Bowie. EMI released it in both regular and deluxe editions. The deluxe version featured the disc housed in a card sleeve featuring a George Underwood painting, four reproductions of old RCA promo photographs, a poster featuring the *Los Angeles Times* original review of the show and a sixteen page booklet filled with Mick Rock photos from the concert. Bowie complimented Mick in this statement quoted on the back cover: "I can tell that I'm totally into being Ziggy by this stage of our touring. It's no longer an act; I *am* him. This would be around the tenth American show for us and you can hear that we are all pretty high on ourselves. We train wreck a couple of things, I miss some words and sometimes you wouldn't know that pianist Mike Garson was onstage with us. But overall I really treasure this bootleg. Mick Ronson is at his blistering best."

In late 2008 it was announced that a Mott the Hoople documentary was in the works. Led by Mike Kerry at Start Productions, they've interviewed most of the original members and have encouraged fans to get involved. Rumours of a Mott the Hoople reunion concert were also circulating; a secret that quietly rumbled throughout the holidays. Then, on January 9, 2009 it was officially announced that Mott the Hoople would reunite for two nights, their first performance together in thirty-five years. Scheduled at the HMV Hammersmith Apollo (formerly the Odeon), the line-up consists of the original band and marks a 40th Anniversary celebration. Mott the Hoople, Hunter and Ronson fans from all over the world rushed to attend. Both shows sold out and before the end of January, another show was added which also sold out shortly thereafter.

In February, Spontanuity delivered a promo show reel for review and with one glance it was evident that they represent a diverse roster of clients. The reel showcases twelve feature shorts, three of which are associated with the Ronson documentary, clocking in at nearly fourteen minutes. First, there's the David Bowie *Ziggy Stardust* clip that includes the full 'Ziggy Stardust' from the Civic Hall in Dunstable June 21, 1972 overdubbed with the audio from Santa Monica, Civic Auditorium, October 20, 1972. This footage varies slightly from the previous 1994 Griffin promo. The other clip is the infamous *Only After Dark* promo video that Sony music issued during the promotion of *Heaven and Hull*. Turns out, Spontanuity's Mark Coker directed that promo, which was a welcome surprise. "Yes, he was the one that originally transferred the old footage from the 1970s so he's a very interested party!" says Suzi.

The third clip features footage from the Ziggy Stardust Tour and most notably, the solo Rainbow performances. Suzi has the pro-video footage for both Rainbow shows but sadly the audio is missing. As Cherry Vanilla indicated earlier, there's a chance that the master tapes were wiped but some believe otherwise. Until it surfaces, this remains a mystery.

A montage of aged tickets and passes mark the era and watching long time photo stills come to life is just short of breath taking. Video of both the Hunter Ronson Band and the Rolling Thunder Tour nicely represent the mid-to-later part of the 1970s; with the Bob Dylan clip being especially comical. Mick is smoking hot on guitar (wearing a hippie hat) playing a riff that even takes Dylan somewhat off-guard. It's priceless.

Rare, vintage footage of Mick and Suzi dining and enjoying life are cut between other personal clips including shaving and laying in a bed relaxing. Quick to tug on the heartstrings are the clips from the crystal clear *Slaughter on 10th Avenue* promo video, although it seems unlikely that this will be used in its entirety.

New interviews with Ian Hunter, Tony Visconti, Mick Rock, Alice Cooper, Bob Neuworth, Mike Garson and Joe Elliott embellish Ronson's story. Backed with a sea of music and crystal clear video footage, the tastefully layered interview clips validate the impact that Ronson had on people, personally and professionally. Ian Hunter is right on when he reminds us "real good friends don't grow on trees."

Originally, *Access All Areas* and *Unsung Hero* were the titles associated with the documentary and that plan consisted of cutting a fifty-five minute film with possibilities of a bonus (interactive) disc accompanying it. Due to the wealth of material, plans for a more detailed, two-part documentary went into motion, resulting in a title change. The working title *...And Ziggy Played Guitar* has been chosen for part one of the documentary.

The first release plans to cover Mick's early life and career up through mid-1975 and promises to feature 90 minutes of fantastic material. The second release plans to tell the story of the Rolling Thunder Revue and forward. "I'm finding it fascinating the deeper we go. Some of these stories will really make you laugh. Mick was amusing and his take on things really funny," says Suzi.

Joe Elliott has recorded a version of 'This Is for You' (the Laurie Heath song Ronson covered on *Play Don't Worry*) exclusively for the documentary. Laurie, aware of Joe's version kindly shares this comment: "Mick was a very special person indeed, and one I have never forgotten to this day. I still have in front of me Mick's *Teach Yourself Book – Orchestration* by King Palmer that he gave to me on his way to the studio to overdub the first orchestration he'd ever written. Mick was unpretentious, kind, sincere and generous. God ... I wish he were around today so I could tell him how much I loved him."

In regards to the Les Paul replica, we discussed how Ronson's (random) records would one by one disappear as promised in the aforementioned guitar package. A road trip was planned to document the remaining vinyl collection while it was still, for the most part, intact. We felt it of mammoth value to list the records that he enjoyed, played a part of and that inspired him in one way or another. Rick generously granted our request and the list of Mick's record collection is printed in its entirety later in this book.

There were only three boxes of albums but the dust, the wax and the sweet smell of a vinyl treasure was magnified by the fact that these records once belonged to Mick Ronson. Every flip of a title seemed capable of raising suspicion or stirring up mysterious wonder or curious disbelief. A gasp here was followed by a question mark there and then there's the smirk that kindly follows finding a copy of Eddie Murphy's *Comedian* record. Surely, some of these titles landed in his collection by accident and perhaps some of the good ones are missing or forever lost? Still, what remains are the platters once owned by someone with a fine and eclectic taste. This isn't about fondling somebody's records or looking at a list – instead it's an opportunity to look, listen and seek out some of the same titles that Mick felt worthy of keeping in his personal collection.

Apparently, after Ian Hunter looked through the boxes, he told Rick Tedesco that "Mick nicked this one (and that one) from me!" which left them both laughing. Nearly ten random titles had the classic promo MainMan sticker stuck on them, which makes one question did someone have a heyday with some promo stickers or were these titles taken directly from the office? One might ask why his Mae West record looked a lot more played than his Jimi Hendrix record or why there was a self-titled *Whitney Houston* LP stuck inside the Theatre Of Hate sleeve? We found a wealth of Reggae, Elvis and NRBQ amongst several Roy Harper records and a bunch of Creedence Clearwater Revival. Then to find his original Annette Peacock records? Jackpot.

The [NYC street musician and former beat poet] Moondog LP stood out immediately with his Viking image, in full gatefold glory. Ronson check marked three songs on the Dr.

John *Desitively Bonnaroo* title while his Animals' *Animals* was trashed, missing its cover sleeve entirely but oozing with a mysterious sentiment. The Bob Neuwirth debut featured some artistically carved eyes on the cover sleeve while the Dalbello and Payolas Masterdisks were obviously of special interest.

Mick's personal copies of *Slaughter On 10th Avenue* and *Play Don't Worry* were framed at the bottom of a stairway and added to the glamour of the rock 'n' roll hallway that led to a room full of 24-track master tapes. These [Bearsville Sound Studio] two-inch reels stretched across the length of two bookshelves. Notations on the back of the boxes indicate that Sony had sorted through the majority of them, using only the songs that they felt worthy.

In addition to the guitar shop, Tedesco has a home studio where in one room, Mick's Ensoniq keyboard is set up adjacent to the small Marshall Amp and large speaker cabinet used during *Heaven and Hull*. Yet, nothing shined as bright as the Ziggy Stardust Amp, the Bowie-head or 'The Pig' as it's called, stationary on the floor, near the doorway. Well labeled, in bright yellow lettering, it reads: 'DAVID BOWIE', and that little Marshall Major 200 watt head had the presence of an electric warrior. A recent web-post by Keith (Ched) Cheesman indicates that this amp dates back to the Rats era. Upon closer observation you can also see in small black letters, the words: 'Ian Hunter', so clearly, this amp has been around. Due to the agreement made between Rick and Suzi, these reels, records and the other artefacts are all together now, secured and in the hands of someone who understands their value.

All three of Mick's children are doing well and somewhat active in music. We were unable to reach his oldest son Nick for a comment but he's in music production and living in the UK. His daughter Lisa is based in NYC and while continuing her education has found herself fronting a band called The Secret History. Consisting of six other members, their six-song EP is available on Le Grand Magistery and she's the dark, sultry vocalist. Her sweet voice is complemented with a textured sound reminiscent of Belle and Sebastian but with more of an edge. There's a definite nod to Dad, when 'Mark & John (Bring On The Glitter Kids)' starts out with the riff from 'Hang On To Yourself'. This song quickly turns into a real Blondie-esque number and its melody is more than memorable. Another track 'Our Lady Of Palermo' features the lyric 'the man who stole the world' which was another added surprise.

Joakim Ronson (his family call him Kim) was only three years old when Mick passed away. He kindly responded when asked to share facts about himself and voice an opinion on his Dad's music. When prompted to choose a favourite song or piece, here's what he said:

Hi,

To begin with, I'm eighteen years old and I study music at a local school in Stockholm. Though I changed from dancing to music after a year and a half in school I have been playing music since I was seven/eight years old. I have also been dancing different styles for about twelve years. My head instrument is drums but I have guitars at home and I play piano, bass and guitar when there is an instrument in my hand. I play and write my own songs and I like to compose new things. I am working on some acoustic songs at the moment. I live with my grandmother now but have lived alone a while and before high school I went to school in Uppsala. I have two sisters on my mother's side and we come along pretty well except for incident that has been hard, five years back. I spend a lot of my time on music, friends, at my computer and school on weekdays. I don't often go out and drink but I do it sometimes in my home or at friends. I'm not working right now but

THE SPIDER WITH THE PLATINUM HAIR

I'm planning to work with a Swedish festival "Peace & Love" and perhaps with music also. This summer 2009 I'm going to become a bartender. I'm leaving for Mallorca on July 4. It is a three-week course, besides what I do in my spare time I like to do different things and try out new interests. When it comes to what kind of music I listen to, I listen to all kinds of music. I don't judge music or any art. I see it as an expression or a feeling. I can say I see music as a piece of art, forming from what I sense and feel. I like to travel and I've been outside of Sweden a lot. I also have a new band (I had one before this one) but we don't have a name yet. My favourite holiday is summer. I enjoy ice cream a lot and especially at summer. My favorite is Ben and Jerry's.

My favourite piece (song) is 'Empty Bed' and 'All the Young Dudes' with Mick Ronson and Ian Hunter. One more thing about me: I have a myspace if people want to ask anything or listen to songs I'm about to upload. Best wishes and keep on rock'n.

Best wishes,
Joakim Ronson, March 2009

On March 7, 2009, two more Mott the Hoople shows were added in London, making it a five-night concert extravaganza for the first week of October 2009. News continues right up to press time, with Angel Air re-issuing the Rats material and EMI UK planning a 30th Anniversary deluxe edition of Ian Hunter's *You're Never Alone with a Schizophrenic.* The disc features five bonus tracks and a live disc culled from (Hammersmith, Berkeley and Cleveland) the YNAWAS tour. Last but not least, plans for an annual Mick Ronson convention (Ohio) are currently in motion and you're all invited.

Years later, life goes on and though it feels like nothing has changed (we know it has) here we are, still standing and still staring, at The Spider with the Platinum Hair.

CONCLUSION

AND LITTLE LORD FAUNTLEROY – WHO LET HIM OUTTA HIS AMP?

In regard to mourning artists we've never met, a fan once said: "We don't cry because we knew them, we cry because they helped us know ourselves." That simple and tender quote is loaded with truth and best summarizes the heartache many of us feel in losing the artists involved in Mick Ronson's life.

In 2013 two of Ronson's contemporaries died: Lou Reed and Trevor Bolder. Lou passed on October 27 due to an ailment stemming from his recent liver transplant. Trevor Bolder, his fellow Spider, died on May 21 after undergoing surgery for pancreatic cancer earlier in the year.

On January 8, 2016, David Bowie celebrated his 69th birthday by releasing his new studio album *Blackstar* to critical acclaim. Two days later David succumbed to liver cancer after a long, private battle.

Fans, celebrities and fellow musicians around the world took to social media to express their grief with a succession of tributes. Leave it to Ian Hunter to turn out the best one of all by composing the celebratory hymn 'Dandy'. A sweet and loving tribute to David and the Spiders, it hits the emotional bullseye. Woody and Trevor are given a name check, and Mick is appropriately referred to as Little Lord Fauntleroy! 'Dandy' is included on Ian's latest album *Fingers Crossed*, which maintains the level of high quality songwriting that fans have come to expect after a long string of brilliant albums.

Speaking of those albums, Proper Records recently released *Stranded in Reality*, a mammoth thirty-disc Ian Hunter retrospective featuring all of Ian Hunter's solo work from the first album to *When I'm President*. Also featured is a large selection of studio and live rarities (many featuring the talents of Mick) on both CD and DVD. It's an exciting milestone, but Ian shows no signs of slowing down. He continues releasing new music and doing knockout concerts with his longtime Rant Band. Mick certainly would be proud of his friend and musical partner.

The recently released Mick Ronson *Heaven and Hull* album completes the vinyl trilogy of Ronson's official studio work. Available on the Music On Vinyl label, the 180 gram audiophile vinyl makes the album available for the very first time in this format. Its compact disc counterpart is no match for it with its beautiful large album art. The glossy tones of blue and enlarged photo of the Humber Bridge, complete with full-size, four-page insert, make this a very special piece of wax.

Meanwhile, a Japanese *Heaven and Hull* Blu-spec CD (a compact disc manufactured using Blu-ray technology) has just been released and is said to sound spectacular. Both reissues are a welcome surprise and the timing is ideal for the spotlight to beam brightly on *Heaven and Hull*.

At present, the city is preparing for huge celebrations due to the announcement in 2013 that Hull was the winner of the UK City of Culture 2017 award. This honor is only bestowed on a city once every four years. These events will bring worldwide attention to the tough little town that overflows with history. Finally, the rest of the world will catch up and recognize Hull's largest musical asset, the Spiders from Mars.

In 2013, the last remaining Spider, Woody Woodmansey, came back to the world of music shortly after being invited to speak at the Institute of Contemporary Arts. He was asked to talk about the Bowie records he'd played on decades earlier. The ICA had put together a first-rate band to play Bowie songs, calling the band Holy Holy. Blondie drummer Clem Burke and Spandau Ballet's Steve Norman, joined by some of the Ronson family, paid tribute to the songs they love. Later, when the band took their show to the stage at the Latitude Festival, they invited Woody to sit in but he chose to only play on a few numbers. When commitments to Blondie prevented Clem from touring with Holy Holy, Woody was quick to jump in and became a full-fledged member. As the project evolved, Woody's desire to play *The Man Who Sold the World* album increased as it had never been played live before.

In 2014 Woody asked Tony Visconti to join the band, and the reunion of the original *The Man Who Sold the World* rhythm section took place. This resulted in both musicians playing their original drum and bass parts in the studio and live.

Holy Holy first released a seven inch picture disc single followed up by the double live CD of their 2014 Shepherd's Bush performance. The show now included *The Man Who Sold the World* in its entirety plus a dozen other Bowie songs. In the summer of 2015, the band did a month-long tour of the UK and Dublin which found Lisa Ronson at front and centre stage, performing a beautiful version of 'Lady Stardust'.

After some successful dates in Japan, the line-up, now consisting of Woody, Tony, James Stevenson and Paul Cuddleford with the addition of Glenn Gregory, Bernice

Scott, Terry Edwards and Jessica Morgan, prepared to bring their show to the USA and Canada in the early part of 2016.

The eleven-city tour kicked off in Portland, Maine on January 7, but when the news of Bowie's passing broke, the band had a serious decision to make. They arrived in Toronto on the 12th, playing to an overwhelmingly supportive audience, confirming their choice to carry on with the tour. When they hit Cleveland four days later (on what felt like the coldest night of winter), they were met with a heated enthusiasm that warmed the entire Odeon. It was a highly emotional concert which, in its own magical way, ignited a communal type of healing for the band and the audience. After the show, you could find the group hanging out and chatting with fans, Woody staying until everyone had a chance to get autographs and photos.

Holy Holy have a string of shows planned for 2017 including two sold-out nights in Hull during the City of Culture celebrations. The band have announced they will play *The Rise and Fall of Ziggy Stardust and the Spiders from Mars* in its entirety during the last weekend of March. Woody also has a new book titled *Spider from Mars: My Life with Bowie* on the shelves now, accounting his years with Mick and David during the early seventies. A USA launch of the title will soon follow.

The spotlight continues on our hero from Hull with the upcoming Mick Ronson documentary now titled *Beside Bowie*. Previously, Suzi was working with Spontanuity on a two-part film project but nearly a decade later it's evolved, due to her collaboration with Jon Brewer and Marc Coker from Cardinal Releasing and Content Media. Currently, they're working together in an effort to finalize Mick's story on film and get it launched. Beside Bowie has mammoth potential to introduce Mick to a larger (new) audience while still rewarding the loyal fans. The trailer looks very promising and was posted on the web by Cardinal Releasing in the early part of 2016. There is still no projected date for the *Beside Bowie* release.

In 2015, Lisa Ronson recorded her first solo record, called *Emperors of Medieval Japan*. The album is varied in topics and sounds thanks in part to Reeves Gabrels. It's a very interesting listen and is highly recommended. Lisa supported Reeves during his tour, and since then, she's found herself touring with and supporting Earl Slick and Bernard Fowler, who performed Bowie's *Station to Station* album in full during their brief tour of the UK. Lisa is back out on the road in 2017 for her *Tales of the City Tour*, which features special guest Morgan Fisher on keyboards.

Mick's sister Maggi released her own recording in 2013 called *Sweet Dreamer*. On it, she pays tribute to her brother by covering songs he'd written or covered himself. She cleverly recreated the drag cover of Bowie's *The Man Who Sold the World* for her artwork and did a marvelous job of it.

Suzi Ronson is active, participating as a special guest on radio and TV both here and abroad. She's shared her stories publicly, even speaking at the Moth Ball 2016 in New York. She is currently writing her own book, which promises to be special, given her unique position as Bowie's hair stylist and personal assistant.

Mott The Hoople returned in 2013; reuniting for the second time, to play five nights in November at different UK venues. Commemorating the event, the Manchester gig was recorded, filmed and released in various formats, including a limited edition yellow vinyl set. Dale 'Buffin' Griffin did not play on the tour, but The Pretenders' drummer (and Herefordshire mate) covered for him. It should be noted that 'Buffin' was so very pleased about the reformation of Mott The Hoople. It was something he had worked diligently towards for a very long time. On January 17, 2016 Dale 'Buffin' Griffin passed away, having struggled with Alzheimer's for many years. On January 22, 2017, bassist Pete 'Overend' Watts succumbed to throat cancer at age 69. Overend's passing clearly marks the end of an era and it's a very sad time for generations of fans worldwide.

A few notable Bowie-era recordings have slipped out in recent years. In 2014, David Bowie issued his career-spanning collection *Nothing Has Changed*. For fans of Ronson, the appearance of the shorter, punchier stereo mix of the Spiders performing 'All the Young Dudes' was a much welcome addition.

The BBC's practice of wiping tapes has been a nightmare for fans of sixties and seventies rock. Many performances were lost due to this practice. One such performance was David and the Spiders' January 4, 1973 appearance on *Top of the Pops* performing their hit 'The Jean Genie'. It turns out that cameraman John Henshall had saved a copy for himself, and in 2011 the footage aired as part of a *Top of the Pops* Christmas special on BBC 2. What a delight it was for fans to see this classic piece of Spiders history. It gives fans hope that a copy of their appearance performing 'Starman' on *Lift Off with Ayshea* will one day surface!

In other BBC news, David's *Bowie at the Beeb* collection was finally issued on vinyl in 2016. This four-LP box set features David and Ronno's performance of 'Oh! You Pretty Things' recorded for *The Sounds of the Seventies* programme on September 21, 1971. This was previously available only on the Japanese CD edition. New to the box set and an incredible find is an earlier appearance on *Sounds of the Seventies*, recorded on March 25, 1970, of them performing 'The Supermen'. This one had never been broadcast and was discovered when the original CD edition was put together. One can only hope for a full set of David's BBC sessions including a full good quality version of Mick's debut session from February 5, 1970 on *The Sunday Show*.

In April 2014, Rick Tedesco, the owner of Mick's original Les Paul, shared a story on his blog entitled *Saying Goodbye to an Old Friend*. He retells the story of how he acquired the guitar and his difficult decision to part with it. We recommend searching out the article for the full report, but in short, Rick was offered a "stupid enormous" price to sell the guitar. Though it pained him greatly, he was made an offer that he just couldn't refuse. After playing it one last time, he cried, saying goodbye and packing it up for its new caretaker. Both historic and beloved, the Les Paul is now "across the pond and in very good hands", says Rick.

In parting, let us remind you that the Little Lord Fauntleroy character that Ian mentions during 'Dandy' is much like Ronson, in that he was good and kind and understood that his nobility was defined by his actions. Unlike the fictional character, Ronno had a guitar and platform boots that put him on a whole other level. In 'Dandy' Ian asks the question, "And Little Lord Fauntleroy – who let him outta his amp?" We all did and we continue to do so every time we play one of the many classic albums he left his unique stamp on.

Long live RONNO!

APPENDICES

'THAT'S ALL I CAN SAY...'
MICK RONSON IN HIS OWN WORDS

Guitar playing: As long as a guitar player can play good melodies he's a good musician. It's got nothing to do with technical abilities. Fancy solos just make you wonder what it is they're trying to prove. I was influenced by the Shadows, Duane Eddy and – surprising, as it may seem – George Harrison. I can still remember the guitar solos as well as the songs. If I can walk down the street and whistle the solos from those records, there's got to be something there. Jeff Beck and Neil Young are also great players at that level. Neil can play one note for five minutes and though he doesn't really do anything, he takes you through many different feelings. There are many good guitar heroes nowadays too, but I don't listen to them. I'm not interested in them. I'm after all, more interested in listening to the music itself than the guitar. Personally I don't practice at all. It's because I used to play classical piano and violin and I learned to hate practicing the scales. When I took up the guitar I decided not to practice anymore, just play. (*Music Maker* 1988 Holland)

Success: I think everybody that's in a group, when they start out that's what they dream about. I mean I used to go to bed and dream. I remember one night I dreamed I was on stage with the Rolling Stones. There I was, in Keith Richards' place and I was playing and the audience was going crazy and it felt so good and I never felt anything like it in my life before and I always remember that. I guess every kid who starts off playing guitar or drums, or piano, or whatever it is, must go through all that and dream about it and keep striving for it and that's why people buy new guitars and bigger amplifiers. For about five years I had one pair of shoes a year, if that, and I used to get one pair of trousers. I've really been through all that. I was really scraping a bit. I was doing that for a long time and I thought, well, I'm getting older, is this ever going to end? Then, it just happened, three years ago. It's good fun when you look back on it, but at the time, it's so depressing sometimes I sat down and cried because I thought well what am I going to do and why can't I do this and why can't I do that and why won't this happen, and why should it happen to me? You get so depressed with it all. (*Hit Parader* March 1975)

Guitar Influences: George Harrison, he influenced me a lot. Harrison was a great guitarist, really excellent. I told you about my classical background; so the beautiful melodies he was playing really grew on me. Every time George Harrison is playing, he does exactly the right thing for the song. He never had a 'big guitar sound' he didn't play everywhere, just in the right sections. So you can easily remember all his solos, while some other guitarist would play melodies you forget the next minute. Jeff Beck is a great melodical guitarist, too. Regarding rhythm guitarists, Pete Townshend influenced me a lot with the full chords of his. I learned some things here and there. Duane Eddy is another guitarist that still makes great melodies. So, after years of listening to all these guys, I finally got my own style. (*Hit Parader* March 1975)

Feeling: Feeling has an important role in music. You might say, the music is in your heart. I think to play the scales fast or practice like mad is not what a good musician should do. Of course, this is my opinion. Being a technician is similar to that of being a monkey; they only repeat what someone tells them to do. (*Fare Musica #68* November 86)

THE SPIDER WITH THE PLATINUM HAIR

Rejoining Bowie in 1971: I considered it for two weeks. I had got out of a few debts and had a steady job. I wasn't making any money but I wasn't in debt, either. I thought 'Should I go? Am I going to have this happen to me all over again?' After two weeks I reached the decision I HAD to go because if something good happened with David I would kick myself for the rest of my life. I think the reason I made it possibly better than anyone else from Hull is that I took a lot of chances when I was younger. I don't see anybody getting on if they don't take gambles. They have got to put up with a bit of trouble and a bit of debt but if they keep struggling then they will do something for themselves. I was very determined and also quite lucky. The two go hand in hand. (*Hull Daily Mail* April 18, 1975)

Mick's Spiders From Mars Equipment: On stage I use two Gibson Les Paul Custom guitars, with another as spare, placed on a convenient stand. I use Rotosound strings and the gauges are: 00.09 (1st), 00.11 (2nd), 00.14 (3rd), 00.25 (4th), 00.35 (5th) and 00.44 (6th). My amplifier is a Marshall 200-watt with one 120-watt Marshall cabinet containing four 12-inch Celestion speakers. I use a Cry Baby wah-wah pedal and an American Tonebender – which used to belong to Pete Townshend. He sold it to someone else about seven years ago and I bought it for £5. It is the only one of its kind I have ever seen. Other guitars I possess are a Yamaha acoustic, a Brazilian Carlos Robelli acoustic, a Gibson black SG Special and a Fender Mustang. My advice on lead guitar playing is to suggest that you do what I did when I was starting. I listened carefully to my favorite guitarists on stage and records, notably Jeff Beck, Jimi Hendrix, Keith Richards and George Harrison, and watched exactly how they played, where they put their fingers, and how they got the sounds. I put two and two together, went home and practiced until I could do it myself. (*Melody Maker* June 9, 1973)

Sounds on a Bowie album: We like changes. In a way, the new album *Aladdin Sane* has a much heavier variety of sounds than before. We consider it to be a new aspect that we have put the avant-garde sound up front this time. Yet we do not prepare for these changes in our minds prior to the recording. The changes are created from the happenings in the studio, or I'd rather say that while we are trying different ways to vitalize the number, the sound on the album is gradually created and decided. (*Music Life*, April 1973 Japan)

I'm not denying that I was chiefly responsible for the sound of the David Bowie records from the seventies. I'm not trying to brag about it, it just so happens that I was an integral part of the band, as well on the stage and in the studio. With another guitarist it would all have sounded different. (*Sounds* February 1990 Finland)

Bowie's bisexual image: I took it quite seriously because he wasn't kidding. I didn't like it at first, but then you get used to it. You got used to so many people around being bisexual that you got used to it for yourself. But it shook me up. I felt 'wow, what are people going to say?' (*Circus* August 1975)

Ziggy Stardust: The Motion Picture: Once they got the rights then they could put the film together, chop it up and release it. I haven't seen it. I'm more interested in the future than the past. (KLBS Austin Texas radio interview October 1988)

Parting with Bowie: David and I really never broke up, we grew apart, sort of went our own ways. At some stage David wanted to do something else. He had plans for a Broadway play and I didn't want to tour anymore. At the same time, I was offered a solo deal, so I went off to record an album, after that I was always busy with different things. (*Music Maker* 1988 Holland)

Bowie reunion: David didn't contact me for the (1990) tour but I wouldn't have been interested in it anyway. I already once turned down the chance to reform (1978) the Spiders From Mars. (*Music Maker* 1988 Holland)

Transformer: Yeah, that album gave me a lot of satisfaction and I love Lou. (*Nineteen* January 1976)

USA versus UK: If I had to make a choice of making it either in Britain or America, then I'd have to choose the States, because the scope there is so much greater. There'd be more for me to do in America, but I could never live there. America is all right just as long as you know you can come home to England again. (*Disc* October 20, 1973)

Slaughter on 10th Avenue: It's come quicker than I thought, which is probably why I've only written three numbers for this album. I wouldn't write a stack of stuff for the album and record it simply because it's my material. I don't care who wrote the number. As long as I present it properly, that's all I'm interested in. I will write more numbers and on my next album I'll have more of my own numbers and on the album after that ... I'll be five things, singer, guitarist, producer, arranger and composer. There's a lot of ground to cover and I'll be into doing it. That is if I *can* do it ... I'll just keep going. (*Scene* 1975)

Vocals: I'm not the best of vocalists. There are a lot of good vocalists around but I'm certainly better than a lot of 'em and

I'm going to get better as I get more experience as a front man. I've been practicing a lot by myself. When me and David (Bowie) sing together we sound very much alike. I'll sound like David on some parts, but at other times I'll sound like different people. But I'll be singing well, or else I wouldn't be singing at all. I don't want to be doing anything unless it's perfect. I don't want any rough edges. It'll sound rough – but gutsy and tight, but not so tight it's as tight as Yes, where every note's been worked out. Every single note, so that they become like computers on stage.(*Scene* 1975)

Solo live shows: When we get out on the road, the numbers are gonna sound different. They're going to sound even fuller than they do already. They'll be heavier and more exciting than they are now. They always are when you play 'em on the stage anyway. If people buy the album and like something, then when they come to see us on the road, they'll say, 'The album's great, but wait until you see 'em on stage.' 'Hang On to Yourself' was very bouncy on the record, but when we did it live it was really grinding, very heavy. Really chunky. (*New Musical Express* October 6, 1973)

Slaughter **billboard Times Square:** Yeah, it was pretty funny. I looked like a doll on there, like a doll that you would buy in a store with bright red rosy cheeks. Of course I thought it would be a photograph, but it was this painting. There was one side of it that looked like a touched–up photograph but the other side looked like a painting to me because my face was very round and I don't have a round face. I remember looking up at it from the cab window and thinking it looked funny. (*Circus* August 1975)

Recording with Mott the Hoople: It worked out very well. We were in there last Friday and we laid the B-side down which was like a jam and playing away and it felt very good. (*Rock Scene* March 1975)

Playing with Mott the Hoople: It really was a bad trip. When I left David, I had some problem in finding musicians for my own band so I soon accepted their offer to join when they asked me. I needed a band but soon realized that things weren't good. We played together on stage, but off stage everyone was on his own. (*Ciao 2001* July 25, 1976–Italy)

Playing with Bob Dylan: Lots of times, like when I was recording the solo stuff, I was very self-conscious about what I was playing, and it was getting too complex. After Rolling Thunder, I had more faith in meself. What I do, I can do really well, and not because I look a certain way and dress a certain way. In a lot of ways, I thought image was all I was by then. I can go out onstage now and do anything I want. I can dress up how I want and play any type of music I want. Nobody will even know what I'm gonna do until I get up there. I don't even really know, because I could change me mind next week and change it again the week after. (*CREEM* February 1977)

It doesn't matter what the public thinks about my playing, whether it's Dylan or anybody, as long as I'm enjoying myself. Some people will like it and some people won't. Some will probably think, 'Why is he playing that hillbilly stuff?; why doesn't he just go back to what he was doing?' and that is a good thing to do now and again. It's always good if you can keep up what you've done in the past as well as develop yourself in the present. It may really come in handy – you never know when you'll want to use what you've learned before some time in the future. Of course I hope everyone will like my music but either way, I have to keep moving on. (*Guitar Player* December 1976)

(Dylan) *Renaldo & Clara:* You know, I never saw the film! (*Ronson Ablaze!* #3)

Groupies: Groupies are nice people … I like them. (*Good Times* August 12, 1975)

Jeff Beck: Oh, I love what Becky does. There are lots of good guitarists around but none can get it on like him. I used to spend days listening to his records, copying his ideas, when I was younger. (*Nineteen* January 1976)

Being a musician: It's very hard. It may look like gold but sometimes it ain't so. The friends you have are the players in your band, the technicians, and the band supporters. You are always traveling in different cities, different countries. The boys and girls you meet somewhere; they can't be your good friends. If I have to tell the truth, I really don't like this. I have no normal contact with school friends, parents, cousins etc. but right now, I'm lucky. I've got a woman to love and she's Suzi Fussey and she's my best friend, too. Sometimes I think that the day will come when I'll be 40 or 50 and maybe I'm not in the music business, then I will recall all the things I've lost … but now I'm just playing and that's all I wanna do. Good things. (*Ciao* 2001 July 25, 1976 Italy)

Welcome to the Club: The album sounds like you're sitting in the audience and I find that quite exciting. We used the room's ambience a lot on the recording. If you sweeten live recordings too much, you should've just done it in the studio in the first place. (*Beat Instrumental* March 1980)

Who's the boss? You can't really tell. Ian and I seem to have the same opinions about everything after we've kicked it around for a while, that is. We've never had a real fight although I did once throw something at Ian. I think it was in Ohio in '79 or something but we've been friends ever since the beginning. The friendship has lasted all through the times when we didn't play together. Besides, our children love each other. (*Music Maker* 1988 Holland)

Italy 1986: It ain't easy getting used to Italy, the language was the first problem. I still enjoy recording in different countries, I like that very much because basically I'm a big tramp. (*Metro* October 1986)

Style: I can do any kind of music – I like lots of different kinds of music. So when I do me own stuff I tend to record anything. It's not in any kind of style. I think that's what confuses record companies because they like to put a stamp on something and say 'Well, it's this kind of style and this is the video that goes with it and this is how we're going to market it' but with me they don't know how to do that because I don't know myself. So if I don't know myself, how are they gonna know so it makes it more difficult for them. To me it's all the same thing, to me it's all music. To everybody else they have to be able to put it into a bag, they have to label it in some way and I can't do that. I've never done that. As a musician I've always done different things. (*Metro* October 1986)

Getting into the music business: I would say pack it in – give up! It's pretty tough. I'm pretty lucky, really. It's not a nice business. If you can do something else for a living I think you should try it. It's always good to try different things. I think it's just faith; you do something that you believe in. I'd like to be able to do something else for a living. I used to be a gardener, so I always had this passion for being a landscape gardener. I also would like to be a chef, so I always had this passion to be a chef. It just so happens to be that I have a passion for music too. It's just what I do – I like doing it but what I'm talking about is having the option to do something else, because sometimes things don't work out the way you expect them to work out. I see a lot of people around that try and do one thing for years and years and it doesn't work out. At the end of it they don't know what else to do and they just end up being lost. If you have another area to go in, another interest, it's always good to keep up that interest. It's a form of expression whatever it is, whether in my case it's in gardening or whether it's in cooking or whether it's in music, it's all the same thing. It's a form of expression. To some other people it might be painting or it might be poetry, or it might be digging the roads, I don't know what it is but it's another form of expression. I'll tell you something else I wanted to be: a gymnast. I was good at gymnastics. (WDTX Detroit, Michigan Radio Interview June 13, 1986 courtesy Cody Melville)

Reuniting with Ian: We're always friends but we sort of get together here and there. That's how it's been the past fifteen, sixteen years or something. We get on to doing other things and wander off, then we come back together and work. It's been a few years since we worked together and it feels real good. (KOME San Diego California radio interview October 1988)

Working with Ian: Ian basically writes the stuff and then I come along and say, 'Well, I like this bit' or 'I don't like that bit, I think that song's good or I don't think that's very good.'

That's pretty much how most of it comes about. (Promotional television interview for YUI ORTA)

Recording *YUI ORTA*: We worked twelve hours everyday, from recording to mixing. We have finished fifteen songs out of sixteen songs recorded. It was all recorded in twenty days. (Guitarist, 1990 Japan)

Producing *YUI ORTA*: We're discussing some outside production. I think that when you get involved with it yourself sometimes you can't see the wood for the trees. You can go so far with something and maybe some other objective point of view might come in real handy along the line. (KLBS Austin Texas radio interview October 1988)

'Sweet Dreamer': It was not as good as it sounded through my amp when it was mixed. Maybe few people realize this but it made the sound change. I made the song when I was in Amsterdam for some production work. I play the solos a little different on stage than on record. If I play the same things everyday, it makes me bored. Though I play better now since I started playing guitar again, playing style doesn't change – like a man's personality rarely changes. (KLBS Austin Texas Radio interview October 1988)

Guitar sound: Sounds which come first are often the best. There's no time to think (laughs). We were really productive, it was like 'Take 1, OK, Next!' but it really doesn't matter. I made many mistakes playing but I never replayed the thing. I didn't want to lose the feeling at that moment. So for this reason, it's a very basic album (*YUI ORTA*). (*Guitarist* 1990 Japan)

Live 1989 solo intro to *Slaughter on 10th Avenue*: It's mine all right. I just played around. (*Ronson Ablaze!* #3)

Guitar effects: Right now, I like the combination of Mesa-Boogie's head and Marshall cabinet. If possible, I don't want to use any effects. Sometimes they change the guitar tone. To get the best sound you have to link the guitar directly to the amp. (*Guitarist* 1990 Japan)

Playing in a band: The main thing with me and I think with all of us, is I never wanted it to be like a job where you go along and do your job and get your weekly pay. When it ends up like that you might as well get a regular job. (*Rave Up* Issue#16 1989)

The future: The music business is a very odd way of life. I've met a lot of great people and have been involved with some great music but basically the business side of it all sucks. I can't wait to go back on the road, I miss it so much. Also, the more you play live the better you get and it's a waste for me and Ian not to be playing. (*Beat Instrumental* March 1980)

Bootlegs, live tapes and videos: Depends from which night it was (laughs). (*Ronson Ablaze!* #3)

Producing: Being a producer is such a strange thing. Today, there's such a technical production; people just want to make 'that' sound. That's not for me. I think it's more down to musical problems. (*Fare Musica* #68 November 86)

Being a well-rounded musician: I can't say that I'm just a guitarist. I think if I was just a guitarist I would think I was a bit of a loser, because I think I've got more knowledge about music. I first studied on the piano, then recorder and violin. The guitar came much later. I got thrown out a lot in my violin class because I kept holding it like a guitar and plucking the strings. I was playing those kinds of things on the violin and the teacher threw me out, and I mean I was playing good violin but as soon as his back was turned I was plucking and I was thinking like The Shadows and The Beatles or anything you know, and then after that, I thought, I've got to get a guitar and I put my violin away and got a guitar and I stopped playing piano and was just playing guitar. So guitar became a big part of my life for a long while, but for the past three or four years I've started realizing that I was being very sort of narrow-minded in my music. Then I started playing the piano again and every instrument that I saw, I wanted to pick up and play and record because I like doing arrangements. I thought, now if I can write the notes on a piece of paper and then people can play it, I thought, well, if I write this, if I dish it out to them, then it can sound like this, so I did. The first thing I did was 'Andy Warhol' for Dana Gillespie. You know I wrote the parts out and said, it should sound like this, and it did. I thought 'good', and I started to do it. (*Rock Scene* March 1975)

Learning from Tony Visconti: When I was working with David, Tony Visconti used to be down at the studio, and I'd say to him, 'Can I come and watch what you're doing?' and he'd say 'Sure.' I was really impressed with what Tony did – I thought he was great. I still think he is. He's got a really good ear for sound. I thought to myself 'I could do that as well.' (*Beat Instrumental* March 1980)

Getting production jobs: I don't really have a card that I hand out to all the record companies. People just kind of find me. (*Beat Instrumental* March 1980)

Recording live in the studio: It's all a matter of attitude. I want the band members to feel proud of what they are doing, adopt a kind of 'it's now or never' attitude. The rest is simple; you look at the band's strong sides and try to make these even better while at the same time you try to get rid of their weak points. Fatal Flowers are a guitar-band so it makes no sense to let them sound like a keyboard band. I don't want to use things that they cannot use on stage because then you are cheating the audience. I'm going to start recording drums first, then bass, two guitars, organ and last, but not least, the vocals. Then I will listen to see what I might add. Many producers start with drums and bass and then put keyboards on top of it, but then there will be no more space left for the guitars. You have to record the characteristic things of the band before you add any extras. It is also very important that you record the vocals on tape as early as possible. If you spend a lot of time recording the music, there will be little time left for the vocals and the vocals are very important. Another reason to record the vocals early is that you know exactly where you can and where you cannot add the little extras. (*Beat Instrumental* March 1980)

Technical perfection: It must be good in an emotional way; it must have the right feeling. Jimi Hendrix sometimes played terribly out of tune but what he did was very convincing. Everybody is listening to records with 'hi-fi-ears' these days and we want this album [Fatal Flowers] to have as good a sound as possible. The equipment in any average studio is okay nowadays and I strongly believe in recording live in a studio. I hate it when I have to stop the tape during a song. When the guitarist plays, I'll make him play the whole song not only the solo. The same goes for the vocals. I don't believe in singing the same short piece for hours at a time. It might be technically perfect but the emotion will be gone. I prefer to compare a couple of takes and choose the best parts from them. Of all the records I've made the most exciting ones are those that, almost by accident, were recorded in one take. (*Beat Instrumental* March 1980)

Studios: I don't believe in good or bad studios, it doesn't matter what they got there. What's important is what you do with what's there. I have seen people going to the best studios in the world and coming out with terrible records and vice versa. The Eurythmics recorded some of their best albums on an 8-track. In addition, I don't forget that it's important to work undisturbed. In New York you will easily be distracted; in Woodstock however, there is nothing else to do but record. (*Music Maker* 1988 Holland)

Mick's Advice: Whatever you do, please do it from your heart. Be faithful to yourself and do what you want to do. That's all I can say. (*Guitarist* 1990 Japan)

Thanks to Cody Melville, mickronson.com and all the great media folks (radio, television and print) who helped make this appendix possible. English translations courtesy: Naomi Fujiyama, Pasquale Truglia, Peter Hornberg, Martijn Dierkx and Jari Rasanen, for Sven Gusevik's *Ronson Ablaze!* series.

MICK RONSON MEMORABILIA

A six-page handwritten bio of himself.

(1.)

Left School at 15. played classical piano, violin and Recorder. Stopped playing the violin because I wanted to be a Cello player, Started playing guitar at age 17 after getting hooked on duane eddy the Yardbirds Stones played in a band in Hull Yorkshire. called the Rats a blues based Band, met David Bowie at the end of 1968, then joined David, along with Tony Visconti; and drummer from the Hull john Cambridge. We played a few gigs and then We went into the Studio to Record (The man who Sold the World) after that a few odd gigs Tony Visconti left I brought down other Rats member Woody Woodmansey drums + Trevor Bolder Bass. To form a new band with David, David + myself played a few Solo gigs both playing accoustics + Bass guitars Ex for one duet gigs. then We asked Rick Wakeman to Join us on some gigs, The Next Album to be Recorded after that was Hunky Dory, I was the Band leader + musical arranger writing Orchestration etc. at the Same time we were working with Dana Gillespie which we produced together and I wrote arrangements then We met Lou Reed + Iggy Pop. David + myself produced Lou Reeds Transformer Album: the Single was walk on the wild Side; I knew this fellow Bob Ring whom I met in New York. when David + myself flew to New York. to Sign Davids New Deal with R.C.A Records. Bob was working at R.C.A. in A+R. He was producing Annette Peacock and I fell in love with Her music Bob Asked me if I would like to fly to Toronto where He was going to Produce a New Act on R.C.A. Pure prairie deegue. I flew to Toronto to write orchestration on the Album and Hang out for a Couple of Weeks also I played Bass + Sang on Amy Aters hit Single.

(2.)

We then went on to make Ziggy Stardust + the Spiders from mars being more electric because we had more of a permanent band in between tours these days. I worked with the New Seekers and various other people like Elton John Simon phillips Al Stewart and an assortment of other folks

the Next Album we did after Another American Tour + Japan was Aladin Sane and then yet Another Tour. the Next Album after that was pin ups. David & myself worked with and produced Lulu. Also David produced Mott the Hoople - and I worked with them on Arrangements for their album wrote string parts etc. the Single was All the young Dudes I think at that point I started to work on my 1st Solo Album "Slaughter on 10th Avenue". David worked on lyrics for the Album on 3 Songs, I believe. Tony Defries had this Idea that I was to become another David Cassidy or Something like that a total money making venture and being able to split us up and being able to manage two Hit Recording Stars Anyway, David Started to work on some broadway Ideas for a musical which Never made the light of day And we Started the Recording of Diamond Dogs at that time I think I started working on my Second Solo Album "Play Don't Worry" At that time I Started Hanging out with Ian Hunter from Mott the Hoople. We were good mates from the office. Anyway I decided that Solo Vocal projects for me wasn't quite right. I felt uncomfortable

(3)

Singing as I didn't quite believe in what I was singing
So I decided to finish my recording career on the Road,
Ian asked me to work with Mott on a European tour which
lasted around Six weeks. which had its problems on the Road
Not musically but personally. wise. This lead up to Ian
wanting to leave the band + pursue his own Solo Album which
I worked with him producing + arranging the Album.
the Album was Called Simply (Ian Hunter) We Went on
the road with this Album + Started Hanging out in New York.
When I first moved into New York I Started Hanging out in the
Village where I met people like Bob Dylan   Bobby Neuritt
T. Bone Burnett   Rambling Jack Elliot, Joan Biaz Joni mitchell
and a Hundred others.   Bob Asked me out on the Road with
Him So I Said Yes, A Very good tour meeting and playing
with lots of musicians, + name people, "After that 1st
tour I Started Hanging out in London again working with
(John Couger mellencamp) Who was managed by Tony Defries,
also my manager.   Another tour with Bob Dylan was
going on the road ~~going~~ So I played the next tour with Him
after that tour I went Back to London to check out the
Sex pistols / Clash / Generation X   Etc,   I dived back in
London for a while producing the Rich Kids / Glen Matlock bass
for the Sex pistols + mudge vile (Ultravox) And I produced
another punk band Called (Dead fingers Talk)   I also played
from time to time Jumping up on Stage in pubs etc.

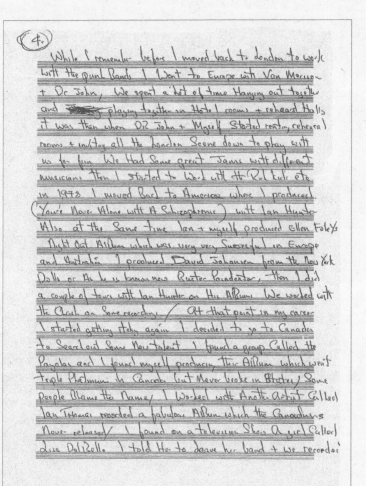

(4.)

While I remember before I moved back to London to work with the punk bands I went to Europe with Van Morrison + Dr John, We spent a lot of time Hanging out together and playing together in Hotel rooms + rehearsal Halls it was then when DR John + Myself started renting rehearsal rooms + inviting all the London Scene down to play with us for fun We Had Some great Jams with different musicians then I started to Work with the Rich Kids etc in 1978 I moved Back to America where I produced (You're Never Alone with A Schizophrenic) with Ian Hunter Also at the Same time Ian + myself produced Ellen Foley's Nich Out Album which was very very Successful in Europe and Australia I produced David Johansen from the New York Dolls or As he is known now Buster Poindexter, then I did a couple of tours with Ian Hunter on His Albums We worked with the Clash on Some recording / At that point in my career I started getting Itchy again I decided to go to Canada to Search out Some New talent I found a group Called the Payola's and I found myself producing this Album which went triple Platinum In Canada but Never broke in States Some people Blame the Name / I Worked with Another Artist Called Ian Tohmas recorded a fabulous Album which the Canadians Never released / I found on a television Show A girl Called Lisa DalBello. I told Her to leave her band + we recorded

⑤

a very Successful Album for Canada Yet again it never broke in the United States / it was then Capitol Records Asked me to work with Tina Turner. We met + talked a lot, I booked the Studio but it all fell through / I then went down to texas where I worked with Charlie Sexton in Austin-texas / I was getting tired again of working with all these people and Nobody knowing about what was going on I mean the public coming up to me and Saying Things like Hi Mick Are you Still in the music business meanwhile Ive been working my balls off producing good music but never quite getting to the public on a wide enough Scale I Was fed up So I went Back to England And I Started to head for European Artists, I spent time in Paris and Florence in Italy producing Some different artist Over there, I Had a great time but yet again Nobody knows about it. I then got a Call from an Old friend in Nashville Singer (Ronno) my Nickname What the fuck are you doing in London get your Ass back over to the States and Come Stay with me in Nashville. So I Went - there I met lots of Artists musicians etc And I met David dyan Jones whom I am producing right Now. We Are on the Second Album the first Album which I produced with Ritchie Albright (Waylon Jennings drummer is Still in the charts,

6.

We have Willie Nelson on the Album & Waylon Jennings but We had to take Willie off because of Record Company politics, the Second Album is almost Complete So before this tour we might have it (finished)

Stepping back a few dines after I got itchy again after Ian Hunters Couple of tours I worked with John Cougar on Jack + Diane I went to Miami with him and worked on arrangement for that Album I played the accoustic guitar on Jack + Diane and while I was working with disc dal Bello I played with David Bowie again in toronto on this Serious moonlight tour

I can't remember Anymore right Now

Also worked on the Who tour in 88 with T Bone Burnette produced a mexican Band called dos illegals for A + M Records recording Some in Spanish and Some in English

THE

BIOGRAPHY

Born in Hull, a fishing port in Yorkshire, England on May 26, 1949, Mick chose at an early age to use his hands making music rather than trouble in the tough and salty town. He began playing piano at age 5, and though not encouraged by his parents, by age 11 had added violin and recorder.

He worked in a grocery store, hung out in bowling alleys and coffee bars, rode a motorcycle and dreamed of becoming a concert pianist. At age 17, he bought himself a guitar and formed his first band appopriately named The Mariners. He managed to survive the fights, the broken glass in the dance halls and three more bands; The King Bees, The Cabaret Band and the Cresters before moving to London to seek his fame and fortune. He worked in a garage, a paint factory, a construction company and three starving bands; Voice, Wanted and The Rats before returning home to Hull and a job as a gardener at the Andrew Marvel School for Girls.

A friend brought him over to David Bowie's house one day and he wound up playing guitar for him that evening on the Top of the Pops TV show. He's been Bowie's arranger and lead guitarist ever since.

Mick has a passion for California beaches and lady-liek females. He loves to cook, swim, watch television, rise early and see his body turn brown in the sun. His first solo album, "Slaughter on Tenth Avenue", will be released by RCA records in January.

A MAINMAN ARTISTE

THE SPIDER WITH THE PLATINUM HAIR

THE

EVERYTHING YOU'VE ALWAYS WANTED TO KNOW ABOUT RONNO -
BUT NEVER DARED TO ASK..

Real Name: Michael Ronson
Nickname: Mick, or Ronno "People just call me that"
Born: 26th May, 1949 in Hull, Yorkshire
Height: 5ft 8ins Weight: 9st 7lbs Hair: Fair Eyes: Green
Family: George & Molly Ronson (parents)
      Margaret Rose (younger sister) David (even younger brother)
Family's Home: In Hull - council house with back garden and front garden -
      lots of trees
Schools Attended: Park Grove Primary School, Wyvern Road School and
      Maybury School "by which time I was very fed up..."
Married or Single (the million dollar question.): Single "Still hunting."
Musical Instruments Played: Violin, Cello, Piano, Recorders, Guitar
Favourite Groups: ·Slade, Jackson 5, Beatles, Stones, Roxy Music, Jeff Beck,
      Wishbone Ash, etc., etc., etc...
Favourite Singers: Annette Peacock, David Bowie, Roy Harper, Melba Moore,
      Michael Jackson, Mick Jagger
Favourite Actor: Paul Newman
Favourite Actress: Bette Davis
Favourite TV Shows: Please Sir, Star Trek, The Johnny Carson Show, Top
      of the Pops
Favourite Colours: Green, red, white
Favourite Food: Everything "From a tin of baked beans to caviar..."
Hobbies: Painting, Gardening, entertaining pretty young ladies...
Favourite Sport: Swimming
What he looks for in a girl (wait for it...): "That twinkling eye...", a nice
      personality, someone interesting to talk to
What he likes to do on a date: Eat dinner, watch Sesame Street on TV and go
      to sleep
Professional Ambition: Carry on what doing now, produce records, go into films
Personal Ambition: Buy a house and some horses and a few ducks. Market tour
      of the world.
Address: Mick Ronson.
      Assorted Hotels,
      Worldwide.

WEIRD & GILLY

An extract from Mick's early studies in landscape gardening

Once Bitten 60
Lookin' at Me 144
Tell it 112
Cool Jerk 104
Standing IN MY Light
Just Another
Pain 104
Beg 138
American Music 86
Sweet Dreamer 127
White Light.
Bastard 96
Loner 117
Womans Intuition 135
Big Time 173 →176
*IRENE   * Memphis
* Dudes
* CleveLand

Hunter Ronson Band set list

WEIRD & GILLY

```
                                                        13,000
                                                    13,500

Guest Name Search: + (dn), - (up), number (to select), or name:
 #  Last Name  First   Conf Num   R     Sec    Type      Grp   page
 1  BRYSON     KEI     61047718   703           IN-HOUSE  389
 2  GOETSCH    CRA     61052268   719    S      IN-HOUSE  389
 3  HELM       HOW     61052268   718    S      IN-HOUSE  389
 4  HUNTER     IAN     61047718   803           IN-HOUSE  389
 5  JOHNSON    TRE     61052268   816    S      IN-HOUSE  389
 6  KILBRIDE   PAT     61052268   816           IN-HOUSE  389
 7  MASTER ACC                    18            Master    389
 8  MORRONGIEL TOM     61052268   824           IN-HOUSE  389
 9  POTTS      MOE     61052268   718           IN-HOUSE  389
10  RONSON     MIC     61047718   810           IN-HOUSE  389
11  SLOPER     BAR     61052268   719           IN-HOUSE  389
12  STEVENS    MAR     61052268   824    S      IN-HOUSE  389
```

Hotel room info for Hunter/Ronson tour, November 1989

334

Hunter/Ronson logo

Japanese advert

MICHAEL RONSON
1946 - 1993

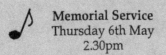 **Memorial Service**
Thursday 6th May
2.30pm

Church Of Jesus Christ Of Latterday Saints
64-68 Exhibition Road
London SW7

Order of Service for Mick's funeral

THE SPIDER WITH THE PLATINUM HAIR

Memorial Concert poster

*All-areas pass for the 1997
Hull Memorial Concert*

The Landmark
LONDON

I think about my dad
everyday. A lot of people
list him as an influence,
but no one was more influenced
by him than me.

To this day when I meet
people who have met him,
they usually don't talk
about his guitar solos, or
his production skills.

222 Marylebone Road London NW1 6JQ
Telephone: (44) (0)20 7631 8000 Facsimile: (44)

Handwritten speech by Mick's daughter Lisa, on accepting the 'Tommy Vance Inspiration Award' at the 2007 Classic Rock ceremony. Note the omission of the "but it's more important to be nice" closing line. Lisa didn't need to write that one down, it was the powerhouse part of her message and one she'd never forget.

They talk about what a
decent, funny, down-to-earth
person he was. If ever
someone felt out of place, he
had a way of making them
feel liked, or loved, or accepted
because to him, they were.

He taught me to be strong and
courageous, but most of all
he taught me to be kind. A
rather small and gentle lesson
to receive from someone who
appeared so much larger than
life, wearing more makeup than
I ever have. He taught me
it's nice to be important...

MICK RONSON US/UK ALBUM DISCOGRAPHY
BY SVEN GUSEVIK

NOTE: First time releases only are listed, unless re-issues came with extra material.

SLAUGHTER ON 10TH AVENUE

Love Me Tender / Growing Up and I'm Fine / Only After Dark / Music Is Lethal / I'm the One / Pleasure Man – Hey Ma Get Papa / Slaughter on 10th Avenue
CD bonus tracks: Solo on 10th Avenue / Leave My Heart Alone / Love Me Tender / Slaughter on 10th Avenue
1974 LP (UK) RCA APL1-0353
1974 LP (US) RCA APL1-0353
1997 CD (UK) Snapper SMMCD 503
1997 CD (US) Snapper 155032

PLAY DON'T WORRY

Billy Porter / Angel No. 9 / This Is for You / White Light, White Heat / Play Don't Worry / Hazy Days / Girl Can't Help It / Empty Bed / Woman
CD bonus tracks: Seven Days / Stone Love / I'd Rather Be Me / Life on Mars / Pain in the City / Dogs / Seven Days / 28 Days Jam / Woman
1975 LP (UK) RCA APL1 0681
1975 LP (US) RCA APL1-0681
1997 CD (UK) Snapper SMMCD 504
1997 CD (US) Snapper 155042

YUI ORTA
(credited to Hunter/Ronson)

American Music / The Loner / Women's Intuition / Tell It like It Is / Livin' in a Heart / Big Time / Cool / Beg a Little Love / Sons 'n' Lovers / Sweet Dreamer
1989 CD bonus tracks:
Following in Your Footsteps / Pain / How Much More Can I Take
2003 CD additional bonus

tracks: Fourth Hour of My Sleep / Powers of Darkness

1989 LP (US) Mercury 838 973-1

1990 LP (UK) Mercury 838 973-1

1989 CD (US) Mercury 838 973-2

1990 CD (UK) Mercury 838 973-2

2003 CD (UK) Cherry Red Lemon CDLEM06

HEAVEN AND HULL

Don't Look Down / Like a Rolling Stone / When The World Falls Down / Trouble With Me / Life's a River / You And Me / Colour Me / Take A Long Line / Midnight Love / All the Young Dudes

1994 LP (UK) Epic EPC 474742 1

1994 CD (UK) Epic EPC 474742 2

1994 CD (US) Epic EK 53796

BBC LIVE IN CONCERT (credited to Hunter/ Ronson)

Once Bitten Twice Shy / How Much More Can I Take / Beg a Little Love / Following in Your Footsteps / Just Another Night / Sweet Dreamer / (Give Me Back My) Wings / Standin' in My Light / Bastard / The Loner / You're Never Too Old to Hit the Big Time / All the Way

from Memphis / Irene Wilde

1995 CD (UK) Windsong WINCD 078

1995 CD (US) ROIR/Windsong WINCD 078

JUST LIKE THIS

Just Like This / I'd Give Anything to See You / Takin' a Train / Hard Life / (I'm Just a) Junkie for Your Love / Crazy Love / Hey Grandma / Is That Any Way / I've Got No Secrets / Hard Headed Woman / Roll like the River / Angel No. 9 **Bonus disc:** Crazy Love / I'd Give Anything to See You (Right Now) / Takin' the Next Trrain / Hard Life / Junkie / Hey Grandma / Just like This / Ronno's Bar & Grill

1999 CD (UK) NMC Pilot 50

[first 2000 with bonus 'outtakes' CD]

SHOWTIME

Crazy Love / Hey Grandma / Takin' A Train / Junkie / I'd Give Anything to See You / Hard Life / Just Like This / Sweet Dreamer / FBI / White Light, White Heat / Darling Let's Have Another Baby / Slaughter on 10th Avenue **Bonus disc:** FBI / Take A

THE SPIDER WITH THE PLATINUM HAIR

Long Line / Trouble With You,
Trouble With Me / Don't Look
Down / Interview / Angel
No.9
1999 CD (UK) NMC Pilot 16X
[first 5000 with bonus 'live in Sweden ' CD]

INDIAN SUMMER
Indian Summer / Tinker Street
/ Satellite 1 / Get On With It
/ Ballad Of Jack Daniels / Blue
Velvet Skirt / Midnight Love /
Satellite 1 / Blue Velvet Skirt /
Plane To England / China / I'd
Give Anything to See You
Bonus disc: film screen-test
dialogue
2000 CD (UK) NMC Pilot 57 *[first
2000 with bonus CD]*

MICK RONSON US/UK SINGLES DISCOGRAPHY

(* credited to Hunter/Ronson)

1974 UK/US –
Love Me Tender /
Slaughter on 10th Avenue
(RCA 11474XST – flexidisc)

1974 UK –
Love Me Tender /
Only After Dark
(RCA APBO 0212)

1974 US –
Love Me Tender /
Only After Dark
(RCA APBO 0212)

1974 UK –
Slaughter on 10th Avenue /
Leave My Heart Alone
(RCA LPBO 5022)

1974 US –
Slaughter on 10th Avenue /
Leave My Heart Alone
(RCA APBO 0291)

1974 UK -
Billy Porter / Seven Days
(RCA 2482)

1974 US -
Billy Porter / Hazy Days
(RCA PB 10237)

1985 UK –
Billy Porter / Slaughter on 10th
Avenue (RCA GOLD 546)

***1989 US –**
–American Music /
Tell It like It Is
(Mercury 874 934-4 – cassette single)

***1989 US –**
Women's Intuition /
Following in Your Footsteps
(Mercury 876 478-4 – cassette single)

***1990 UK –**
American Music / Tell It like It
Is (Mercury MER315 – 7" single)

***1990 UK –**
American Music / Tell It like It
Is (Mercury MERX315 – 12" single)

***1990 UK -**
–American Music / Tell It like
It Is / Sweet Dreamer
(Mercury MERCD315 – CD single)

THE SPIDER WITH THE PLATINUM HAIR

*1990 UK -
American Music /
Tell It like It Is
(Mercury MERMC315 - cassette single)

1994 UK -
Don't Look Down /
Slaughter on 10th Avenue
(Epic 660358 4 - cassette)

1994 UK -
-Don't Look Down /
Slaughter on 10th Avenue /
Billy Porter /
Love Me Tender
(Epic 660358 2 - CD single)

1994 UK -
Don't Look Down /
Slaughter on 10th Avenue /
Billy Porter /
Love Me Tender
(Epic 660358 6 - 12" single)

MICK RONSON SESSION
DISCOGRAPHY
BY SVEN GUSEVIK

**IMPORTANT –
How to read the
discography:**

Records issued before 1987 will be listed with their original vinyl catalogue number, even if a CD re-issue exists. For post-1987 releases, compact disc catalogue numbers will be listed. If an album was made available in both formats, a (@) symbol will be printed next to the album title (although only one format will be listed - usually CD). The same symbol (@) is also used on older titles to indicate that CD re-issues exist.

Compilation albums are included only if they have non-album tracks. Promo pressings are listed only when no stock copies exist. Albums are listed in CAPITAL LETTERS to easily separate them from singles.

The catalogue numbers are prefaced with a country code:

(UK) = England
(US) = USA
(CAN) = Canada
(FRA) = France
(GER) = Germany
(HOL) = Holland
(ITA) = Italy
(NOR) = Norway
(SWE) = Sweden

ARCO VALLEY

[see also Andi Sexgang]
1986
LOVE AND DANGER
(ITA) IRA 508005-1

JOHNNY AVERAGE BAND

[see also The Falcons, The New York Yanquis]
1980
SOME PEOPLE
(GER) Bearsville 203289320 -
(US) Bearsville BRK 3514

1981
Ch Ch Cherie / Gotta Go Home
(UK) Island WIP 6676 – (US) Bearsville
49761

LISA BADE
1982
SUSPICION
(US) A&M SP-6-4897
1982
–Ain't No Way to Treat a Lady /
Pile-Up on the Highway
(US) A&M AM-2437

DAVID BOWIE
[see also Arnold Corns]
1969
–*DAVID BOWIE* @ –
(UK) Philips SBL 7912 –
(US) Mercury 61246
(renamed "Man of Words,
Man of Music")
1970
–*THE MAN WHO SOLD
THE WORLD* @ –
(UK) Mercury 6338 041 – (US)
Mercury 61325
1971
HUNKY DORY @ –
(UK) RCA SF 8244 – (US) RCA LSP
4623
1972
Various Artists:

GLASTONBURY FAYRE (UK)
Revelation Records 001
1972
–*THE RISE AND FALL OF
ZIGGY STARDUST* @ –
(UK) RCA SF 8287 – (US) RCA LSP
4702
1972
*THE MAN WHO SOLD
THE WORLD* @ –
(UK) RCA LSP 4816 – (US) RCA LSP
4816
1973
ALADDIN SANE @ –
(UK) RCA RS 1001 – (US) RCA LSP
4852
1973
PINUPS @
(UK) RCA RS 1003 – (US) RCA LSP
0291
1979
CHANGESONEBOWIE @ –
(UK) RCA RS 1055 – (US) RCA
APL1 1732
1983
BOWIE RARE
(UK) RCA PL 45406 – (US) RCA PL
45406
1983
–*ZIGGY STARDUST
– THE MOTION PICTURE* @ –
(UK) RCA PL 84862 – (US) RCA CPL
2-4862

1989

SOUND AND VISION @ -

(US) Rykodisc 90120/21/22

1993

-BLACK TIE WHITE NOISE @ -

(UK) BMG 74321 13697 -

(US) Savage 7478550212 2

1994

-SANTA MONICA '72 @ -

(UK) Trident Music GY002 -

(US) Griffin GCD-392-2

1995

RARESTONEBOWIE @ -

(UK) Trident Music GY014

1996

BBC SESSIONS 1969-1972 SAMPLER

(UK) NMC NMCD 0072

1997

-THE BEST OF DAVID BOWIE 1969/1974

(UK) EMI 7243 8 21849 2 8 -

(US) EMI/Capitol 72438-21320-2-8

2000

BOWIE AT THE BEEB

(UK) EMI 7243 528629 2 4

2008

LIVE SANTA MONICA '72 @ -

(UK) EMI BOWLIVE 201072

1970

–Memory of a Free Festival Part 1 / Part 2

(UK) Mercury 6052 026 - (US) Mercury 73075

1971

Holy Holy [#1] / Black Country Rock (UK) Mercury 6052 049

1971

All the Madmen [mono/stereo promo] (US) Mercury 73173

1972

Changes / Andy Warhol

(UK) RCA 2160 - (US) RCA 74-0605

1972

Starman / Suffragette City

(UK) RCA 2199 - (US) RCA 74-0719

1972

John I'm Only Dancing [version #1] / Hang Onto Yourself

(UK) RCA 2263

1972

Jean Genie / Hang Onto Yourself

(US) RCA 74-0838

1972

Jean Genie / Ziggy Stardust

(UK) RCA 2302

1973

John I'm Only Dancing [version #2] / Hang Onto Yourself

(UK) RCA 2263

1973

Life on Mars? / The Man Who Sold the World

(UK) RCA 2316
1973
Drive In Saturday / Round and
Round (UK) RCA 2352
1973
Space Oddity /
The Man Who Sold the World
(US) RCA 74-0876
1973
Sorrow / Amsterdam
(UK) RCA 2424 - (US) RCA APBO
0160
1973
Time / Prettiest Star
(US) RCA APBO 0001
1973
Let's Spend the Night Together /
Lady Grinning Soul
(US) RCA APBO 0028
1974
Rock 'n' Roll Suicide /
Quicksand
(UK) RCA LPBO 5021 - (US) RCA
LPBO 5021
1974
Diamond Dogs /
Holy Holy [version #2]
(UK) RCA APBO 0293 - (US) RCA
APBO 0293
1975
Space Oddity / Changes /
Velvet Goldmine
(UK) RCA 2593

1983
White Light White Heat [live] /
Cracked Actor [live]
(UK) RCA 372
1989
(CDV single) John I'm Only
Dancing / Changes / Supermen
/ Ashes to Ashes (US) Rykodisc
RCDV 1018.
Only available with the "Sound &
Vision" boxed set
1989
(CD promo) Round and Round
(US) Ryko RCDPRO 0120
1990
(CD promo) Growing Up
(US) Ryko RCDPRO 9005
1994
(CD) Ziggy Stardust /
Waiting for That Man / The
Jean Genie
(FRA) Trident GYCD S002 -
and (US) Griffin GCD-382-2.
The French CD was used as a UK
promo as well.
1994
-(7") Ziggy Stardust /
Waiting for That Man
(US) Griffin [no catalogue # issued].
Only available with the digipack version
of "Santa Monica" CD

BROKEN HOMES
1989
studio sessions – *not released*

T-BONE BURNETT
1983
-PROOF THROUGH THE
NIGHT @ -
(UK) Demon FIEND 14 –
(US) Warner Brothers WB 23921
1983
-(12" promo) Radio Sampler:
The Murder Weapon / Fatally
Beautiful / Baby Fall Down
(US) Warner Brothers PRO-A-S074

JOHN CALE / CORKY
LAING / IAN HUNTER
[see also Corky Laing]
1978
studio sessions – *not released*

CARELESS TALK
1977
studio sessions – *not released*

DAVID CASSIDY
1976
GETTIN' IT IN THE
STREETS
(US) RCA RVP 6108
1976
Gettin' It in the Streets /

I'll Have to Go Away
(UK) RCA 2749 - (US) RCA PB
10788

MICHAEL CHAPMAN
1970
-FULLY QUALIFIED
SURVIVOR
@ - (UK) Harvest SHVL 764 – (US)
Harvest 816
1977
-THE MAN WHO HATED
MORNINGS
@ - (UK) Decca SKL-R 5290 – see
below
1994
-DOGS GOT MORE SENSE:
THE DECCA YEARS 1974-
1977
(UK) Shakedown Shakebox 124Z
[2CD set includes the full "The Man
Who Hated Mornings" album]

ARNOLD CORNS
(aka David Bowie & The
Spiders from Mars)
1971
Moonage Daydream /
Hang Onto Yourself
(UK) B&C CB 149
1971
Hang Onto Yourself /
Man in the Middle

(UK) B&C CB 189
1974
Hang Onto Yourself /
Man in the Middle
(UK) Mooncrest MOON 25
1985
-(12") Looking for a Friend /
Hang Onto Yourself /
Man in the Middle
(NOR) KrazyCat PAST2

DALBELLO
1984
WHOMANFORSAYS @ -
(GER) Capitol 2401 3814 -
(US) Capitol ST 12318
1984
-Gonna Get Close To You /
Guilty By Association
(GER) Capitol 20 01627 - (CAN)
Capitol 72942

1984
-(12") Gonna Get Close to You
[two versions]/Guilty By
Association
(GER) Capitol 2002046
1984
Animal / Target, My Eyes Are
Aimed at You
(CAN) Capitol B72954
1984
(12") Animal [two versions] /

Cardinal Sin
(HOL) Capitol 20 04706
1984
(12") Animal [three versions]
(US) Capitol V-8619 - (CAN) Capitol
75074

ROGER DALTREY
1977
ONE OF THE BOYS @ -
(UK) Polydor 2442 146 - (USA) MCA
MCA 2271
1977
One of the Boys /
You Put Something Better
Inside
(UK) Polydor 2058 896
1977
(12" promo) One of the Boys
[long/short promo]
(US) MCA L33-1967
1977
Avenging Annie
[long/short promo]
(US) MCA 40800
1977
Say It Ain't So, Joe
[long/short promo]
(US) MCA 40765
1978
Say It Ain't So, Joe / Prisoner
(UK) Polydor 2058 986
1978

Written on the Wind / Dear
John
(UK) Polydor 2121 319

DEAD FINGERS TALK
1978
-*STORM THE REALITY
STUDIOS* @ -
(UK) PYE NSPH 24
[2002 CD re-issue adds 8 bonus tracks]
1978
Hold On to Rock 'n' Roll /
Can't Think Straight
(UK) PYE 7N 46069

SANDY DILLON
1985
Flowers / Heavy Boys
(UK) Mainman SANDY 1
1985
*DANCING ON THE
FREEWAY* - *unreleased album*

LISA DOMINIQUE
1986
-(tape) Act Tuff / The Big Kiss
/ Dreammaker
(UK) Scorpio Records [no catalogue #]

DR. JOHN
1977
Studio sessions - *not released*
(see Van Morrison)

BOB DYLAN
1976
HARD RAIN @ -
(UK) CBS 86016 - (US) Columbia PC-
34349
1985
BIOGRAPH @ -
(UK) CBS 66509 - (US) Columbia
C5X 38830
1991
THE BOOTLEG SERIES @ -
(UK) CBS 4680862 - (US) Columbia
C3K 47382
2002
-*LIVE 1975*
(US) Columbia Legacy C2K 87047 -
(UK) Columbia Legacy 510140 2
[BONUS DVD (only available with CD):
Tangled Up in Blue / Isis / It Ain't Me,
Babe]
1978
(12" promo) 4 songs from
RENALDO & CLARA movie
(US) CBS XSM 164035
1995
Dignity / Dignity / John Brown
/ It Ain't Me Babe (UK) Sony
662076 5

EC²
1990
You're My Man /
Communication

(SWE) Mercury 875560-7
1990
I'm So Sorry / Kiss Me
(SWE) Mercury 876922-7
1990
Passion / I'm Forever Blowing
Bubbles
(SWE) Mercury 878500-7
1990
MR produced album – *not
released* ("Koshima", "Not My Day"
and "Summertime" from the unreleased
album are available at www.myspace.
com/ec24u)

THE FALCONS

(see also Johnny Average, The
Phantoms)
1980
Studio sessions – *not released*

THE FALLEN ANGELS

1973
Studio sessions – *not
released*

THE FATAL FLOWERS

1988
JOHNNY D. IS BACK! @ -
(GER) WEA 242 333-2 - (US) Atlantic
7 81872-2
1990
PLEASURE GROUND @ -

(HOL) Mercury 842 581-2
1988
Second Chance /
Second Chance
(HOL) WEA 247 269-7
1988
Movin' Target / Johnny D Is
Back
(HOL) WEA 247 761-7
1988
(7") Rock 'n' Roll Star /
No Expectations (live)
(HOL) WEA 247 875-7
1988
(CD) Rock 'n' Roll Star / No
Expectations (live) / Younger
Days
(HOL) WEA 247 875-2
1988
(12" promo, also on CD)
Rock 'n' Roll Star [two
versions]
(US) Atlantic PR 2483
1990
(7") How Many Years / Speed
of Life (HOL) Mercury 875 074-7
1990
(CD) How Many Years / Speed
of Life (HOL) Mercury 875 074-2
1990
(7") Both Ends Burning /
Burning
(HOL) Mercury 875 542-7

1990

(CD) Both Ends Burning /
Burning

(HOL) Mercury 875 542-2

1990

(CD) Better Times /
Better Times (acoustic) /
Heroes

(HOL) Mercury 878 205-2

THE FENTONS / PAUL
FENTON

1988

studio sessions – *not released*

1991

VARIOUS ARTISTS:
*A COMPILATION OF
CANADIAN NEW MUSIC*

(CAN) Intreprid CD-4

1997

PAUL FENTON: *BINSON'S
BLUES* (CAN) Compact Music

CMCD 0971

2007

*RED HOT SLIDE 1995-2002
(THE OFFICIAL BOOTLEG)*

(CAN) Jealous Monk Records

DAG FINN

1991

*THE WONDERFUL
WORLD OF D. FINN*

(SWE) Mercury 848 494-2

ELLEN FOLEY

1979

NIGHTOUT @ -

(UK) Epic EPC 83718 - (US) Epic JE
36052

1979

We Belong to the Night /
Young Lust (UK) Epic EPC 7847

1979

What's a Matter Baby /
Hideaway

(UK) Epic EPC 7999 – (US) Epic
9-50770

1979

Stupid Girl / Young Lust

(UK) Epic EPC 8122 – (US) Epic
9-50770

1979

Sad Song / Don't Let Go

(UK) Epic EPC 8561 - (US) Epic
9-50839

1982

MR produced studio demos -
not released

STANLEY FRANK

1982

-studio sessions – *not released*

["Canadian Boy", "Scum Heaven" and
"Run for the Sun" are available from
www.stanleyfrank.com]

KINKY FRIEDMAN
1976
LASSO FROM EL PASO @ -
(UK) Epic EPC 81640 - (US) Epic 34304

FUNHOUSE
1991
(Tape) Gotta Let Loose /
World on Fire / Twisted Heart
(US) Rainbow RC-101

DANA GILLESPIE
1974
WEREN'T BORN A MAN
(UK) RCA APL1-0354 - (US) RCA
APL1-0354
1994
ANDY WARHOL
(UK) Trident Music GY001 -
(US) Griffin GCD-355-2
1974
Andy Warhol / Dizzy Heights
(UK) RCA 2466

GIRLS NEXT DOOR
(featuring Daryl Hannah)
1984
Studio sessions - *not released*

GUAM
(Ronson & Roger McGuinn
with friends)
1976

Studio sessions - *not released*
(see entry for McGuinn)

STEVE HARLEY
1986
EL GRAN SENOR - *unreleased*
album
1985
Irresistible / Lucky Man
(UK) RAK RAK 389

MARY HOGAN
1976
Studio sessions - *not released*

IAN HUNTER
(see also Hunter/Ronson)
1975
IAN HUNTER @ -
(UK) CBS 80710 - (US) Columbia PC
33480
1979
YOU'RE NEVER ALONE
WITH A SCHIZOPHRENIC
@ - (UK/US) Chrysalis CHR 1214
1980
LIVE / WELCOME TO THE
CLUB @ - (UK) Chrysalis CJT6 -
(US) Chrysalis CHR 1269
1981
SHORT BACK N' SIDES @ -
(UK/US) Chrysalis CHR 1326
1983

ALL OF THE GOOD
ONES ARE TAKEN @ -
(UK) CBS 25379 - (US) Columbia PC
38626
1984
VARIOUS ARTISTS:
TEACHERS [with "(I'm) The
Teacher"] @ -
(UK) Capitol 2402471 – (US) Capitol
SV 12371
1984
VARIOUS ARTISTS:
FRIGHT NIGHT [with "I'm A
Good Man In A Bad Time"] @ -
(UK) Epic EPC 70270 - (US) Private
SZ 40087.
2000
MISSING IN ACTION -
(UK) NMC Pilot 52
2001
ONCE BITTEN TWICE SHY
(UK/US) Sony 496284-2
2006
THE JOURNEY:
A RESTROSPECTIVE OF
IAN HUNTER AND MOTT
THE HOOPLE
(UK) Columbia 82876 890022
1975
Once Bitten Twice Shy /
3000 Miles from Here
(UK) CBS 3194 - (US) Columbia
3-10161

1975
Who Do You Love / Boy
(UK) CBS 3486
1979
When the Daylight Comes /
Life After Death
(UK/US) Chrysalis CHS 2324
1979
Ships / Wild East
(UK) Chrysalis CHS 2346
1979
Just Another Night / Cleveland
Rocks (US) Chrysalis 2352
1979
Cleveland Rocks / Bastard
(UK) Chrysalis CHS 2390
1979
We Gotta Get Out of Here /
Once Bitten Twice Shy /
Bastard / Cleveland Rocks /
Sons and Daughters / One of
the Boys
(UK) Chrysalis CHS 2434
1980
We Gotta Get Out of Here /
Sons and Daughters
(US) Chrysalis 2405
1981
Lisa Likes Rock 'n' Roll / Noises
(UK) Chrysalis CHS 2542
1981
I Need Your Love / Keep On
Burnin'

(US) Chrysalis 2542
1981
Central Park N' West / Rain
(US) Chrysalis 2569
1983
All of the Good Ones… /
Death 'n' Glory Boys
(UK) CBS A3541 - (US) Columbia
38-0329
1983
(12") All of the Good Ones Are
Taken / Death 'n' Glory Boys
/ Traitor
(UK) CBS TA3541
1984
(12" promo) I'm the Teacher
[two versions]
(US) Capitol SPRO-9244

**IRON CITY
HOUSEROCKERS**
1980
*HAVE A GOOD TIME
(BUT GET OUT ALIVE)* @ -
(US) MCA MCA-511
1980
Junior's Bar [stereo/stereo
promo]
(US) MCA MCA-51002
1980
Hypnotised / Old Man Bar
(UK) MCA 651

DAVID JOHANSEN
1979
IN STYLE @ -
(UK) Blue Sky SKY-83745 - (US) Blue
Sky 36082
1978
Funky But Chic / Let Go
Strong
(UK) Blue Sky SKY-6663
1979
Melody / Wreckless Crazy
(US) Blue Sky 2781
1979
Swaheto Woman /
She Knew She Was Falling in
Love
(UK) Blue Sky SKY-8125 – (US) Blue
Sky 2789

ELTON JOHN
1992
RARE MASTERS
(US) Polydor 314514138-2
1994
CLASSIC ELTON JOHN
(US) Polydor 521 17955
1995
*TUMBLEWEED
CONNECTION*
re-issue - (UK) Mercury 528 155-2 -
(US) Rocket 12-28155
1989
-(CD promo) Madman Across

the Water [long/short versions]
(US) Polydor CDP 819

KISS THAT
1986
KISS AND TELL
(UK) Chrysalis CHR 1513
1986
(12") March Out / Simple Girl
(UK) Chrysalis CHS 122966

CORKY LAING / FELIX PAPPALARDI / IAN HUNTER
1999
THE SECRET SESSIONS
(US) Pet Rock PETCD 60042

MARIE-LAURE ET LUI
1987
(7") C'est pas le Pérou / Sam Me Glace (FRA) Wea 248107-7
1987
-(12") C'est pas le Pérou (two versions) / Sam Me Glace
(FRA) Wea 248962-0

THE LEATHER NUN
1991
(CD) Girls / I Ain't Turning Back / Girls (SWE) Wire WRCDS 034
1991

NUN PERMANENT
(SWE) Wire WRCD 018
1994
-A SEEDY COMPILATION
(SWE) MGV MGV 117
[includes unreleased "Save My Soul"]

LENNEX
[see also Perfect Affair, Rick Rose]
1981
(one sided flexi disc) Struggle
(CAN) Evatone 81382XS
1982
MIDNIGHT IN NIAGARA -
unreleased album
1982
-VARIOUS ARTISTS:
Q107 HOMEGROWN VOL. 4
(CAN) Basement Records BASE X6008
[includes "She's Got It" by Lennex]
2004
-VARIOUS ARTISTS:
WHEN CANCON ROCKED
Vol.1
(CAN) Bullseye BLR-CD-4015)
[includes "She's Got It" by Lennex]

LES FRADKIN
2006
GOIN' BACK (US) RRO RRO-1009

LOS ILLEGALS
1983
INTERNAL EXILE
(US) A&M SP-4925
1999
*AY CALIFAS! RAZA ROCK
OF THE 70s* (US) Rhino R2 72920

LULU
1973
-The Man Who Sold the World
/ Watch That Man
(UK) Polydor 2001490 - (US) Chelsea
3001
1976
*HEAVEN AND EARTH
AND THE STARS*
(US) Chelsea CHL-518
1994
*FROM CRAYONS TO
PERFUME:*
Best Of Lulu
(US) Rhino 71815

DAVID LYNN JONES
1987
*HARD TIMES ON EASY
STREET* @ -
(UK/US) Mercury 832 518
1987
Bonnie Jean /
Valley of a Thousand Years
(US) Mercury 888-733-7

1987
The Rogue (stereo/stereo promo)
(US) Mercury 8705257
1988
MR produced a new album –
not released

ROGER McGUINN
1976
-*CARDIFF ROSE* @ -
(UK) CBS 81369 - (US) Columbia
34154
[the 2004 US re-issue CD includes
unreleased demo of "Soul Love"]
1976
Take Me Away / Time
(US) Columbia 10385

BENNY MARDONES
1978
THANK GOD FOR GIRLS
(US) Private Stock PS 7007
1978
-(12" promo EP) All for a
Reason / Thank God for Girls /
I Started a Joke / Timeless
(US) Private Stock PS 1000

MEAT LOAF
1981
DEAD RINGER @ -
(UK) Epic EPC 32692 - (US) Epic FE
36007

1981

Dead Ringer For Love /
More Than You Deserve

(UK) Epic EPC 1697

JOHN COUGAR
MELLENCAMP

1976

*–CHESTNUT STREET
INCIDENT @ –*

(UK) Mainman MML 602 - (US) MCA
2225

1982

–AMERICAN FOOL @ –

(UK) Riva RIVA RVLP 16 -
(US) Riva RIVA 7501

1982

(7") Hurts So Good / Close
Enough (UK) Riva RIVA 36

1982

(7") Jack & Diane / Danger List
– (UK) Riva RIVA 37

1982

(12") Jack & Diane / Danger
List / Need A Lover –

(UK) Riva RIVA 37T

1982

(7") Jack & Diane / Can You
Take It

(US) Riva R210

1982

(12" promo) Jack & Diane (two
versions) (US) Polygram MK-209

1983

(7") Hand to Hold On To /
Hurts So Good

(UK) Riva RIVA 38

1983

(12") Hand to Hold On To /
Hurts So Good

(UK) Riva RIVA 38T

CODY MELVILLE

1986

*–studio sessions – unreleased
["One More Goodnight", "Voices",
"International Appeal" and "Drop
The Needle On" are available from
www.myspace.com/session86]*

MILKWOOD

1972

Watching You Go / Here I
Stand

(UK) Warner Bothers K16141

MODA

1986

CANTO PAGANO (ITA) IRA

508 009

MORRISSEY

1992

YOUR ARSENAL @ –

(UK) EMI CDCSD3790 - (US) Sire 9
26994-2

1993

-(video) *THE MALADY LINGERS ON*

(UK) HMV MVR4900063 -

(US) WB/Reprise 3-38359

1992

-We Hate It When Our Friends Become Successful / Suedehead / I've Changed My Plea To Guilty / Pregnant For The Last Time @ -

(UK) EMI CDPOP 1629

1992

-We Hate It When Our Friends Become Successful / Suedehead / I've Changed / Pregnant For The Last Time / Alsatian Cousin @ -

(US) Sire 9 405 60-2

1992

-You're the One for Me Fatty / Pashernate Love / There Speaks a True Friend @ -

(UK) EMI CDPOP 1630

1992

-Tomorrow / Let the Right One Slip In / Pashernate Love @ - (US) Sire 9 40580-2

1992

-Certain People I Know / You've Had Her / Jack the Ripper @ - (UK) EMI CDPOP 1631

1992

Glamorous People [1-track CD promo] (US) Sire PRO-CD-5752

MOTT THE HOOPLE

1972

ALL THE YOUNG DUDES @ -

(UK) CBS 65184 - (US) Columbia KC 31750

1976

GREATEST HITS @ -

(UK) CBS 81225 - (US) Columbia PC 34368

1993

-*THE BALLAD OF MTH*

(UK) Columbia CD 46973 -

(US) Columbia 2CK 46973

1974

Saturday Gigs / Jerkin' Crocus-Sucker-Violence

(UK) CBS 2754

THE MUNDANES

1982

Studio sessions - *not released*

DAVE NERGE

1990

Studio sessions - *not released*

**THE NEW YORK
YANQUIS**
[see also The Falcons,
Johnny Average Band]
1981
Studio sessions – *not released*

ONE THE JUGGLER
1985
SOME STRANGE FASHION
(UK) RCA PL 70606
1985
(7") Hours and Hours / Secret
of Love (UK) RCA RCA 482
1985
(12") Hours and Hours
[extended] / Secret of Love
(UK) RCA RCAT 482

THE PAYOLA$
1982
-*NO STRANGER TO
DANGER*
(UK) A&M AMLH 64908 – (US) A&M
SP6-4908
1983
HAMMER ON A DRUM
(UK) A&M AMLH 64958 – (US) A&M
SP6-4958
1987
*BETWEEN A ROCK
& A HYDE PLACE*
(CAN) A&M CD 9134

1982
Eyes of a Stranger / Where Is
This Love (CAN) A&M AM576
1982
(12") Eyes of a Stranger /
Soldier
(CAN) A&M SP 23502
1982
Never Said I Loved You /
Soldier
(UK) A&M AM 164 – (CAN) A&M
AM623
1982
Romance / Mystery to Me
(UK) A&M AMS 8241
1983
-I'll Find Another / Christmas Is
Coming
(CAN) A&M AM627 – (US) A&M
AM-2589
1983
-(12" promo) Christmas Is
Coming / I'll Find Another (US)
A&M SP-12084
1983
Where Is This Love / I Am a
City
(CAN) A&M AM635
1983
You're the Only One /
Eyes of a Stranger
(US) A&M AM-2733

THE PHANTOMS
1987
(tape) *THE PHANTOMS*
(US) Opaque Productions OPC1
1987
-(tape) *VARIOUS ARTISTS:*
A WOODSTOCK SAMPLER
Vol 2
(US) Wildlife Records 410

ANNETTE PEACOCK
1978
X-DREAMS @ -
(UK) Aura AUL 702 -
(US) Tomato 7025
1978
Don't Be Cruel /
Dear Bela
(UK) Aura AUS 102

PERFECT AFFAIR
[see also Lennex, Rick Rose]
1983
PERFECT AFFAIR
(UK) Attic LAT 1182 - (CAN) Attic
LAT 1182
2001
VISIONS
(CAN) Pacemaker PACE 036
1983
On The Edge / Visions
(CAN) Attic AT303
1984

She's Got It / Crazy
(CAN) Attic AT304

THE PROOF
1981
Unreleased Session

PURE PRAIRIE LEAGUE
1972
BUSTIN' OUT @ -
(UK) RCA SF 8417 - (US) RCA LSP
4769
1972
Amie / Memories
(US) RCA 101184
1975
Amie / Angel No. 9
(GER) RCA YHPBO-0900

THE RATS
1995
- *THE RISE AND FALL OF*
BERNIE GRIPPLESTONE
@ - (UK) Tenth Planet TP012
2009
THE FALL AND RISE –
A RAT'S TALE
(UK) Angel Air 165

GENYA RAVAN
1979
-*AND I MEAN IT!* @ -
(GER) 20th Century Fox 6370 296 -

(US) 20th Century Fox T595
1979
Junkman / Love Isn't Love
(NOR) 20th C Fox6162 168

PHILIP RAMBOW
1977
studio sessions / demos – *not released*
["Fallen" available at www.mickronson.com]

AXELLE RED
1985
studio sessions – *not released*

LOU REED
1972
–*TRANSFORMER* @ –
(UK) RCA LSP 4807 – (US) RCA LSP 4807
[2004 CD re-issue includes demo versions of "Hangin' Round" and "Perfect Day"]
1972
Walk on the Wild Side / Perfect Day (UK) RCA 2303 – (US) RCA 0887
1972
Vicious / Satellite of Love
(UK) RCA 2318
1972
Walk and Talk It / Satellite of Love
(US) RCA 0964

RICH KIDS (see also Midge Ure)
1978
–*GHOSTS OF PRINCES IN TOWERS*
@ – (UK) EMI EMC 3263 – (US) EMI 5-1010
1998
BURNING SOUNDS
(UK) Rev Ola CREV 051CD
1978
Rich Kids / Empty Words
(UK) EMI 2738
1978
Marching Men / Here Comes the Nice
(UK) EMI 2803
1978
Ghosts of Princes in Towers / Only Arsenic
(UK) EMI 2848

RONNO
1971
The 4th Hour of My Sleep / Powers of Darkness
(UK) Vertigo 6059 029
1971
–The 4th Hour Of My Sleep
mono / stereo (promo)
(US) Vertigo VEDJ1
1990
–*VARIOUS ARTISTS:*

VERTIGO CLASSICS AND RARITIES vol 1 @ -
(UK) Vertigo 846 522-1
2003
-HUNTER RONSON: YUI ORTA
(UK) Cherry Red Lemon CDLEM06

RICK ROSE
[see also Lennex, Perfect Affair]
1987
Gypsy Jewelry /
Under the Sky, Under the Moon
(CAN) CBS CODA87

BOB SARGEANT
1974
FIRST STARRING ROLE
(UK) RCA LPL1 5076
1974
Situation / The Waiting Game
(UK) RCA LPBO 5038

SECRET MISSION
1991
STRANGE AFTERNOON @ -
(NOR) EMI 777-7961122
1991
You Can Run / Follow Me
[promo only]
(NOR) EMI 1375447
1991

(7") Silent Spring / Walking on Glass (NOR) EMI 1375447
1991
(CD) Silent Spring / Walking on Glass / Stay On
(NOR) EMI 1375442
1991
-(CD) Call Out Her Name (2 versions) / Stay by My Side
@ - (NOR) EMI 1375542

ANDI SEXGANG
(see also Arco Valley)
1989
ARCO VALLEY @ -
(UK) Jungle FREUD 24
1995
WESTERN SONGS FOR CHILDREN
(US) Triple X 51186-2
1988
(7") Seven Ways to Kill a Man / Jesus Phoned
(UK) Jungle JUNG 42
1988
-(12") Seven Ways to Kill a Man [2 versions] / Jesus Phoned
(UK) Jungle JUNG 42T
1989
(7") Assassin Years / Power Waits
(UK) Jungle JUNG 48
1989

(12") Assassin Years /
Power Waits
(UK) Jungle JUNG 48T

CHARLIE SEXTON
1984
Studio sessions – *not released*

**SLAUGHTER AND THE
DOGS**
1978
DO IT DOG STYLE @ -
(UK) Decca SKL 5292
1978
Quick Joey Small / Come on
Back
(UK) Decca F13758

SONIC WALTHERS
1992
MEDICATION
(SWE) MNW/Radium RA91782
1991
On The Wall / Time
(SWE) Radium Records RA 070

THE SPARKS
1976
Studio sessions – *not released*

**THE SPIDERS FROM
MARS**
1976
Studio sessions – *not released*

CHRIS SPEDDING
1989
Jam session – *not released*

SPLIT ENZ
1982
Jam session – *not released*

AL STEWART
1973
Studio sessions – *not released*

CASINO STEEL
1991
*-CASINO STEEL & THE
BANDITS feat. Mick Ronson*
(NOR) Revolution REX CD 03
1992
OH BOY (NOR) Revolution REX
CD 04
1991
-(7" promo) Heroine /
When You Walk in the
Room
(NOR) Revolution REXS 4720

IAN THOMAS
1983
STRANGE BREW
[soundtrack]
(CAN) Anthem Records ANR-1-1042
1984
RIDERS ON DARK HORSES
(CAN) Anthem Records ANR-1-1044
1983
Strange Brew / Another Strange
Brew (CAN) Anthem Records ANS-055
1984
I'll Do It Right / Riders on
Dark Horses (CAN) Anthem ANS-058
1984
-Picking Up the Pieces /
She Don't Love You
(CAN) Anthem Records ANS-061

THE TOLL
1988
-*THE PRICE OF
PROGRESSION* @ -
(GER) Geffen 924 201 - (US) Geffen
GHS 24201

TOPAZ
1977
TOPAZ (US) Columbia 34934

MIDGE URE
1985
(12") That Certain Smile / The
Gift / Fade to Grey (UK) Chrysalis
602125
2000
NO REGRETS (UK) EMI 7243 5
2759125

URGENT
1985
CAST THE FIRST STONE @ -
(US) Manhattan ST 53004
1987
-*THINKING OUT LOUD* @ -
(UK) Manhattan 74 6680 -
(US) Manhattan MLT 46680
1987
IRON EAGLE [soundtrack] @ -
(UK) Capitol 24 04981 - (US) Capitol
SV-12499
1985
Running Back / Dedicated to
Love (US) Manhattan B-50005
1985
Love Can Make You Cry /
Dedicated to Love
(US) Manhattan B-50022
1985
(12" promo) Pay Up [two
versions]
(US) Manhattan SPRO 40350

WEIRD & GILLY

RANDY VANWARMER
1994
THE VITAL SPARK
(UK) Alias ALCD 194

XDAVIS
studio sessions – *not released*

TONY VISCONTI
1998
VISCONTI'S INVENTORY
(US) TVP Records ORCH 5276

VISIBLE TARGETS
1982
studio demos – *not released*
1983
AUTISTIC SAVANT
(US) Park Avenue PA82803

THE WILDHEARTS
1993
-EARTH VS THE
WILDHEARTS
(UK) Eastwest 4509-94859-2 –
(US) Eastwest 923 15-2
1993
-(12") Suckerpunch /
My Baby Is a Headfuck [promo
only]
(UK) Eastwest SAM1212

MARS WILLIAMS
1985
studio sessions – *not released*

MICK RONSON'S RECORD COLLECTION

"Music is music – whatever label it falls under."
Mick Ronson WDTX Detroit, Michigan Radio 1986

The slash (/) indicates a b-side whereas the dash (-) notes a special interest.

Mick Ronson's 7" Singles
Clash – *The Call Up* / *Stop the World*
Dillon, Sandy – *Flowers* / *Heavy Boys*
Easton, Sheena – *Sugar Walls* / *Double Standard*
Furs, The – *Love My Way* / *Aeroplane*
Harrison, George – *Give Me Love Give Me Peace on Earth* / *Miss O'Dell*
Hot Chocolate – *I'll Put You Together Again (from Dear Anyone)* / *West End of Park Lane*
Hot Chocolate – *Sex Appeal*
Kramer, Billy J – *Ships That Pass in the Night* / *Is There Any Home like You*
Laure Et Lui, Marie – *C'est pas le Pérou*
Lindisfarne – *Run for Home* / *Stick Together* - D.Ronson is hand written in top corner of label
Quatro, Suzi – *Devil Gate Drive* / *In the Morning*
Wonder, Stevie – *All Day Sucker* / *Easy Goin' Evening (My Mama's Call)*

Mick Ronson's 10" Singles / Extended Plays
Carmichael, Hoagy – *Stardust Road*
Clash – *Black Market Clash* – Promo
Hagen, Nina – *TV Glotzer (White Punks On Dope)* – Promo
Morrissey – *We Hate It When Our Friends Become Successful*
Nelson, Rick - *Four You* – Promo

Mick Ronson's 12" Singles / Extended Plays
Ayers, Roy – *Hot* / *Hot Dub Mix*

Big Audio Dynamite – *Bottom Line* – Promo

CCCP – *Ortodossia II – Red Vinyl*

Clash – *Rock The Casbah* - Promo

Cliff, Jimmy – *Peace Officer / Special* – Promo

Laure Et Lui, Marie – *C'est Pas Le Pérou – Remix*

Sexgang, Andi – *Ida–ho*

Sexgang, Andi – *Les Amants D'Un Jour*

Third World – *Now That We Found Love / One Cold Vibe*

Turner, Tina – *Let's Stay Together* – Promo

XDavis – *Dancing In The Dark*

Mick Ronson's Long Plays

Alpha Band – *Alpha Band*

Animals – *The Animals*

Atkins, Chet – *Picks On The Hits*

Battisti, Lucio – *Il Mio Canto Libero*

Beatles, The – *The Early Beatles*

Beatles, The – *The Beatles (White Album)* – Promo

Beatles, The – *Yesterday and Today*

Beck, Jeff – *Wired*

Bowie, David – *Aladdin Sane*

Bowie, David – *Scary Monsters*

Interview – Promo

Boxer – *Below the Belt*

Brigati – *Lost in the Wilderness*

Briggs, Brian – *New Bigger* – autographed to Suzi, Mick and Lisa

Burnett, T-Bone – *Trap Door*

Burtnick, Glen – *Heroes and Zeroes* – Promo

Bush, Kate – *The Dreaming* – Promo

Bush, Kate – *The Kick Inside* – Promo

CCCP – *Fedeli alla Linea - 1964-1985*

Ciletti, Eddie – *3B Cats* – handwritten note to Mick on cover sleeve

Clapton, Beck, Page – *Guitar Boogie* – Promo

Clapton, Eric – *No Reason to Cry*

Clash, The – *Sandinista*

Colter, Jesse – *Diamond in the Rough*

Cooder, Ry – *Jazz*

Cream – *Best Of*

Creedence Clearwater Revival – *Cosmos Factory*

Creedence Clearwater Revival – *Creedence Clearwater Revival*

Creedence Clearwater Revival – *Green River*

Creedence Clearwater Revival – *Pendulum*

Creedence Clearwater Revival – *Willie and the Poor Boys*

Dagradi, Tony – *Oasis*

DalBello – Masterdiscs – *Sterling Sound – 1-26-1984 – Two Disc Set – Side A and B*

Davis, Miles – *Fat Time* – Promo

Davis, Miles – *The Man with the Horn*

Deburgh, Chris – *The Getaway*

Delaney, Bonnie & Friends - *To Bonnie from Delaney*

Dr. John – *Desitively Bonnaroo*

Dr. John – *Dr. John's Gumbo*

Duran Duran – *Seven and the Ragged Tiger* – Promo

Dury, Ian and the Blockheads – *Laughter* – Promo

Dylan, Bob – *Blond On Blonde*

Dylan, Bob – *Slow Train Coming*

Essex, David– *Rock On*

Everly Brothers – *Born Yesterday*

Faces – *Long Player*

Faithfull, Marianne – *Broken English*

Falco – *Einzelhaft*

Fatal Flowers – *Johnny D Is Back* – eleven copies of this title

File Series – *Lonnie Donegan* – Two Record Set

Flash and the Pan – *Lights in the Night* – Promo

Gordon, Peter – *True Love Ways*

Gorl, Robert – *Night Full Of Tension*

Grant, Eddy – *Can't Get Enough*

Guthrie, Woody – *Greatest Songs*

Haggard, Merle – *Epic Collection Recorded Live*

Hall, George and His Taft Hotel Orchestra 1933-1937

Harper, Roy – *Flashes from the Archives of Oblivion*

Harper, Roy – *Folkjokepus* – two copies of this title

Harper, Roy – *HQ* – two copies of this title – one is a Promo

Harper, Roy – *Lifemask* – Promo

Harper, Roy – *Stormcock*

Harris, Sugarcane – *Sugarcane*

Hartley, Ray – *The Trembling of a Leaf*

Heads Hands and Feet – *Old Soldiers Never Die* – Promo

Heads Hands and Feet – *Tracks* – Ronson's name written on front cover

Holland, Amy – *Amy Holland* – Promo

Houston, Whitney – *Whitney Houston*

Idol, Billy – *Rebel Yell*

Jacksons, The – *Triumph*

Jimi Hendrix Experience – *Electric Ladyland*

Joplin, Janis – *Janis* – Promo

Knack – *Round Trip*

Knight, Gladys and the Pips – *That Special Time of Year* – (Christmas)

Laws, Hubert – *Quincy Jones – Chick Corea & Blanchard – New Earth Sonata*

Loggins, Dave – *Country Sweet*

Los Illegals – *Internal Exile* – Promo

McCartney, Paul – *Pipes of Peace*

Meglio, Del Mio - *N.2 – Mina*

Moda – *Canto Pagano* – two copies

Moondog – *Moondog*

Motown Story – Four Record Set

Murphy, Eddie – *Comedian* – Promo

Neuwirth, Bob – *Bob Neuwirth*

NRBQ – *At Yankees Stadium*

NRBQ – *Scraps and Workshop* – Two Record Set

NRBQ – *Tiddly Winks* – two copies of this title

Oglesby, Carl – *Going to Damascus* – Demo

Original Motion Picture Soundtrack - Annie

Original Motion Picture Soundtrack - Lenny

Original Motion Picture Soundtrack - Midnight Express

Oskar, Lee – *Lee Oskar*

Otis, Johnny – *Rock 'n' Roll Revue*

Payolas – *Masterdisk* – A&M – 16th, March 1982 – Two Disc Set – Side B only

Peacock, Annette – *I'm the One*

Peacock, Annette – *I'm the One* – Re-issue

Peacock, Annette – *X-Dreams*

Perkins, Carl and NRBQ – two copies of this title

Pop, Iggy – *Idiot/Passenger* – Two-Disc LP Set

Pop, Iggy – *Instinct*

Porter, Cole – *Cole Porter's Can Can*

Presley, Elvis – *Back in Memphis*

Presley, Elvis – *Elvis (1973)*

Presley, Elvis – *For Everyone!*

Presley, Elvis – *G.I. Blues*

Presley, Elvis – *Is Back!*

Presley, Elvis – *Return of the Rocker* – Sealed

Presley, Elvis – *That's the Way It Is*

Presley, Elvis – *Worldwide 50 Gold Award Hits, Vol. 1 Boxed Set*

Pretenders – *Learning to Crawl*

Pukwana, Dudo & Spear – *In The Townships*

Rainey, Gertrude 'Ma' – *Queen of the Blues*

RCA August 1975 Red Seal Classical Sampler – Promo

RCA Test Pressing – white label - unknown

Reed, Lou – *Metal Machine Music* – Promo

Reed, Lou and the Velvet Underground – Collection

Robinson, Smokey – *Quiet Storm*

Rolling Stones – *Black and Blue*

Rolling Stones – *Got Live If Ya Want It*

Rolling Stones – *Hot Rocks* – Ronson's name written on back cover

Rolling Stones – *More Hot Rocks*

Ronson, Mick – *Slaughter on 10th Avenue*

Roxy Music – *Siren*

Santana – *Santana*

Screaming Blue Messiahs – *Totally Religious*

Shear, Jules – *When Love Surges*

Spandau Ballet – *True*

Sugarcubes – *Life's Too Good*

Swaggart, Jimmy – *Presents the Sweetest Sacred Music This Side of Heaven*

Tarantellas – *Featuring Nordini's Mesette Orchestra*

Temptations – *Sing Smokey*

The 60's (Various) – *The File Series* - Two Record Set

Theatre Of Hate – *Nero*

Third World – *Prisoner in the Street* – Promo

Traffic – *Traffic*

Tremulis, Nicholas – *Nicholas Tremulis*

U2 – *The Unforgettable Fire*

UB40 – *Live in Moscow*

Utopia – *Utopia*

Ventures – *Guitar Genius Of*

Vincent, Gene – *Ain't That Too Much*

Vincent, Gene – *Born to Be a Rolling Stone*

Visible Targets – *Autistic Savant*

Wailers – *Burnin'*

Warrior – *Ipi 'n' Tombia*

Warwick, Dionne – *Collection*

Waterfront – *Waterfront*

West, Mae – *The Fabulous*

Who, The – *Face Dances*

Who, The – *Meaty Beaty Big and Bouncy*

Wolf, Howlin', Muddy Waters and Bo Diddley – *The Super Super Blues Band*

Wreckless Eric – *Big Smash* – Promo

Zevon, Warren – *Warren Zevon*

THE SPIDERWEB

Mick Ronson – http://www.mickronson.co.uk
Weird and Gilly – http://www.weirdandgilly.com

Angel Air Records – https://www.angelair.co.uk
Annette Peacock – http://www.annettepeacock.com
Benny Marshall – https://www.facebook.com/ben.marshall.127
Beside Bowie Teaser https://vimeo.com/159204101
Bob Harris – http://bobharris.org
Billy Corgan – https://www.facebook.com/BillyCorgan
Cherry Vanilla – http://cherry-vanilla.com
Chris Carter – http://breakfastwiththebeatles.com
Chrissie Hynde – http://chrissiehynde.com
Cleveland Rocks – https://www.facebook.com/search/
    top/?q=vive%20le%20rock%20wjcu
Cody Melville – https://codymelville.bandcamp.com
Dagmar – http://www.dagmarfotos.com/dagmar1.html
David Bowie – http://www.davidbowie.com/news
David Bowie – http://www.bowiewonderworld.com
Def Leppard – http://www.defleppard.com
Dennis Dunaway – https://www.dennisdunaway.com
Easy Action Records – http://www.easyaction.co.uk
Ellen Foley – https://www.ellenfoley.com
Eric Bloom – http://www.ericbloom.net
George Underwood – http://www.georgeunderwood.com
Glen Matlock – http://www.glenmatlock.com
Graham Parker – http://www.grahamparker.net/Home.html
Ian Hunter – http://ianhunter.com
Independent Publishers Group – http://www.ipgbook.com
Joe Elliott – http://www.downnoutz.net
John Blake Books – https://johnblakebooks.com

WEIRD & GILLY

Just A Buzz Online - http://www.justabuzz.com

Les Fradkin - http://www.lesfradkin.com/news.html

Lisa Dalbello - https://www.facebook.com/dalbellofanpage

Lisa Ronson - https://www.facebook.com/LisaRonsonMusic

Lou Reed - http://www.loureed.com

Madeline Bocaro - http://madelinex.blogspot.com

Maggi Ronson - http://www.maggironson.com

MainMan Records - http://mainmanrecords.com

Michael Chapman - http://www.michaelchapman.co.uk

Mike Garson - http://www.mikegarson.com

Mick Rock - http://www.mickrock.com

Mott The Hoople - http://mottthehoople.com

Mott The Hoople Film - http://ultimateclassicrock.com/ballad-of
mott-the-hoople-film

Rick Tedesco - http://guitarhangar.com

Mick Ronson - https://www.facebook.com/pages/Mick-
Ronson/106072969423868

Mick Ronson Club - https://www.facebook.com/
groups/488317961255687/

Mick Ronson Gear - https://www.facebook.com/MickRonsonGear/

Mick Ronson TSWTPH Book Launch - https://www.youtube
com/watch?v=KwkZIrKDO7Q

Morgan Fisher - http://www.morgan-fisher.com

Phil Collen - http://www.philcollenpc1.com

Quonset Hut - http://www.qhut.com

Rodney Bingenheimer - http://kroq.cbslocal.com/show/rodney-
on-the-roq/

Roger McGuinn - https://www.facebook.com/roger.mcguinn.3/

Slaughter And The Dogs - http://www.satd.band

Sparks - http://allsparks.com

Steve Harley - http://www.steveharley.com

Suzi Ronson - https://www.facebook.com/suzi.ronson

Spontanuity Promo Clip Access All Areas - https://www.youtube.com/watch?v=B4hz0fsXA8w

Teenage Wildlife - http://www.teenagewildlife.com

The Exchange - https://www.theexchange.com

The Mott Archive - http://home.lyse.net/mott

The Yellow Monkey - https://www.facebook.com/FanpageWeLoveTheYellowMonkey

The Ziggy Stardust Companion - http://www.5years.com

Tony Visconti – www.tonyvisconti.com

Turn And Face The Strange - https://www.facebook.com/groups/1868755410035821

Vote For Mick https://www.ipetitions.com/petition/ronno

Welcome To Kingston Upon Hull - http://www.hull.gov.uk

Woody Woodmansey - http://www.woodywoodmansey.com

Worn Free - https://www.wornfree.com

REFERENCES/SOURCE MATERIALS:

DIRECT QUOTES FROM VARIOUS SOURCES:

All the Young Dudes – Campbell Devine

Alternative Press – Lorraine Ali – February 1993

Chris Charlesworth – NY – David Cassidy quote – Magazine unknown

Circus magazine – Ron Ross – April 1975

Creem Magazine – John Mortland

David Bowie – *Black Tie White Noise* – World Premier Weekend (printed) interview

David Bowie A Chronology – Kevin Cann

George Bertovich – Sons of the Silent Age – *Sons of Sound* – Part 1

Guitar Player Magazine – December 1976

Heaven and Hull Liner Notes: Sham Morris

Japanese Play Don't Worry In Heaven – Memorial Programmes –#1 thru #3

WEIRD & GILLY

John Oreskovich – Sons of the Silent Age –*Sons of Sound* – Part 1
Just A Buzz Fanzine/Justin Purington – Issues #4 & #5

Melody Maker – 14th, June 1975
Mick Ronson – Radio Interview w/ Rodney Bingenheimer –
    Chris Carter – Jan. 1993
Mick Ronson Ablaze: Issues #1 thru #5 – Sven Gusevik
Mick Ronson Discography – Sven Gusevik
Morrizine – Morrissey Fanzine – 3rd August, 1992 Rockline
Musical Express – Ian Penman – September 1978
Pure Prairie *Greatest Hits* Liner Notes – Joseph F. Laredo
Rolling Stone – Mick quote (F. Mercury) from Obituary/
    Tribute Article
Sounds – Linnet Evans
The Cleveland Plain Dealer – Jane Scott
The David Bowie Story – Edwards and Zanetta
The Ziggy Companion – Mike Harvey
Tony Parsons – Mick's last interview–newspaper/magazine–title
    unknown
UK – *Making Music* – March 1995 –Wildhearts
Ziggy Stardust – Mick Rock

BOOKS REFERENCED:

Alias David Bowie – Peter & Leni Gillman
All the Young Dudes – Campbell Devine
Backstage Passes – Angela Bowie with Patrick Carr
Bob Dylan – *Rolling Thunder Logbook* –Sam Shepard
David Bowie – *A Chronology* –Kevin Cann
David Bowie – *The Concert Tapes* – Pimm Jal de la Parra
David Bowie – *The Pitt Report* – Kenneth Pitt
David Bowie World 7" Records Discography 1964–1981 –
    Marshall Jarman
Moonage Daydream – Dave Thompson

The David Bowie Story – Henry Edwards and Tony Zanetta
The End of Innocence – Scallo
The Freddie Mercury Tribute – International Music Publications
Ziggy Stardust – Mick Rock

FANZINES -TOUR PROGRAMMES-LINER NOTES-MISC. REFERENCED:

Annette Peacock – *X–Dreams* – Liner Notes

Billboard Ad – Morrissey
BowinMan – Faxed Materials – 1999
BowinMan – Robin Davis – All Three Memorial Programmes
Cybernauts – *Live* – Liner Notes
David Bowie – *Black Tie White Noise* – Retail One Sheet
David Bowie – *Starzone* Issue #13 & #15
David Cassidy – *When I'm A Rock 'n' Roll Star* – *The Collection* – Liner Notes
Freddie Mercury Tribute Programme
Goldmine Magazine – Issue #388 – June, 1995
Johnny Cougar – *Chestnut Street Incident* – Liner Notes
Just A Buzz – Justin Purington – Issues #4 – #5
Melody Maker – Obituary 1993
Mick Ronson – *Just Like This* – Liner Notes
Mick Ronson – *Play Don't Worry & Only After Dark* – Liner Notes
Mick Ronson Memorial Programme – Kevin Cann
Mick Ronson Memorial Programme II – Kevin Cann
Naomi Fujiyama – Japanese Reports – 1999
Personal Notes – Diary – 1988 – 1997
Pure Prairie League – *Greatest Hits* – Liner Notes

Roger McGuinn – *Cardiff Rose* Liner Notes
Ronson Ablaze – Sven Gusevik – Issues #1 thru #5
Slaughter & the Dogs – *Do It Dog Style* – Liner Notes

WEIRD & GILLY

Spiders from Mars – *Spiders From Mars* – CD Liner Notes
The Outsider – Sven Gusevik – Issues #1 – #8
The Rats – *The Rise and Fall Of Bernie Gripplestone* – Liner Notes
Various Bootleg Tapes and Videos referenced

WEBSITES REFERENCED:

All Music Guide
Angel Air Records
Artists Direct
Just A Buzz Online –Justin Purington
Mick Ronson's Official Site –Justin Purington
Only After Dark – John Slaven
Slaughter & The Dogs
Sparks
The Mott Archive –Sven Gusevik
The Ziggy Companion – Mike Harvey

MEMORABILIA SECTION

From the authors' personal collection apart from Treacle
businesscard and Hype artwork, courtesy of David Wells; and
Mick's gardening studies, courtesy of Maggi Ronson.